D1121202

Beyond Apathy

Beyond Apathy

A Theology for Bystanders

Elisabeth T. Vasko

Fortress Press
Minneapolis

BEYOND APATHY

A Theology for Bystanders

Copyright © 2015 Fortress Press. All rights reserved. Except for brief quotations in critical articles or reviews, no part of this book may be reproduced in any manner without prior written permission from the publisher. Visit http://www.augsburgfortress.org/copyrights/ or write to Permissions, Augsburg Fortress, Box 1209, Minneapolis, MN 55440.

Substantive portions of this book were previously published in Elisabeth T. Vasko, "LGBT Bullying at the Crossroads of Christian Theology: Girard, Surrogate Victimage, and Sexual Scapegoating." In *Violence, Transformation, and the Sacred: They Shall Be Called Children of God*, College Theology Society Annual Volume 57, ed. Margaret R. Pfeil and Tobias L. Winwright, 38–53. Maryknoll, NY: Orbis, 2012.

Cover design: Tory Herman

Cover image © Nik_Merkulov/iStock/Thinkstock

Library of Congress Cataloging-in-Publication Data is available

Print ISBN: 978-1-4514-6929-5

eBook ISBN: 978-1-4514-9419-8

The paper used in this publication meets the minimum requirements of American National Standard for Information Sciences — Permanence of Paper for Printed Library Materials, ANSI Z329.48-1984.

Manufactured in the U.S.A.

This book was produced using PressBooks.com, and PDF rendering was done by PrinceXML.

Contents

Acknowledgments

A book is never the work of one person. There are many who helped me along this journey. I would like to thank Duquesne University for the research sabbatical that allowed for the completion of this project. Colleagues in the department of theology and across campus have been an invaluable source of support and friendship. James Bailey, Gerald Boodoo, Lori Koelsch, Aimée Upjohn Light, Anna Floerke Scheid, and Elochukwu Uzukwu assisted with this project in numerous ways, including providing me with resources, thinking through the material with me, and reading chapters of the text. Heartfelt gratitude goes to Maureen O'Brien for the time and energy that she has devoted to my development as a teacher-scholar. I also wish to thank Arlene Montevecchio, my graduate assistant, for her help in preparing the final stages of this manuscript. Most of all, I wish to acknowledge the role my students played in the formation of this book. In a large part, the impetus for this project arose out of their courageous witness to experiences of violence, bullying, and passive bystanding.

I also would like to recognize the support of colleagues and friends outside of Duquesne. Jon Nilson, Kate Ott, Susan Ross, Karen Teel, and Rachel Hart Winter have been particularly helpful: reading chapters of the manuscript, providing me with references, and "hearing me to speech" over the years. Throughout this process, Paula Drass has not only inspired me to keep going when I did not feel like it, but she has been instrumental in teaching me to find grace in the ordinary. I also wish to acknowledge the many individuals at Fortress Press who helped to bring this project to fruition, including Michael Gibson, Marissa Wold, and Carolyn Halvorson.

Writing a book is often a family affair. This was certainly the case here. Over the past year, members of my family have read far more theology than they probably would ever care to do. Without Michael Stevens's editing assistance, this project would surely be less clear. I am also grateful to Therese Stevens, who has been my cheerleader throughout this entire process, celebrating my accomplishments along the way. Finally, I want to thank Scott Vasko, my partner in life, for his patience through the ups and downs of writing and for his willingness to learn alongside me. Your unconditional love has given me new eyes to see beauty—in people and in myself.

Elise, this book is for you. Not only do you bring me great joy, helping me to realize the depths of my own capacity for love, but you have further instilled in me the importance of creating a more peaceful and just world. As you grow, may you find your own place within this journey.

Introduction: Bystanders as a Critical Locus for Theological Reflection

In the fall of 2010, the country witnessed a string of teen suicides. Pictures of fifteen-year-old Billy Lucas, thirteen-year-old Seth Walsh, and eighteen-year-old Tyler Clementi flashed across every news media outlet in the United States.[1] While there can be many causes of teen suicide, a common thread held all of these deaths together: LGBTQ bullying. Billy Lucas, Seth Walsh, and Tyler Clementi took their own lives after enduring daily harassment and torment by their peers because of their sexual orientation. Several years later, the deaths of these young men remain little more than a distant memory to most.

The next winter, we watched intoxicated members of The Big Reds, a football team in Steubenville, Ohio, boast about the rape of an unconscious sixteen-year-old girl at a party. When the district attorney finally decided to press charges, instead of rallying around the young woman, the town rushed to the defense of her attackers, "who were athletes for the town's pride and glory, the high school

---

1. Cody J. Sanders cites many of these examples in *Queer Lessons for Churches on the Straight and Narrow: What All Christians Can Learn from LGBTQ Lives* (Macon, GA: Faithlab, 2013), 117.

football team."[2] This story is hardly an isolated incident. In January 2012, two high school freshwomen were invited to a house party by a senior star of the football team in Maryville, Missouri. Once there, they were encouraged to drink by popular students. As reported by the *Kansas City Star*, the next morning one teen's mother found her daughter, alone on the front lawn of the house in tears.[3] While helping her daughter clean up, she discovered red marks on her daughter's genital area. A medical examination along with the video recording of the event (taken by a friend of the perpetrator) verified that Daisy Coleman had been raped.[4] Within days, the students involved were taken in for questioning and arrested. Yet, similar to the Steubenville case, the town itself turned on the family of the young woman. Daisy not only received threats at school, but "her mother, a veterinarian, was fired from her job two weeks after the incident without so much as an explanation, only later learning that her boss feared that her presence 'was putting stress' on her other employees."[5] The family moved out of the area. Later that spring, "their old house burned down mysteriously."[6] Since then, the charges against the perpetrators have been dropped.

In July 2013, an all-female and mostly white jury acquitted George Zimmerman, a neighborhood watch volunteer who fatally shot unarmed black teenager Trayvon Martin, of second-degree murder and manslaughter. The confrontation between Zimmerman and Martin, which took place in residential community in Sanford,

2. Adam Peck, "Victim's House Burned Down after She Accuses Football Star of Rape," *Think Progress*, http://thinkprogress.org/health/2013/10/14/2777431/maryville-missouri-rape/.

3. Dugan, Arnett, "Nightmare in Maryville: Teens' Sexual Encounter Ignites a Firestorm Against Family," *The Kansas City Star*, October 12, 2014, http://www.kansascity.com/news/special-reports/maryville/article329412/Nightmare-in-Maryville-Teens'-sexual-encounter-ignites-a-firestorm-against-family.html.

4. Ibid. Names of victims of sexual violence are usually not released to the public. In this, case Coleman's family made the exception because they wanted her story to get out.

5. Peck, "Victim's House Burned."

6. Ibid.

Florida, "began with Zimmerman's non-emergency dispatch call, a call that was racially assaultive in its discourse, one that used the tropes of anti-black racism."[7] The socio-cultural link between blackness and criminality contributed to Zimmerman's assumption that a seventeen-year-old black teenager wearing a hoodie and carrying a pack of Skittles and an Arizona Iced Tea, was "up to no good or he's on drugs or something."[8] Abuse of Florida's Stand Your Ground law and racially marked police missteps in the case led to Zimmerman's acquittal.[9]

Rarely do we engage in serious conversation about violence in the United States. We have a propensity to avoid so-called hot button issues: sexual and domestic violence, the denigration and violation of LGBTQ persons, and white racism. When we do attempt to speak about the "unspeakable," our focus tends to be on the victim and the perpetrator. "Why did he do that to her?" "How could the jury acquit him?" Such responses not only do little to resolve the issue at hand, but they also obscure the way in which violence touches us all. In the events involving Tyler Clementi, Trayvon Martin, and Daisy Coleman, responsibility did not lie solely in the hands of their accused perpetrators. In each case, the violence experienced (racial, sexual, or homophobic and heterosexist) was tied to the tacit (and sometimes overt) acceptance of cultural norms that allow for the denigration of entire groups of people.[10] The idea that women's bodies are objects for male sexual consumption participates in the normalization of

---

7. George Yancy, "Walking While Black in the 'White Gaze,'" September 1, 2013, *The New York Times*, http://opinionator.blogs.nytimes.com/2013/09/01/walking-while-black-in-the-white-gaze/?ref=trayvonmartin.

8. Ibid. Yancy is quoting George Zimmerman.

9. And as I review the final draft of this manuscript, Michael Brown has just been laid to rest in Ferguson, Missouri. Brown, an unarmed eighteen-year-old black young man, was fatally shot in broad daylight by a white police officer in August 2014. Trayvon Martin's death was neither the first nor last of its kind.

10. Traci C. West, *Wounds of the Spirit: Black Women, Violence, and Resistance Ethics* (New York: New York University Press, 1999), 1.

violence against women. Stereotypes about the criminality of black men undergird racial inequality and racial bias within the criminal justice system in the United States. Religious and cultural ideation that regards same-sex unions and gender-variant behavior as sick, distorted, and unnatural can compound depression and psychological distress. Violence does not always have visible wounds and complicity does not always entail wielding a weapon or physical assault. Violence impacts everyone and leaves very few spaces of innocence. Until Christians privileged by virtue of race, gender, class, or sexual orientation begin to see the anguish and suffering of those who are marginalized as something for which we are responsible, the *basileia* of God (reign of God) lies beyond our grasp.[11]

My own theological journey with questions about violence began when I was working as a youth minister in a very wealthy parish in a suburb outside of Chicago. I had just completed a master's degree in pastoral ministry and, at the age of twenty-three, was idealistically enthusiastic about the power of the gospel to transform young hearts and minds. Yet my idealism quickly came to a halt when the parish I worked for decided to convert its gym into an overnight shelter for homeless families once a week. In response, homeowners across the street threatened to sue, fearing the site and the regular appearance of its nonwhite guests would lower their property values. When the shelter was finally cleared to open, I was faced with another conflict: the guests at the shelter would meet in the same building at the same time as teen confirmation classes that I ran. Parents, who were once willing to serve and volunteer at the shelter, now refused to allow their children to be in the building at the same time. As

---

11. According to Elisabeth Schüssler Fiorenza, the central symbol of the movement named after Jesus is the *basileia*, the kingdom or commonwealth, of God. This term expresses a Jewish religious-political vision that signifies freedom from domination and is marked by a "praxis of inclusive wholeness." See *In Memory of Her: A Feminist Theological Reconstruction of Christian Origins* (New York: Crossroad, 1983), 118–30.

registration fell and catechists dropped out, my job became incredibly stressful. Under pressure from parents, the church installed locking gates within the building that separated our homeless guests from the "rest of the church." One evening, while I was walking the halls during class, it all became clear to me. Not only did the members of this parish not "get it," I did not either. I had isolated myself in a world where I did not have to see anything that I did not want to see or do anything that I really did not want to do. I was able to hide from the realities of economic and racial injustice. I did not have to see poverty, much less deal with it. As much as I yearned to cry out that year, I was too afraid of those who had money and power.

At times, we have all witnessed injustice and felt powerless to help. There are also times in which we have seen injustice and remained silent, missing opportunities for connection. My situation in Chicago provided an occasion for reflecting about power from the vantage point of a privileged bystander. On the one hand, as an employee of the parish staff, I had access to a public platform in which I could voice concern over the gates and what they symbolized. Looking back, I wish I could say that I organized an educational campaign examining poverty and its effects on families. But I did not. Instead, I left the position. This would be an example of unethical passivity, wherein I relinquished my own power unnecessarily. Yet, passivity in this case must also be contextualized in view of the gender stratification and clericalism that continue to function within Roman Catholicism. As violence is a collective phenomenon, so is social change. Efforts to resist social injustice are never the result of a single individual's actions. They require the support of a community. As a young female working in large parish, my voice was often muted. To some degree, I was powerless to effect change.

Human violation can span a range of intensity, from social exclusion to war. Yet, when violence is institutionalized and coded in cultural mores and prejudices, the abuse of power can become so subtle that it is difficult to detect our own complicity. One of the most unsettling aspects of violence, as manifest within a twenty-first-century Western context, is the persistent failure of elites (a term used by Mary Hobgood) to reckon with their participation in violence.[12] Elites (or privileged people) work pretty hard to protect our innocence, to maintain a sense of ourselves as morally good people. As I will discuss in chapter 2, one of the ways in which privileged people maintain a sense of moral innocence is through systemic unknowing. Systemic unknowing is a form of selective attention, wherein entire groups of people fail "to extend to a minority the same recognition of humanity, and hence the same sympathy and care, given as a matter of course to one's own group."[13] Selective attention has appeared in various modalities throughout history: whites have ignored the plight of nonwhites; members of the upper and middle classes have relegated the concerns of poor to the margins; men have dismissed the credibility of women's experiences of domestic and sexual abuse; heterosexuals have shunned LGBTQ persons. The problem with ignorance is that it breeds arrogance and indifference.

The issue isn't that people aren't aware of human suffering. Rather, the issue, as articulated by Jon Sobrino, is that "people do not want to acknowledge or face up to the reality of a crucified world, and even less do we want to ask ourselves what is our share of responsibility for such a world."[14] Ignorance is a form of the entitlement of abuse. It is that which suggests one is entitled to economic, social, cultural,

12. Mary Elizabeth Hobgood, *Dismantling Privilege: An Ethics of Accountability*, rev. and updated ed. (Cleveland: Pilgrim, 2009), 17. Elites benefit more from social privilege than they suffer social oppression.

13. Bryan N. Massingale, *Racial Justice and the Catholic Church* (Maryknoll, NY: Orbis, 2010), 32. Massingale is quoting Charles R. Lawrence III, "The Id, the Ego, and Equal Protection: Reckoning with Unconscious Racism," *Stanford Law Review* 39 (January 1987): 317-88 at n. 135.

racial, or gender advantage even when these advantages come at great cost to others.[15] From a theological perspective, ignorance actively denies the heart of the Christian religion: that we are persons created to be in relation. Ignorance encourages isolation and, ultimately, escapism from our very humanity. When privileged people protect our innocence, we bypass possibilities for participating in God's redeeming work in the world, and, as such, resurrection is stymied. This soteriological conviction holds special relevance for bystanders to violence.

As the term is used in this book, *bystanders* are those who aid and abet perpetrators (oppressors) through acts of "omission and commission."[16] While bystanders can occupy a range of social locations from margin to center, many occupy social sites of privilege to some degree. It is important to note that I write this book as a privileged person and am primarily concerned about bystanders who "enjoy more dominance than [they] suffer subordination" by virtue of their race, class, ethnicity, sexual orientation, or gender.[17] In other words, implicated in my use of the term *bystander* are assumptions about social privilege.[18] Occupying a social location marked by privilege creates conflict, internal and external. Many who occupy sites of privilege are uneasy with the injustice it causes, and some even feel guilt about their own complicity in it. Yet, few are willing to relinquish the unearned entitlements and advantages that come with it. Those who are willing to work to eradicate the system may be intimidated by the social cost that comes with doing so.

14. Jon Sobrino, *The Principle of Mercy: Taking the Crucified People from the Cross* (Maryknoll, NY: Orbis, 1994), 5.

15. Hobgood makes this point in *Dismantling Privilege*, 20.

16. This definition of *bystander* is found in Barbara Coloroso, *The Bully, the Bullied, and the Bystander*, rev. ed. (New York: HarperCollins, 2008), 62.

17. Hobgood, *Dismantling Privilege*, 17

18. It is possible to be a bystander and to occupy a nondominant social site. This has happened throughout history. However, this would be the subject matter for a different book.

We live in a world where success is predicated upon the use of power as domination, creating a situation of divide and conquer in which no one dares to get singled out. As the dynamics of power take hold and social boundaries are created, many feel the need to distance themselves from subordinated groups in order to maintain social acceptance. Consider, for example, the increased scapegoating of those who hold a lower socioeconomic status by the religious and political right wing during the economic downturn at the beginning of the twenty-first century in the United States.[19]

The contested space that bystanders inhabit is an important locus for theological reflection since in many instances it is the space that many in the Western world occupy in relation to violence. The majority of human beings are not the ones to initiate harm, nor do they intend to do so. Rather, we are born into a world where patterns of human violation—racism, violence against women, heterosexism, imperialism, and classism—are already set in motion. Yet, regardless of intent, we are responsible. Injustice that is overlooked or ignored is dangerous. It can become "a contagion that infects even those who thought they could turn away."[20] The habit of ignoring suffering bodies is difficult to break. Our humanity is defined by our relationships with others. In the words of Archbishop Desmond Tutu, "'My humanity is caught up, is inextricably bound up, in yours.' We belong in a bundle of life."[21] Violence rends the very fabric of our common humanity, dehumanizing us all. This capacity to objectify fellow human beings is a part of the human condition. I don't say this in order to excuse the behavior of those who benefit from systems of privilege. Rather, I mention it in order to

---

19. Hobgood first made this point in *Dismantling Privilege*, 22. It remains relevant, as evidenced by the political rhetoric surrounding fiscal reform in the 2012 presidential election, wherein critics of welfare reform chanted "no free hand-outs."

20. Coloroso, *The Bully*, 63.

21. Desmond Mpilo Tutu, *No Future without Forgiveness* (New York: Doubleday, 1999), 31.

acknowledge that evil is both chosen and imposed.[22] Evil "can and does take on a life of its own and accrue a power that rivals God and the good."[23] We are pressured into participating in forces that do tremendous harm, even when we are aware of this harm. Yet, at the same time, we are responsible for our actions. One of the questions that drives the research behind this book is how can a group of well-intentioned, and sometimes, socially aware individuals repeatedly bypass opportunities for resisting violence? In part, this is a question about the dynamics of groupthink or group behavior. But it is also a question about the nature of Christian discipleship.

Like Jesus, Christians are called to contest "that which thwarts the power of human personal and communal becoming, that which twists relationship, which denies human well-being, community, and human solidarity to so many in our world."[24] For privileged persons, embodying this call will mean "break[ing] through the 'lies, secrets, and silences' that mask the prevailing distortions and manipulations in relationship and the power or relations."[25] Christians, therefore, need to not only recognize the damage done by violence in its various forms, but they also must contend with their own complicity in violence. Too often, Christians, especially those who occupy social sites of privilege, have been bystanders to violence, conforming to racial and gendered mores of our society. This is not to suggest that Christians actively seek out the role of bystander. Nor is it my presumption that bystanders are intrinsically bad people. Doing so would imply that bystanders (and perpetrators) are "monsters and demons," instead of "moral agents to be held responsible" for their

22. Darby Kathleen Ray, "Tracking the Tragic: Augustine, Global Capitalism, and a Theology of Struggle," in Constructive Theology: Classical Themes in Contemporary Perspective, ed. Serene Jones and Paul Lakeland (Minneapolis: Fortress Press, 2005), 141.
23. Ibid., 137.
24. Beverly Wildung Harrison, "The Power of Anger in the Work of Love," in Making the Connections: Essays in Feminist Social Ethics, ed. Carol S. Robb (Boston: Beacon, 1985), 18–19.
25. Ibid., 19.

action and inaction.[26] More importantly, such a perspective renders bystanders incapable of conversion, personal and communal.

Disrupting indifference requires the transformation of individuals and social structures. Apathy must be interrogated in view of patterns of social conditioning that support and even reward indifference to suffering. While the concept of apathy will be further developed in a later chapter, it suffices to note that the term comes from the Greek word *apatheia*, meaning "nonsuffering, freedom from suffering, or a creature's inability to suffer."[27] For Dorothee Sölle, apathy "is a social condition in which people are so dominated by the goal of avoiding suffering that it becomes a goal to avoid human relationships and contacts altogether."[28] To be apathetic is to lack compassion.

Theology has played a role in the social conditioning of privileged apathy. In particular, I will argue that models of redemption wherein divine justice is accomplished by means of penal substitution affirm patterns of relationality undergirding white supremacy and heteropatriarchy in the United States today, erasing them from the consciousness of dominant elites.[29] When paired within individualized notions of sin-talk, such theological language works to further privileged apathy. As such, new ways of speaking about sin and redeeming grace are sorely needed.

Intended Audience

This book is written for an academic audience: students, professors, and those who wish to further engage questions of Christian tradition

---

26. Tutu, *No Future without Forgiveness*, 83.
27. Dorothee Sölle, *Suffering*, trans. Everett R. Kalin (Philadelphia: Fortress Press, 1975), 36.
28. Ibid.
29. My reflection on these two issues is not apart from consideration of the role of economic injustice and Western imperialism. Given the limited scope of this project and the large-scale effect of these two issues, theological reflection on passive bystanding in the purview of economic injustice and Western imperialism merits their own projects.

and violence. Yet I write with the recognition that academic audiences are not monolithic and extend beyond those who sit in the proverbial "ivory tower." Consonant with the principles and practices of feminist, womanist, and liberation theologies, I believe that theology, as a discipline, has a responsibility to engage as broad of an audience as possible, including members of churches and the general public. Therefore, whenever possible, I have tried to use terminology accessible to the nonspecialist. In particular, I write this book to and for Christians who, like me, have struggled with the ways in which our own participation in systems of power and privilege renders us complicit in violence.[30] As a woman, I have experienced the ill effects of sexism firsthand. Yet, my race, socioeconomic background, geographical location as an American citizen, and heterosexual orientation have given me access to significant social advantage, an advantage that precipitates violence against those who are not white, middle-class, Western, or straight. While my own experiences of gender discrimination have informed my view of injustice, as a member of a number of privileged social groups, I also must acknowledge that my own awareness of the subjugation others experience is limited in view.[31] In the context of white racism, Karen Teel articulates this well: "As a member of the oppressor group, I need to listen to black women in order to recognize the part I have played in their suffering, to repent that role, and to be transformed."[32] This is because of the blinding nature of social privilege itself. Social privilege works to normalize patterns of

---

30. Throughout this book, the intermittent use of the first person plural is to indicate my own complicity in the structural injustices of which I speak, as well as the need for the collective whole to work toward justice. While roles and responsibilities may differ in relation to violence, the project of justice is one that involves work of all parties: victim-survivors, perpetrators, and bystanders.
31. Karen Teel, *Racism and the Image of God* (New York: Palgrave MacMillan, 2010), 11.
32. Ibid.

social dominance and entitlement, such that those who benefit most often miss its power.

As members of dominant cultural and social groups, the goal for privileged bystanders is to become allies or advocates in the struggle for justice, in the work of bringing about the kin-dom of God.[33] Ada María Isasi-Díaz says it best when she states, "To become aware that one is an oppressor does not stop with individual illumination but requires the oppressor to establish dialogue and mutuality with the oppressed. The first word in the dialogue that can bring awareness to the oppressor is uttered by the oppressed."[34] In the work of justice, allies do not set the agenda for reform. Rather, allies listen "to what priorities and needs are expressed by those who know the experience of injustice from the inside out. To be an ally is challenging work: taking risks, making mistakes and admitting them, staying open to dialogue even though it sometimes hurts."[35]

To be an ally is to have your subjectivity marked by what feminist philosopher Kelly Oliver terms *address-ability* and *response-ability*.[36] To be address-able is to listen; it is to be open to the voice of another. To be response-able is to respond to the world around you: ethically, politically and morally. In this context, it is to hear the cries of those who are suffering. Both characteristics in tandem bear the marks of compassionate witnessing. Compassionate witnessing is a hopeful behavior that allows for remembering. "Life circumstances, troubling interactions, oppressive conditions, common shock, negative relationships—our reactions to any of these—can produce

33. Ada María Isasi-Díaz uses the phrase *kin-dom* to avoid the sexist and elitist connotations of the word *kingdom* and to denote the communal aspects of God's vision for the world. See *Mujerista Theology: A Theology for the Twenty-first Century* (Maryknoll, NY: Orbis, 1996), 65n14.
34. Ibid., 95–96.
35. Pamela Cooper-White, *The Cry of Tamar: Violence against Women and the Church's Response*, 2nd ed. (Minneapolis: Fortress Press, 2012), 50.
36. Kelly Oliver, *Witnessing: Beyond Recognition* (Minneapolis: University of Minnesota Press, 2001).

disconnectedness from our feelings, beliefs, values and commitments and then disconnection from others and our communities. When we are witnessed, or when we witness ourselves, we are remembered."[37] That which has been "scattered, shattered, or forgotten" by violence is brought back together.[38] This is not to suggest that the shards of broken glass can be put back together in the same form or that the glass will ever serve the same purpose again. Rather, the process of remembering, of witnessing, is more like creating a mosaic from the broken glass. It creates a new possibility through which light can be refracted.

Why Bystanders?

Scholars in a cross section of disciplines have recognized that addressing community health and social justice issues requires the engagement of bystanders.[39] To date, bystander intervention programs have been developed and studied in relation to bullying, sexual violence, and racial violence, the rationale being that relationship violence will only be eliminated when social norms are challenged and a wide range of audiences reached.[40] In particular,

---

37. Kaethe Weingarten, *Common Shock: Witnessing Violence Everyday* (New York: Penguin, 2003), 196.

38. Ibid.

39. As first documented by the research of Latané Bibb and John Darley, the bystander effect refers to the phenomenon that an individual's likelihood of helping decreases when passive bystanders are present in a critical situation. In examining why this is the case, psychologists have identified three facets of human behavior that increase bystander inhibition: 1) diffusion of responsibility, 2) evaluation apprehension, and 3) pluralistic ignorance. See *The Unresponsive Bystander: Why Doesn't He Help?* (Englewood Cliffs, NJ: Prentice-Hall, 1970), 121–28.

40. All major bullying prevention programs are targeted at changing the behavior and value systems of bystanders. For a summary of the research, see Dan Olweus, "Bullying at School: Basic Facts and Effects of a School Based Intervention Program," *Journal of Child Psychology and Psychiatry* 35, no. 7 (1994): 1171–90. Bystander intervention programs are also being studied and implemented in relation to sexual violence and racial violence. For example, see Jacqueline K. Nelson, Kevin M. Dunn, and Yin Paradies, "Bystander Anti-Racism: A Review of the Literature" *Analyses of Social Issues and Public Policy* 11 (2011): 263–84 and Victoria L. Banyard, Elizabeth G. Plante, and Mary M. Moynihan, "Bystander Education: Bringing a Broader

bystander approaches seek to transform harmful social norms that silence marginalized members of the community and render violence invisible.[41]

From a theological vantage point, focusing on bystanders is a helpful heuristic tool for naming sin and redeeming grace within violent contexts. First and foremost, the category of *bystander* works to disrupt victim–perpetrator and oppressor-oppressed binaries and the hierarchal dualisms often accompanying it: good/evil, innocence/guilt, men/women, white/nonwhites, God/creation, mind/body—to name a few. Hierarchical dualisms have played a pivotal role in theological justification of hegemony.[42] (*Hegemony* is a term that refers to "the social, cultural, ideological, or economic influence exerted by a dominant group."[43] This influence works to silence or discredit other forms of knowing.) Moreover, the perpetrator-victim split shuts down conversation through an ill-balanced propensity to place blame. As psychologist Sharon Lamb illustrates, this propensity to place blame, to seek out the guilty party, often reinforces victim-blaming.[44] Most potential perpetrators do not see themselves as perpetrators and often deny their own participation in violence. In contrast, victim-survivors of sexual abuse tend to take too much

Community Perspective to Sexual Violence Prevention," *Journal of Community Psychology* 32 (2004): 61–79.

41. For more on the bystander approach in relation to sexual violence prevention, see http://www.ncdsv.org/publications_bystander.html. In particular, see the three-part series by Jackson Katz, *The Bystander Approach* (Enola, PA: National Sexual Violence Resource Center, 2011), starting with "Penn State: The Mother of All Teachable Moments," accessed at http://www.ncdsv.org/images/NSVRC_PennStateTheMotherOfAllTeachableMomentsFor TheBystanderApproach_12-1-2011.pdf.

42. This point is central to theses of Ivone Gebara, *Out of Depths: Women's Experience of Evil and Salvation*, trans. Anne Patrick Ware (Minneapolis: Fortress Press, 2002) and Kelly Brown Douglas's *What's Faith Got to Do With it? Black Bodies/Christian Souls* (Maryknoll, NY: Orbis, 2005).

43. Merriam-Webster Dictionary, "Hegemony," http://www.merriam-webster.com/dictionary/hegemony.

44. Sharon Lamb, *The Trouble with Blame: Victims, Perpetrators, and Responsibility* (Cambridge, MA: Harvard University Press, 1996), chapter 1.

responsibility for what has been done, engaging in self-blame.[45] The category of *bystander* is helpful to the degree that is shifts the locus of responsibility, suggesting that to some degree we are all involved in the violation that has happened. Culpability may differ according to the role one takes and the context, but all parties—bystanders, victim-survivors, and perpetrators—are touched by violence. Attention shifts from the individual to the collective. The question is no longer, "Why did you let this happen to you," or, "Why did you do this to him," but, "Why did we let this happen in our community?"[46] This is not to deny the individual responsibility of perpetrators, but it is to situate human violation within a structural and social context. Therefore, the starting point is a relational and communal anthropology that explicitly acknowledges all are impacted by violence.[47]

Such a statement can be risky, especially when one considers the fluid and sometimes overlapping nature of the categories of bystander, victim-survivor, and perpetrator. For example, research in the area of relational aggression suggests that many bullies have been bullied themselves.[48] Moreover, when the analysis of violence is

45. In contexts marked by individual trauma such as sexual violence or bullying, I follow Traci C. West and use the term *victim-survivor* to refer to those "who have been both victimized by violent assault and have survived it." See *Wounds of the Spirit: Black Women, Violence, and Resistance Ethics* (New York: New York University Press, 1999), 5. As West suggests, the language of *victim-survivor* acknowledges the harm done as well as the resilience and agency of those harmed (ibid.). When speaking of community trauma or collective violence, I use terminology that describes the practice or group being discussed (for example, white supremacy, white people, and so on). Where appropriate, I will use the terms *oppressor* and *oppressed* in order to delineate the roles of those involved in collective acts of violation. The category of bystander will be applied to both collective and individual contexts.

46. Joan Tabachnick, "Engaging Bystanders in Sexual Violence Prevention," *National Sexual Violence Resource Center* (Enola, PA: NSVRC, 2008), 5.

47. Marjorie Hewitt Suchocki speaks about violence and the human person in this manner in *The Fall to Violence: Original Sin in Relational Theology* (New York: Continuum, 1995).

48. For example, see David Schwartz, Laura J. Proctor, and Deborah H. Chien, "The Aggressive Victim of Bullying: Emotional and Behavioral Dysregulation as a Pathway to Victimization by Peers," in *Peer Harassment in School: The Plight of the Vulnerable and Victimized*, ed. Jaana Juvonen and Sandra Graham (New York: Guilford, 2001), 147–74. Some studies also indicate

expanded to include the category of the bystander, the lines between perpetrator, bystander, and victim-survivor become blurred. This is particularly true when we examine the problem of normative or structural violence. To the degree that social institutions, sacred and secular, have "decisively allied themselves through acts of omission and commission" with cultural forms of domination such as racism and heterosexism, all who participate in these institutions without questioning violence are complicit in violence.[49] In this sense, to be a bystander (individual or institutional) is to be a perpetrator of violence insofar as one "promotes, defends, and partakes—however, unwittingly—of the culture of dominance."[50] To some degree, regardless of intent, to be a bystander is to align oneself with cultural structures of domination. Bystanders do not occupy neutral moral states. Bystanders participate in perpetrating social evils.

Assertions about the complicity of an entire group of people in violence have been critiqued primarily on two grounds: "the disappearing problem" and "the equalizing problem."[51] As educational philosopher Barbara Applebaum explains, the former objection reasons that when responsibility is "shared by so many people," not only is it difficult to place blame on a particular individual, but "it loses its potency and effectiveness."[52] The statement that all are complicit "could function to excuse those who are personally guilty."[53] The second critique is related to the first. If all

a similar phenomenon in the context of domestic partner violence. See Charles L. Whitfield, Robert F. Anda, Shanta R. Dube, and Vincent J. Felitti, "Violent Childhood Experiences and the Risk of Intimate Partner Violence in Adults: Assessment in a Large Health Maintenance Organization," *Journal of Interpersonal Violence* 18, no. 2 (2003): 166–85.

49. Massingale, *Racial Justice*, 80. He makes this statement in reference to the Roman Catholic Church's participation in white racial domination in the United States. Yet I would argue that the principle has much broader application.

50. Ibid.

51. Barbara Applebaum, *Being White, Being Good: White Complicity, White Moral Responsibility, and Social Justice Pedagogy* (New York: Lexington Books, 2010), 140. Applebaum is summarizing the work of Hannah Arendt.

52. Ibid., 143.

are guilty, does this lead to the conclusion "that everyone is *equally* responsible?"[54] The problem with this assertion is that "accessories will be judged too harshly" and those who initiated violence "get off too easily."[55] While these objections must be considered carefully, both critiques assume a backward looking (also termed a liability) model of responsibility whose goal is the identification of blame. As will be further discussed in chapter 2, juridical notions of responsibility are consonant with classical Christian ideas about atonement. Taking a cue from Applebaum's work, I will argue that theological claims about the nature of bystander complicity in systemic violence require a different model of redemption, one rooted in an understanding of responsibility that is derived from our collective interdependence. Here "responsibility is not primarily about blame or punishment" (backward looking), but focuses on the future, on changing "institutions and processes so that their outcomes will be less unjust."[56] The idea is that collective change is an ongoing practice that does not happen overnight, requiring a future orientation. In Christian terminology, this model resonates with eschatological notions of the present-future, the "already–not-yet" reign of God (chapter 5).

Adopting the category of *bystander* offers the community the chance to change social norms. Social norms—practices and ideas that govern what constitutes acceptable behavior within a given setting—play a key role in violence prevention.[57] Bystanders have the capacity to effect lasting social change for the good, to alter what

53. Ibid., 142.
54. Ibid.
55. Ibid., 143.
56. Ibid., 160. Applebaum is quoting Iris Marion Young's "Responsibility, Social Connection, and Global Labor Justice," in her *Global Challenges: War, Self-Determination, and Responsibility for Justice* (Malden, MA: Polity, 2008), 159–86, at 179.
57. Mary M. Moynihan and Victoria L. Banyard, "Educating Bystanders Helps Prevent Sexual Violence and Reduce Backlash" *Sexual Assault Report* 12 (2009): 49–50, 52, 57, 60–62, 64.

practices and attitudes are considered acceptable. In a theological framework, attending to the locus of the bystander means that responsibility for redemption, for bringing about the reign of God as justice for all, is located within us all.

Some may object that the term *bystander* instead of *perpetrator*, especially in view of racism and heterosexism, functions to ease the discomfort of those who benefit from white privilege and heterosexual privilege. My use of the term *bystander* is not appropriated without critical analysis of structural violence and the historical context in which hegemonic norms have been and continue to be adopted in US culture, a process that continues to generate great affective anxiety in white straight bodies.[58] Affective dis-ease, apart from an acknowledgment of the human person's capacity for growth and change, can leave people frozen, unable to hear anything other than their own shame and guilt. Lamb explains, "You point the finger, and usually the accused points back. The more you blame a person, the more ashamed he feels and the greater his tendency will be to hide his head, deny his wrongdoing, or look outward for causality."[59] The trouble with blame is that it very rarely encourages perpetrators, and those who are complicit with perpetrators, to take responsibility for their actions.[60] As I will argue in chapter 2, guilt is not a particularly effective tool for engendering social responsibility.

Book Overview

Theologians from a wide range of social, economic, and ethnic backgrounds have challenged the ways in which classical christological constructions of dominant elites have contributed to

58. Applebaum makes a similar point in *Being White*, 161.
59. Lamb, *Trouble with Blame*, 11
60. Ibid.

violence.[61] This project builds upon this scholarship and expands it to include an examination of Christian soteriology that brings to the fore the gray moral terrain marking bystander participation in violence.

As Elizabeth Johnson illustrates, the classical Western Christian tradition has "[drawn] imagery and concepts for God almost exclusively from the world of ruling men."[62] Such speech legitimates "structures and theories that grant a theomorphic character to men who rule" and relegates all others to the margins.[63] The exclusive and literal use of kyriarchical (master-centered) language not only justifies the dominance of elites by identifying patterns of "patriarchal headship" and whiteness as divine, but it also diminishes the dignity of women and nonwhites, psychologically and socially distancing them from "from their own goodness and power."[64] In the context of privileged apathy, this vision of Jesus does more harm than help. Such a framework purports holiness as submission and obedience to power

---

61. Examples include Joanne Carlson Brown and Rebecca Parker, "For God So Loved the World?," in *Christianity, Patriarchy, and Abuse: A Feminist Critique*, ed. Joanne Carlson Brown and Carole R. Bohn (New York: Pilgrim, 1989), 1–30; Rita Nakashima Brock, *Journeys By Heart: Christology of Erotic Power* (New York: Crossroad, 1989); Patrick S. Cheng, *From Sin to Amazing Grace: Discovering the Queer Christ* (New York: Seabury Press, 2012); James H. Cone, *God of the Oppressed*, rev. ed. (Maryknoll, NY: Orbis Books, 1997) and *The Cross and the Lynching Tree* (Maryknoll, NY: Orbis Books, 2012); Robert E. Goss, *Queering Christ: Beyond Jesus Acted Up* (Cleveland: Pilgrim, 2002); Jacquelyn Grant, *White Women's Christ and Black Women's Jesus: Feminist Christology and Womanist Response*, American Academy of Religion Series, no. 64 (Atlanta: Scholars Press, 1989); Carter Heyward, *The Redemption of God: A Theology of Mutual Relation* (Washington DC: University Press of America, 1982) and *Saving Jesus from Those Who Are Right: Rethinking What It Means to Be Christian* (Minneapolis: Fortress Press, 1999); Wonhee Anne Joh, *The Heart of the Cross: A Postcolonial Christology* (Louisville: WJK, 2006); Elizabeth A. Johnson, *She Who Is: The Mystery of God in Feminist Theological Discourse* (New York: Crossroad, 1992); Jon Sobrino, *Christology at the Crossroads* (Maryknoll, NY: Orbis 1978) and *Jesus the Liberator: A Historical-Theological View* (Maryknoll, NY: Orbis, 1993); Emilie M. Townes, ed., *A Troubling in My Soul: Womanist Perspectives on Evil & Suffering* (Maryknoll, NY: Orbis, 1993); and Delores S. Williams, *Sisters in the Wilderness: The Challenge of Womanist God-Talk* (Maryknoll, NY: Orbis, 1993).

62. Johnson, *She Who Is*, 18. The term *kyriarchical* is Elisabeth Schüssler Fiorenza's.

63. Ibid.

64. Ibid., 38.

as domination, leaving little room for lament and ownership of one's own role in the work of social transformation.

As questions about the significance of racism, sexism, heterosexism, classism, and imperialism increasingly shape the landscape of contemporary theological discourse on the meaning of Christ and redemption, elites must contend with the social reality of privilege. At stake is not only the premise of intellectual and spiritual honesty within the praxis of theological naming, but also, as Hobgood explains, "there is no subordination without a complementary exercise of domination."[65] Those who occupy a privileged place by virtue of race, economic standing, gender, or ability have a responsibility to question how their privilege advantages them at the expense of others *and* contributes to human violation. George Yancy, editor of *Christology and Whiteness: What Would Jesus Do?*, argues that this interrogation cannot be viewed as an "extraneous and vague problem that exists outside" the church.[66] Rather, the interrogation of white privilege must be located "within the walls of the church itself . . . [as it is] something rooted there and all too often invisible."[67]

Elites have had a great deal to say about pain and suffering; yet relatively little has been done to challenge the theo-ethical imagination with respect to social privilege.[68] In part, this is a

---

65. Mary Elizabeth Hobgood, "White Economic and Erotic Disempowerment: A Theological Exploration in the Struggle against Racism," in *Interrupting White Privilege: Catholic Theologians Break the Silence*, ed. Laurie M. Cassidy and Alex Mikulich (Maryknoll, NY: Orbis, 2007), 40.

66. George Yancy, "Introduction: Framing the Problem," in *Christology and Whiteness: What Would Jesus Do?* (New York: Routledge, 2012), 4.

67. Ibid.

68. Notable exceptions include Barbara Hilkert Andolsen, *Daughters of Jefferson, Daughters of Bootblacks: Racism and American Feminism* (Macon, GA: Mercer University Press, 1986); Susan Brooks Thistlethwaite, *Sex, Race, and God: Feminism in Black and White* (New York: Crossroad, 1989); James N. Poling, *Deliver Us from Evil: Resisting Racial and Gender Oppression* (Minneapolis: Fortress Press, 1996); Cassidy and Mikulich, *Interrupting White Privilege*; Jon Nilson, *Hearing Past the Pain: Why White Catholic Theologians Need Black Theology* (Mahwah, NJ: Paulist, 2007); Hobgood, *Dismantling Privilege*; James W. Perkinson, *White Theology: Outing White Supremacy in Modernity* (New York: Palgrave MacMillan, 2004); Teel, *Racism and*

reflection of the social status of the majority of those who comprise the academy. This is not to deny the pain experienced by many who occupy social sites of dominance. Rather, it suggests that elites must learn to pay attention to both pain and privilege. This is a difficult task given the high premium placed on innocence within contemporary Western culture. As James Cone once remarked, "America likes to think of itself as innocent. And we are not. No human being is innocent."[69] While Cone is referring to the ways in which white Christians continue to obscure the pain of the US racial history, his claim rings true for Christian participation in hegemony more broadly construed. The separation of Christian identity from violence committed against those on the margins has allowed the dominant elite to claim a Christian identity without opposing the horrors of history and the present.[70]

The purpose of this book is to further challenge Christian interpretations of pain and power, and the corollary between sin and redeeming grace, through an investigation of bystander complicity in patterns of human violation. Drawing upon insights from Christian theologians who occupy marginal and privileged sites, I construct a Christian soteriology for bystanders to violence that foregrounds the significance of compassionate witnessing in the work of redemption. Given the pervasiveness of inaction (whether in the form of willful ignorance, denial, or silent complicity), theological reflection on violence from the vantage point of the bystander is long overdue. This is a complicated task, given the ways in which the dynamics of power and privilege are operative in shaping our own desires, as well as our interpretation of love of God and neighbor.

---

the Image of God; and Jennifer Harvey, Whiteness and Morality: Pursing Racial Justice through Reparations and Sovereignty (New York: Palgrave MacMillan, 2012).
69. "James Cone," Bill Moyers Journal, http://www.pbs.org/moyers/journal/11232007/watch.html.
70. Cone, The Cross and the Lynching Tree, 159.

The next chapter takes a deeper look at the ways in which violence and hiddenness mark central aspects of the human condition within a twenty-first-century Western context. The normalization of social relations of dominance and subjection (via gender, race, and class) renders violence invisible and silences the voices of its victims and survivors. Yet this is only one part of the equation. The other piece has to do with the ways in which hiding in the forms of isolation, individualism, and segregation is generative of violence. Economic and racial privilege plays a pivotal role in segregating entire groups of people from one another. Isolation is exacerbated by social media. This dynamism of hiddenness and violence will be illustrated through an analysis of bullying violence.

Drawing upon the narratives of young people and sociological research, I examine the ways in which bullying violence is a microcosm of patterns of intimidation, coercion, and human degradation operative in society at large. In particular, bullying points to the role of bystanders in supporting the use of power as domination. This is especially evident in view of gay bashing and slut shaming, two of the most common forms of bullying violence. Given the privileging of hegemonic masculinity and "flamboyant heterosexuality"[71] within a Western context, passive bystanders participate in and support heteropatriarchy.

In chapter 2, I argue that unethical passivity, or apathy, manifest by bystanders is learned behavior that must be contextualized in view of the valuation of innocence purported through systems of social privilege and religious ideation surrounding divine perfection and divine suffering within classical Christian atonement tradition. Such narratives reinforce the bystander phenomenon, submitting that

---

71. Sociologist Jessie Klein argues that in a hypermasculine culture, the word *flamboyant* better encapsulates the pressure to conform to heteronormativity than it does the public expression of gender-variant and same-sex behavior. See *The Bully Society: School Shootings and the Crisis of Bullying in American Schools* (New York: New York University Press, 2012), 53.

someone else will take care of the problem. This is a crucial concept for bystanders to violence that must be explicitly examined in view of the ways in which unethical passivity is compounded by social privilege. In order to do so, I take a closer look at the ways in which Christian apathy is manifest in forms of white privilege and white racism. Particular attention is given to the ways in which systemic ignorance, permission to escape, and ineffective guilt inform patterns of white unethical passivity in the United States.

Drawing insight from the work of womanist, black liberation, and feminist theologians, I argue that the divinization of scapegoating (or victim-blaming tactics) within classical Christian atonement tradition functions to erase nonwhite suffering from white consciousness. This is because victim-blaming tactics create confusion about who is responsible for violence and are often used by perpetrators and bystanders in order to minimize the consequences of their actions and to "preserve their sense of themselves as good."[72]

Chapter 3 turns to the question of sin-talk and begins the work of critical reconstruction. Within the history of Western Christian thought, sin has been predominantly defined as an individual offense against God, typically taking the form of pride or disobedience. Such formulations not only obscure the ways in which cultural forms of socialization shape self-understanding (i.e., gender, race, class, nationality), but they also marginalize the structural aspects of sin (sometimes referred to as evil). This is especially pertinent given the ways in which myths of moral innocence allow those who stand out of harm's way by virtue of social privilege—racial, gender, economic, or national—to deny responsibility within violent contexts.

Drawing insight from the work of Bryan Massingale and Denise Ackermann, I maintain sin-talk is best filtered through the language

---

72. Cooper-White, *The Cry of Tamar*, 18.

of lament instead of guilt or disobedience.[73] Lament is "a cry of utter anguish and passionate protest at the state of this world and its brokenness."[74] It is a form of honest reckoning that "holds together both loss and hope" in a way that recenters the plight of those who have suffered injustice as revelatory of divine and social truths.[75] Listening to the critical and constructive lament of feminist, womanist, liberation, black liberation, and queer theologians, I identify four critical markers of sin-talk for bystanders to violence: 1) starting with the relational self; 2) sin as hiding; 3) structural dimensions of sin; and 4) ambiguity in naming sin and grace.

Chapter 4 turns to the story of Jesus and the Syro-Phoenician woman (Mark 7:24-30) as a resource for articulating a theology of redemption for privileged bystanders to violence. Drawing insight from postcolonial and feminist biblical scholarship on the passage, I argue that the narrative speaks to a Christology of "dis-ease" and "dis-comfort,"[76] challenging privileged Christians to take a closer look at the ways in which the body of Christ is complicit in hegemonic violence. In the narrative it is not Jesus who speaks a good word about salvation. Rather, speech about God's *basileia* comes forth from the mouth of a woman who occupies a marginal location in the community by virtue of her gender, religious, and ethnic identity.[77] Her speech becomes a catalyst for healing, as it calls the Christian church to conversion in light of its own complicity in structural

---

73. Massingale, *Racial Justice*, 104–20.

74. Ibid., 105.

75. Ibid., 107.

76. Karen Teel makes this point in "What Jesus Wouldn't Do," in *Christology and Whiteness*, 30. Her phrasing of *dis-ease* and *dis-comfort* are drawn from the writings of M. Shawn Copeland. For one example of Copeland's use of these terms, see "Toward a Critical Christian Feminist Theology of Solidarity," in *Women and Theology*, ed. Mary Ann Hinsdale and Phyllis Kaminski, Annual Publication of the College Theology Society, vol. 40, (Maryknoll, NY: Orbis, 1994), 30.

77. Elisabeth Schüssler Fiorenza makes this point in the introduction of *But She Said: Feminist Practices of Biblical Interpretation* (Boston: Beacon, 1992), 12–13.

injustice. As I will argue, the text, when read through a postcolonial and feminist lens, authorizes a heterogeneous reading of salvation that is otherwise submerged by monolithic christological politics of privileged indifference.

In view of the violence that "surrounds us" and operates within us,[78] privileged Christians and privileged Christologies need a redemptive praxis that moves us beyond apathy and into compassionate witnessing. Such a process will involve a critical examination of the ways that structural sin is operative in the world and inscribed within us. Drawing insight from the interpretative reading of Mark 7:24-30, Christian liberation theologies, and George Yancy's work "theorizing whiteness as ambush," chapter 5 constructs a soteriological praxis for bystanders wherein grace bears the mark of "dis-ease."[79] Within such a theological framework, salvation is best understood as a continuous project rooted in history that is connected to the concrete liberation of those who suffer injustice. Privileged participation in the work of liberation must be rooted in a praxis that 1) is marked by vigilance and uncertainty, 2) embraces vulnerability and demystifies perfection in an effort to 3) cultivate collective and personal maturity within the body of Christ.

This project is a limited endeavor not intended to supplant or replace other models of sin and redeeming grace. While I maintain that the roles of bystander, victim-survivor, and perpetrator are more fluid than static, critical differences must be acknowledged. In the context of domestic violence, it would be inadequate and inappropriate to name hiding as sinful. For victim-survivors of trauma and violence, hiding can be an important survival strategy. Bystanders play only one role within the drama of violence.

---

78. George Yancy, *Black Bodies, White Gazes: The Continuing Significance of Race* (Lanham, MD: Rowman & Littlefield, 2008), 238.

79. Ibid., 227–50.

Therefore, the theological constructions offered here are designed to sit alongside those written from the vantage point of others.

Conclusion

To struggle honestly with one's own participation in the dynamics of power and privilege is not an easy task. It is to reckon with the ways in which the very systems that we struggle against are embedded in our psyche: in our interpretation of the world, of what is right and good and just. This is a long journey that is all the more difficult given Christianity's own participation in imperial hegemony. As Hobgood holds, Christian narratives have functioned to honor those who occupy sites of privilege by virtue of race, sex, and socioeconomic status.[80] We see this in a system of hierarchy and dualism, which marks much of the intellectual history of Western Christian thought, as well as the present-day exclusion of LGBTQ persons, women, criminals, and disabled persons in contemporary ecclesial settings.

To be a Christian is to take sides with those who are marginalized, dehumanized, and subject to violence. Whether we like it or not, neutrality isn't an option. In the face of violent activity, to hide behind the mirror of ignorance is to take a side with the powers that be. Yet the troubling of pain and privilege is also a task that is filled with much hope. As the first thaw always brings signs of early spring, we, too, can note a few cracks in the hegemonic ice. For example, the "It Gets Better Project" has signaled national attention to the problem of violence against LGBTQ youth.[81] The Health Care Reform Act, while far from perfect, has brought about unprecedented reforms in our healthcare system. In the summer of 2013, the Supreme Court declared the Defense of Marriage Act (DOMA) unconstitutional.

80. Hobgood, *Dismantling Privilege*, 37.
81. For more information, visit http://www.itgetsbetter.org/.

These changes are just the beginning, as much work remains ahead of us.

To be a Christian is to hope against hope. It is this narrative that forms the backdrop of the resurrection story. The first disciples, many of whom were bystanders to the violent execution of Jesus, found a way to witness to hope. Yet, this witnessing cannot happen without marked accountability. It means rewriting what has been erroneously deemed the grace of privilege into a new reality that breaks open boundaries.

The brokenness caused by violence calls us to take a long hard look in the mirror and to ask what Christian communities are really doing to create a culture that resists violence and welcomes difference. Dorothee Sölle once remarked, perhaps, the greatest danger in the face of violence lies in "becoming tired and giving up . . . becoming depoliticized because we submit ourselves to the idol of oppression, who whispers to us with a soft voice: 'Nothing can be done about it.'"[82]

---

82. Dorothee Sölle, *Stations of the Cross: A Latin American Pilgrimage*, trans. Joyce Irwin (Minneapolis: Fortress Press, 1993), 94.

1

Violence, Hiddenness, and the Human Condition: A Closer Look at Gay Bashing and Slut Shaming

So when the woman saw that the tree was good for food, and that it was a delight to the eyes, and that the tree was to be desired to make one wise, she took of its fruit and ate; and she also gave some to her husband, who was with her, and he ate. Then the eyes of both were opened, and they knew that they were naked; and they sewed fig leaves together and made loincloths for themselves. They heard the sound of the Lord God walking in the garden at the time of the evening breeze, and the man and his wife hid themselves from the presence of the Lord God among the trees of the garden. But the Lord God called to the man, and said to him, "Where are you?" He said, "I heard the sound of you in the garden, and I was afraid, because I was naked; and *I hid myself.*" (Gen. 3:6–10, emphasis mine).[1]

The biblical narrative of Adam and Eve has played a central role in shaping the Western Christian imaginary, especially in theological

1. All biblical quotations are from the New Revised Standard Version.

formulations of the human condition. As the story goes, Adam and Eve are commanded by God not to eat the fruit of the tree of knowledge of good and evil. Tricked by the serpent, they violate God's command and eat the forbidden fruit. Realizing what they have done and hearing God in the garden, Adam and Eve hide themselves. God finds Adam and Eve and asks them to account for their actions. In responding, Adam places the blame on Eve, saying "The woman whom you gave to be with me, she gave me fruit from the tree, and I ate" (Gen. 3:12). God, then, turns to Eve who also bypasses responsibility stating "The serpent tricked me, and I ate" (Gen. 3:13). In the end, the first humans and their descendants are cast out of paradise, punished by God.

Central to the work of theological anthropology is a wrestling with the place of God and human beings in the brokenness that marks the human condition. Within Christian tradition, the story of Adam and Eve has often been interpreted to name disobedience of divine commands and the ensuing punishment as the root of human suffering. The first humans, created in the image and likeness of God, were given all that they needed in order to be happy. Yet, willful disobedience, the desire to be in control, to be like God, and human fallibility get in the way, ruining paradise for everyone in the future. In the narrative, suffering enters the picture as a consequence of punishment given by God. Adam now must earn his food by the sweat of his brow, as the land has been cursed (Gen. 3:19). Eve's pain greatly multiplies in childbirth (Gen. 3:16). Enmity marks not only the relationships between man and woman (Gen. 3:17), but also among human beings and the natural world (Gen. 3:15). The future is pretty dim in this story. Moreover, the character of divine-human relations is likened to that of punitive parenting of children who are constantly testing the limits. As the parent of a toddler, I can imagine why God might have been a little frustrated with Adam and Eve. (Maybe there was a good reason for asking them not to eat of the fruit of that particular tree. Who knows, maybe God had just cleaned it up and didn't want to pick up the mess again!) Yet, the problem, when we look at the narrative and its implications for theological anthropology, is that we are not all toddlers. Being a "good" Christian, family member, or child can't be chalked up to blind obedience to commands, parental or divine. (This is true even for toddlers.) Moreover, as Patrick Cheng, whose work I will discuss in a later chapter, has argued, the punishment issued forth by God does not fit the crime. As he explains, "To the extent that Adam and Eve were tricked by the serpent to eat of the fruit, they arguably did not intend to commit a criminal act. And even if they did have a criminal intent, it seems unjust to impute criminal intent upon their descendants (that is, all of us) who simply inherited this sin through biological transmission."[2] Such a punitive model for divine–human relations seems to be predicated upon distrust instead of mutuality. Punitive parenting creates a climate of fear, scrupulosity, resentment, and shame—encouraging escapism and mistrust. The same can be said of theologies that depict God as a punitive father more concerned with human infractions of the divine commands than the well-being of God's children. Ironically, such a theologically framework encourages, instead of discourages, radical self-absorption. Carter Heyward notes, "Most of us do not take to heart each day the fact that, in God, our lives are connected at the root of who each of us is and who all of us are."[3] Namely, we have yet to acknowledge the depth of our sacred interdependence. We forget that our own well-being can only be secured in relation to the well-being of others. Fear teaches us to hide vulnerability beneath a masquerade of false

2. Patrick S. Cheng, *From Sin to Amazing Grace: Discovering the Queer Christ* (New York: Seabury, 2012), 37.
3. Carter Heyward, *Saving Jesus from Those Who Are Right: Rethinking What It Means to Be Christian* (Minneapolis: Fortress Press, 1999), 83.

innocence. We tend to our own needs and wants apart from a serious consideration of the flourishing of others. This reaction cannot be chalked up to individual failings. Rather, the problem of unethical passivity must be understood within the current Christian theological and cultural milieu, wherein violence and hiddenness continue to mark the human condition individually and collectively.

As Elizabeth Johnson poignantly reminds us about the function of language for God, "neither abstract in content nor neutral in its effect, speaking about God sums up, unifies, and expresses a faith community's sense of ultimate mystery, the world view and expectation of order devolving from this, and the concomitant orientation of human life and devotion."[4] The symbol of God represents what the community "takes to be the highest good, the profoundest truth, the most appealing beauty."[5] Theological language gives form to the theo-ethical imagination of the community and the individual. God's incomprehensibility serves as a powerful reminder that all God-talk is limited and should not be used literally or exclusively. This does not mean that all symbols for God are equal in value. Rather, it necessitates a careful consideration of the ways in which symbols function to shape what we value and desire in a given context.

As Americans, we inhabit a culture that encourages escapism—from authentic relationships with ourselves, with God, and with another. This is not to say that all relationships are superficial. Rather, as I have suggested, we are not very good at sitting with pain. We tend to engage in a politics of distraction, to shy away from making the really hard decisions (after all, isn't there an app for that?). In doing so, we risk becoming immune to violence happening

---

4. Elizabeth A. Johnson, *She Who Is: The Mystery of God in Feminist Theological Discourse* (New York: Crossroad, 1992), 4.
5. Ibid.

in our midst. The problem of moral indifference is compounded by the relatively sheltered lives we live.[6] We continue to live, work, and worship in largely class and race-segregated environments. Such isolation allows us to maintain the façade that the resources to which we have access are readily available to everyone, and, therefore, tricks us into believing there is no need for change. As such, the question becomes how to speak meaningfully about human participation in violence and the suffering it causes, given the Western valuation of escapism, individualism, and mindless conformity?

I have often wondered whether the story of Adam and Eve is not so much about disobedience of divine commands, but humanity's attempt to hide and the violence that ensues from our hiding.[7] Namely, the narrative in Genesis calls us to ask, to what degree are we hiding—from ourselves, from one another, and perhaps, even from God? This question, and its deep theological roots, is worth keeping in mind in view of bystander participation in violence. In contexts marked by violence, hiding can be risky business, encouraging passivity and escapism, and sapping the world of the vital and creative energy needed for transformation. Genuine care for and nurturing of others is not possible when we are hiding.[8] Compassion only becomes possible when we come out of the shadows and come face to face with vulnerability—human and divine. To the degree that

---

6. Mary Elizabeth Hobgood, *Dismantling Privilege: An Ethics of Accountability*, rev. and updated ed. (Cleveland: Pilgrim, 2009), 21.

7. I am certainly not the first to ask this question. One of the more famous constructions is that of Reinhold Niebuhr. See *Human Nature*, vol. 1 of *The Nature and Destiny of Man* (New York: Charles Scribner's Sons, 1941), 178–79. Niebuhr has been critiqued by feminist scholars of religion: Valerie Saiving Goldstein, "The Human Situation: A Feminine View," *The Journal of Religion* 40, no. 2 (1960): 100–12; Susan Nelson, "The Sin of Hiding: A Feminist Critique of Reinhold Niebuhr's Account of the Sin of Pride," *Soundings* 65 (1982): 316–27; and Judith Plaskow, *Sex, Sin, and Grace: Women's Experience and the Theologies of Reinhold Niebuhr and Paul Tillich* (Washington, DC: University Press of America, 1980). For a contemporary discussion, see the essays that are part of the roundtable discussion in *Journal of Feminist Studies in Religion* 28, no.1 (2012): 75–133.

8. Nelson, "The Sin of Hiding," 325.

violence touches us all and is truly inescapable, a return to paradise is no longer possible. I am not suggesting that healing is impossible. Rather I contend that innocence is a myth, one with which we must reckon in the movement toward healing. Given the pervasiveness of violence, we can no longer afford to hide from ourselves, the divine, and one another. Too much life is at stake.

Our relationship to power is much more complex than dualistic notions of innocence/guilt and good/evil seem to suggest. We continue to need theologies of sin and grace that allow for a greater understanding of the moral ambiguities in which people live their lives. As Alejandro García Rivera has suggested, we walk in the garden of good and evil.[9] Sin, grace, innocence, and guilt cannot always be parsed within lived experience. Dualistic frameworks not only encourage escapism, but they leave us bereft of language to name the ways in which bystanders participate in human violation—as well as their potential to work toward healing.

This chapter begins to draw out implications of unethical passivity for Christian theology by taking a closer look at the problems of violence and hiddenness and their place in a twenty-first-century Western context. In doing so, we will take a closer look at one particular form of violence: bullying. Bullying provides a clear example of the relationship between covert and overt forms of violence and points to the way in which we all (victim-survivors, perpetrators, and bystanders) get caught up in the cycle of violence. In particular, the dynamics involved in bullying violence are a helpful starting point for dissecting the significance of passive bystanding in supporting the use of power as dominance.

Unchecked, bullying normalizes the humiliation and dehumanization of those who are the "least among us," forming the

---

9. Alejandro García-Rivera, *The Community of the Beautiful* (Collegeville, MN: Liturgical, 1999), 142.

building blocks of structural injustice and systemic oppression. It teaches children and reinforces for adults that getting ahead in life means exerting power over those who are vulnerable in society, or at least staying silent when others do. What we learn as children and practice as adults informs our identity and our vision for the future. All too often, we wait to talk about violence until it's too late. Certainly, no analysis of violence can be complete until all the evidence is shown. Yet, one of the aims of this book is to get us talking, from a theological point of view, about violence prevention. In order to do so, we have to examine the assumptions we often carry about what constitutes violent activity and the way in which cultural mores shape these assumptions.

Violence, Hiddenness, and the Human Condition

To speak of violence is to speak of hiddenness. While violence continues to be manifest in overt forms around the globe, most citizens of the Western world do not experience it as such. By and large, war happens on foreign soil, rendering our knowledge and experience of it secondhand through the news media. We do not know the working conditions of those who make most of our clothing. Inhumane and unsafe working conditions are masked behind department store lighting. In the age of online shopping, products arrive at our house in neatly wrapped packages after the click of a button. While women continue to make strides in the workplace and in public leadership, the prevalence of domestic violence reveals that home is one of the most dangerous places for women and children.[10] The distance most white and middle-class

---

10. Women are much more likely to be physically assaulted or sexually violated by an intimate partner than a stranger. As reported by the World Health Organization in 2012, risk factors for being a victim-survivor to intimate partner violence include "low education, witnessing violence between partners, exposure to abuse during childhood and attitudes accepting violence

Americans have from violence allows for what Susan Brooks Thistlethwaite has termed a culture of doublespeak, "where war is named peace and what passes for peace is really war, . . . where economic practice creates poverty and is presented as the cure for poverty, where violence in the home is called family values, and family values are the barest kind of contempt for children, women, and the elderly."[11] Such a culture of doublespeak and doublethink becomes permissible because of the distance most elites keep from violence. "When people starve, they know it is not abundance: when they are abused, they know it is not love, when they are shot, they know it is not peace; and when death is all around, they know it is not life."[12] Such hypocrisy is only possible for those who occupy locations of social power, as wealth affords one the opportunity to purchase an escape from violence. By location of social power and privilege, I am referring to the ways in which one's class, race, gender, ethnicity, or orientation gives a person access to political, social, economic, or cultural advantages that are not shared by all. With economic capital, one can purchase distance from struggling neighborhoods, underfunded schools, and from those who are different by virtue of race, ethnicity, or sexual orientation. To a degree, the ability to flee violence is a marker of social privilege. Hurricane Katrina serves as a poignant reminder of this reality.[13] In the aftermath, the question frequently asked by those who occupied sites of social power and privilege was, why didn't people leave before the storm hit? Leaving

and gender inequality." For more, see "Intimate Partner and Sexual Violence against Women: Fact Sheet," *World Health Organization*, http://www.who.int/mediacentre/factsheets/fs239/en/.

11. Susan Brooks Thistlethwaite, "Militarism in North American Perspective," in *Women Resisting Violence: Spirituality for Life*, ed. Mary John Mananzan et al., (Eugene, OR: Wipf & Stock, 1996, 2004), 123.

12. Ibid., 123–24.

13. Bryan N. Massingale offers a poignant analysis of the aftermath of Katrina in *Racial Justice and the Catholic Church* (Maryknoll, NY: Orbis), 30–33. His analysis will be presented in detail in the next chapter.

requires financial resources (access to a car, gas, and the cash to fund temporary housing) as well as the emotional security that comes with the knowledge that insurance will cover what damage is done to your possessions while you are gone. In the United States, access to financial resources continues to be divided along racial lines. Recent research out of the Urban Institute illustrates that in 2010 the average wealth of whites in the United States was approximately six times that of Hispanics or African Americans.[14]

Violence involves not only personal harm or injury, but it is also structural or systemic. In this book, I use the term *structural violence* or *systemic violence* to name the ways in which social systems exploit some people to the benefit of others.[15] Examples of structural violence include elitism, heterosexism, sexism, racism, poverty, and ethnocentrism. Often, interpersonal violence and structural violence are interrelated. Structural violence creates social injustice. The violence that is rooted in the everyday evils of systemic and institutional oppression is harder to root out because it often escapes recognition.[16] Practices of social exclusion, coercion, and intimidation continue to undergird human relationality within personal, social, and institutional spheres. These practices, which often go unnamed, foster unprecedented levels of social privilege for a select few at the expense of many. Mary Elizabeth Hobgood emphasizes, "Our society has successfully normalized the social relations that comprise class, race, and sex/gender systems and the unshared power arrangements they reproduce. . . . We do not notice how the patterned behaviors that we engage in daily, either as

14. Signe-Mary McKernan, Caroline Ratcliffe, Eugene Steuerle, and Sisi Zhang, "Less Than Equal: Racial Disparities in Wealth Accumulation," *Urban Institute*, http://www.urban.org/UploadedPDF/412802-Less-Than-Equal-Racial-Disparities-in-Wealth-Accumulation.pdf.

15. Johan Galtung, "Violence, Peace, and Peace Research," *Journal of Peace Research* 6, no. 3 (1969): 167–91.

16. Ivone Gebara, *Out of the Depths: Women's Experience of Evil and Salvation*, trans. Ann Patrick Ware (Minneapolis: Fortress Press, 2002), 1.

individuals or as affiliates of institutions, exploit, silence, disable, or marginalize some as they confer status, profits and benefits on elites."[17] Instead, we consider them a normal part of life. Evil of this sort is rarely chosen, yet it continues to form the seedbed of sins of omission, unethical passivity, and blind obedience to forces of hegemony.

The invisibility of structural violence is further compounded by the increasingly covert forms in which present-day racism, sexism, and heterosexism are manifest. The research of renowned Columbia psychologist Derald Wing Sue illustrates that contemporary manifestations of racism, sexism, and heterosexism are more disguised than their predecessors: "It is not the White supremacists, Klansmen, or Skinheads, for example, who pose the greatest threat to people of color, but rather well-intentioned people, who are strongly motivated by egalitarian values, who believe in their own morality, and who experience themselves as fair-minded decent people who would never consciously discriminate."[18] Rather, racism most often appears as unconscious bias, in the stereotypical prejudices that white people hold about people of color. These include assumptions about lower intelligence, presumptions about criminality, assertions that race plays a minor role in life success, and the denial or pretense that a white person does not see race. Because racism is so deeply ingrained in our culture, these understandings are very rarely made explicit. They are tacitly transmitted and often unconscious. Yet, unintentional and unconscious violence is not less harmful. In fact, it is more difficult to address because it goes unnamed. Furthermore, it leaves recipients of racial microaggressions in the pernicious position

---

17. Hobgood, *Dismantling Privilege*, 18.
18. Derald Wing Sue, *Microaggressions in Everyday Life: Race, Gender, and Sexual Orientation* (Hoboken, NJ: Wiley, 2010), 23. In this book, I made the conscious decision to offer in-text descriptors only for those scholars whose expertise falls outside the area of theological and religious studies.

of being perceived as "making a mountain out of a mole-hill," or unable to pinpoint the source of discrimination.[19]

Parallel statements can be made of sexism. "In today's societal climate, it is not politically correct to hold overtly sexist attitudes or engage in obvious discriminatory actions towards women. . . . To be accused of being a sexist or of holding sex-role stereotypes toward women is to be considered unenlightened and a bigot. The strong social sanctions against sexism have changed its face and it has morphed into a more ambiguous, subtle and invisible form."[20] In the workplace, women continue to receive messages (explicit and implicit) that professional advancement is tied to compliance with sexual advances from male superiors or that their worth is defined in terms of physical attractiveness. As Pamela Cooper-White discusses, sexual harassment "is more serious than it seems, because, although it is sometimes more elusive and difficult for victims to prove, and it may not cause physical pain (although prolonged harassment can often cause stress-related illness as in the case of Anita Hill) it has long-term and devastating consequences, both economic and psychological, for victims."[21] Citing a 2005 study conducted by the American Association of University Professors, Cooper-White notes that more than 80 percent of college women report being sexually harassed.[22] The same study reveals that slightly over half of college males report harassing someone. Harassment "creates an environment

19. Ibid., 91.
20. Ibid., 169.
21. Pamela Cooper-White, *The Cry of Tamar: Violence against Women and the Church's Response*, 2nd ed. (Minneapolis: Fortress Press, 2012), 87.
22. Catherine Hill and Elena Silva, "Drawing the Line: Sexual Harassment on Campus," *American Association of University Women Educational Foundation*, 2005, http://www.aauw.org/files/2013/02/drawing-the-line-sexual-harassment-on-campus.pdf. For the incidence of sexual harassment in schools, see Catherine Hill and Holly Kearl, "Crossing the Line: Sexual Harassment at Schools," *American Association of University Women*, 2011, http://www.aauw.org/files/2013/02/Crossing-the-Line-Sexual-Harassment-at-School.pdf. Forty-eight percent of students grades 7–12 surveyed indicated they had experienced sexual harassment at school during the 2010–2011 academic year.

of stress, insecurity, and fear that reduces a woman's identity, role, and worth to her sexuality alone. It erodes her confidence, her initiative, and even her health, with direct consequences for her ability to work competitively and well."[23] As such, sexual harassment directly impacts the material and emotional situation of women. While there are laws against harassment in the workplace, these laws are often undermined by the coding of structural violence in cultural mores and prejudices, which render it invisible to the privileged eye. For example, use of sexual innuendo to put female employees "in their place" in turn has the effect of "silencing" women, making it more difficult for them to speak up at meetings, to offer contributions, and to raise their own questions and concerns. Moreover, as Traci C. West illustrates, sexual violence is often compounded by racism and classism. Stereotypical assumptions about the nature of black womanhood call into question the credibility of victims and survivors of intimate violence, making them less likely to report incidents to authorities.[24] The false presumption that women are liars and temptresses can permeate a victim-survivor's self-perception, further compounding the voicelessness that many experience.

Racism, sexism, and heterosexism are materialized in microaggressions. Racial, gender, and sexual orientation microaggressions "reflect a worldview of superiority-inferiority, albeit in much more subtle but equally harmful manner as overt forms of oppression."[25] These forms of violence often remain invisible because of cultural conditioning predicated upon the normalcy of structural and social inequities that are protected by silence and passivity. "Modern forms of bias, especially, the unconscious kind, are

---

23. Cooper-White, *Cry of Tamar*, 90.
24. Traci C. West, *Wounds of the Spirit: Black Women, Violence, and Resistance Ethics* (New York: New York University Press, 1999), 60.
25. Sue, *Microaggressions*, 132.

more likely to be manifest in a failure to help rather than in a desire to hurt."[26] Research conducted by cultural psychologist John T. Dovidio demonstrated that race played a factor in whether white bystanders helped a stranded motorist with a disabled vehicle. White bystanders, who believed that others also saw the motorist, helped a black person half as often as a white individual (38 percent versus 75 percent).[27] Research has documented that microaggressions can cause significant harm, including assailing the mental health of recipients, creating a hostile and invalidating work or campus climate, perpetuating stereotypes, and contributing to physical health problems.[28]

Thus far we have discussed some of the ways in which violence is hidden, from the invisibility of structural violence to the ways in which violence silences the voices of those in harm's way. Yet, this is only one part of the equation. The other piece has to do with the ways in which hiding, in the form of isolation, individualism, and segregation, generates violence. Hiding only remains permissible in view of the relatively isolated lives we live. Economic and racial privilege play a pivotal role in isolating entire groups of people from one another (e.g., rich from the poor, whites from nonwhites). As Steven Marche writes in *The Atlantic*, "Despite its deleterious effect on health, loneliness is one of the first things ordinary Americans spend their money achieving. With money, you flee the cramped city to a house in the suburbs or, if you can afford it, a McMansion in the exurbs, inevitably spending more time in your car. Loneliness is at the American core, a by-product of a long-standing national appetite for independence."[29] As Marche goes on to say, isolation is exacerbated by the digital age in which we live.

26. Ibid.
27. John F. Dovidio et al., "Why Can't We All Just Get Along: Interpersonal Biases and Interracial Distrust," *Cultural Diversity and Ethnic Minority Psychology* 8 (2002): 88–102.
28. The literature on this point is too numerous to cite here. For a summary, see Sue, *Microaggressions*, 52–56.

MIT researcher Sherry Turkle argues that despite increasing "connectivity," Americans' technology is actually making us lonelier than ever. In *Alone Together: Why We Expect More from Technology and Less from Each Other*, Turkle argues that electronic communication is changing the way we understand ourselves. Turkle paints a picture of the human person as both tethered and markedly absent.[30] Despite the constant companionship offered by social media sites, these relationships are ones of expediency. Technology allows us to respond to friends, family, and coworkers when it is convenient for us. Emailing and texting save us time and the messiness of face-to-face communication. Ignoring others and their feelings is not only easier, but a way of life. A student interviewed by Turkle expresses the problem as follows: "An online apology. It's cheap. It's easy. All you have to do is type 'I'm sorry.' You don't have to have any emotion, any believability in your voice or anything."[31] You don't have to make eye contact with the person whom you have hurt. You can avoid the discomfort of witnessing another person's pain. In this way, the networked world in which we live plays a role in hiding suffering, as it offers a ready escape from our own complicity in the pain of other human beings.

While social media is supposed to free up our time, to unclutter our lives, it is actually making us busier than ever. As most of my students will admit, maintaining an online presence takes a great deal of time and effort. Failure to do so comes at quite a price. When asked to participate in a "Facebook or social media fast," my students protest, saying, "If you aren't online all the time, you are out of

29. Stephen Marche, "Is Facebook Making Us Lonely?," April 2, 2012, *The Atlantic*, http://www.theatlantic.com/magazine/archive/2012/05/is-facebook-making-us-lonely/308930/.
30. Sherry Turkle, *Alone Together: Why We Expect More from Technology and Less from Each Other* (New York: Basic, 2012), 155.
31. Ibid., 196.

the mix." You become a "social leper." In order to stay connected, you have to be connected 24/7. The only way to accomplish this level of connectivity is by multitasking. This is true for teenagers and adults. Multitasking is not always a bad thing. Multitasking is a critical skill in many professions that can lead to creative innovations. It is vital for most parenting. (Truth be told, without multitasking, we would never eat dinner in our house.) Yet, as the saying goes, you can have "too much of a good thing." Constant multitasking rewires our attention span. In so doing, activities requiring patience and long-term dedication seem less attractive. To a degree, the constant pressure to be as efficient as possible pushes us to look for a quick fix. Our drive to get a lot done very quickly has political and social consequences. Most social problems require sustained efforts over time. One has to wonder whether the next generation will have the time or interest to pursue civic and political engagement.[32]

New media creates possibilities for human relationship in ways we could not have imagined a decade ago. Yet, as moral theologians have argued, it is imperative that we ask about the ethical character of these relationships.[33] In particular, we need to consider the ways in which new forms of connectivity shape the human capacity for love: of oneself and others. The case can be made that new media increases opportunities for involvement in social justice campaigns and social awareness, like Kony 2012 or Occupy Wall Street.[34] On the other hand, a constant online presence creates an environment where we are never really focused on one activity or person. We are

32. Christian Smith makes this point in *Lost in Transition: The Dark Side of Emerging Adulthood* (New York: Oxford University Press, 2011), 224.

33. Maureen H. O'Connell, "No More Time for Nostalgia: Millennial Morality and Remixing the Catholic Moral Tradition," paper given at the College Theology Society's Annual Convention, Omaha, NE, May 31, 2013.

34. Kony 2012 was video campaign created by Invisible Children Fund that sought to expose the violence done to civilians in the Sudan by LRA warlord Joseph Kony and his resistance fighters. For more, visit http://invisiblechildren.com/kony/#epic-progress. For more information on Occupy Wall Street visit, http://occupywallst.org/.

always interrupted. We have lost the art of listening—to ourselves and to others.

Though hardly a Luddite, I'll admit that I spend less time on Facebook than most. Too much time on Facebook leaves me anxious or depressed, critical of my own accomplishments or lack thereof, jealous of the exotic vacations others took, and wondering whether my toddler is enrolled in enough extracurricular activities. Too much time on Facebook leads me to determine my own worth in competition with the achievements of others. I am hardly alone in this. As Turkle argues, hyperconnectivity heightens the tendency to rely upon external sources of validation in determining our sense of self-worth and identity.[35] You can ask your friends to weigh in on anything from clothing purchases to what drink you should get at Starbucks. Moreover, the "other" to whom we are turning for validation and comparison is disguised behind a profile. While the "art" of online profile-making allows us to play with our identity, it also teaches us to hide our imperfections and vulnerability. We put our best "face" forward and suppress our failings. People typically don't broadcast on Facebook about a job interview gone wrong or about a comment that truly hurt their feelings.[36] The problems with this are manifold. Not only does constant exposure to a profile, instead of an individual's identity, set up unhealthy expectations about what constitutes the good life, but it voids us of the necessary skills for addressing failure, disappointment, and rejection—all of which are essential to the theo-ethical praxis of self-love.[37] Moreover, one also has to wonder whether compassion, the praxis of suffering

35. Turkle, *Alone Together*, 176.

36. As Turkle points out, the place for this kind of sharing is the online confessional. This is particularly true for those who are thirty-five and older. See *Alone Together*, 231..

37. For more discussion, see Maureen H. O'Connell, "No More Time for Nostalgia: Millennial Morality and a Catholic Tradition Mash-Up," in *Handing on the Faith*, College Theology Society Annual Volume, 59), ed. Matthew Sutton and William Portier (Maryknoll, NY: Orbis, 2014), 75–87.

with another, is even a possibility in a world of profiles. That is, can you really love someone if you only see his or her profile?

Hiding is a multifaceted reality that shapes the relationship we have with one another, ourselves, and the divine. Central to this book is the theological assertion that the relationship we have with God cannot be separated from the relationships we have with other living beings. As Matt. 25:31-46 suggests, love of God and love of neighbor are not distinct realities. When we are alienated from our neighbor, especially those who are suffering, we are alienated from God. So, when we are hiding from ourselves and hiding from our neighbor, we are also hiding from God. The theological implications of hiding need to be further examined, especially given the ways in which violence continues to mark the human condition. In particular, we need to examine the role of bystanders in hiding. In order to begin, let's take a closer look at one particular form of violence: bullying.

Bullying, Bystanders, and Socially Constructed Violence

In the wake of the suicides of Tyler Clementi and Phoebe Prince, a number of news media outlets gave attention to the issue of bullying—*20/20*, *Dateline*, and *Nightline*. In an effort to illustrate that bullying is a widespread public health issue that does not discriminate, the programs highlighted the stories of students from varying backgrounds: racial, socioeconomic, ability, sexual orientation, etc.[38] Certainly, bullying is a common phenomenon. Conservative estimates suggest that one out of five students is bullied at some time during their school career.[39] Yet, a closer look at the data reveals

---

38. For example, "Bullying Tragedy: Amanda Todd's Nightmare," *Nightline*, aired on October 23, 2012, http://abcnews.go.com/Nightline/video/bullying-tragedy-amanda-todds-nightmare -17549647; "Bullied to Death in America's Schools," *20/20*, aired on October 14, 2012, http://abcnews.go.com/Video/playerIndex?id=11879600; or "My Kids Would Never . . . Bully," *Dateline*, aired February 28, 2011, http://www.huffingtonpost.com/2011/03/03/my-kids-would-neverbully-_n_831086.html.

that bullying is not as random as Chris Cuomo and Diane Sawyer might have us think. Students whose gender identity is performed in ways that contradict or call into question traditional definitions of masculinity and femininity are much more likely to be the recipients of bullying violence.[40]

Bullying is a collective form of violence (it rarely happens without a crowd) that is deeply embedded within cultural norms, many of which have been associated with traditional definitions of masculinity.[41] Bullying thrives in environments that prioritize self-interest, winning at all costs, and the unilateral use of power. Such a framework not only leaves people lonely and discourages acceptance of genuine difference (i.e., "you have to fit in to get in"), but it also participates in the invisibility of violence against marginalized persons and communities. Jesse Klein, author of *The Bully Society: School Shootings and the Crisis of Bullying in America's Schools*, explains, "The American expectation to 'stand alone'—the perception that needing help and support is a sign of weakness—plays out in the dynamics of bullying. Bullied students are expected to 'take it'—an attitude directly connected to hegemonic masculinity expectations. Even girls are increasingly encouraged to 'act like a man' and handle

39. U.S. Department of Health and Human Services, "National Youth Risk Behavior Survey 2009 Overview," http://www.cdc.gov/HealthyYouth/yrbs/pdf/us_overview_yrbs.pdf. This estimate is on the conservative side. Some estimates suggest that rates of bullying are as high as one in three students.

40. For example, research by the Gay, Lesbian and Straight Education Network (GLSEN) finds that 71.3 percent of high school students surveyed heard derogatory and homophobic remarks "frequently" or "often" at school, and 84.9 percent heard the term *gay* used generally to imply "someone is stupid or something is worthless." Among those who identified themselves as LGBTQ, over 80 percent had been bullied in the past year. Joseph Koswic et al., *The 2011 National School Climate Survey: The Experiences of Lesbian, Gay, Bisexual and Transgender Youth in Our Nation's Schools* (New York: GLSEN, 2012), 14.

41. Jesse Klein, *The Bully Society: School Shootings and the Crisis of Bullying in America's Schools* (New York: New York University Press, 2012); James Garbarino, *Raising Children in a Socially Toxic Environment* (San Francisco: Jossey-Bass, 1995) and *Lost Boys: Why Our Sons Turn Violent and How We Can Save Them* (New York: Free Press, 1999), and Barbara Coloroso, *The Bully, the Bullied, and the Bystander*, updated edition (New York: Harper, 2008).

things on their own."[42] The notion that bullying or hazing is an inevitable, and even normal, part of life, blinds us from recognizing violence in our midst.

Furthermore, bystander participation in the systemic privileging of hegemonic masculinity continues to go largely unchallenged by the public. In other words, the outcry against gay bashing and slut shaming has not been accompanied by significant acknowledgement of heteropatriarchal complicity in victimization. In view of bullying violence, especially its more sexualized forms, passive bystanders participate in and inadvertently support the cultural linking of masculinity and domination. I am not suggesting that the interpersonal dimension of bullying violence is unimportant or irrelevant. Rather, my point is to offer a critical corrective to the ways in which bullying, and violence more generally, is depicted as random acts distinct from cultural mores, in order to examine the significance of bystander participation in upholding these norms. While this may be painfully obvious to those who have been subject to gay bashing or slut shaming, I am not convinced that those who benefit from gender and sexual privilege have gotten the message. Heteronormativity and LGBTQ bullying are linked.

So, what exactly is bullying and how does one distinguish bullying from teasing and other forms of aggression? According to Dan Olweus, one of the leading experts on peer victimization, bullying

---

42. Klein, *Bully Society*, 236. Hegemonic masculinity is the form of masculinity that embodies a "currently accepted" strategy for dominance. Hegemonic masculinity tends to carry social currency and those who embody it tend to be associated with the top of a given social hierarchy. R.W. Connell, *Masculinities*, 2nd ed. (Berkeley: University of California Press, 2005), 77. As Connell suggests, while the "most visible bearers of hegemonic masculinity" may not always be the most powerful people in society, at an individual level, it is often the case that "hegemony is likely to be established only if there is some correspondence between the cultural ideal [whether symbolic or actual] and institutional power, collective if not individual" (ibid). According to Connell, a successful claim to authority is the mark of hegemony. Hegemonic masculinity must be understood in relation to that which it subordinates or eschews. As expressed in Western context, hegemonic masculinity subordinates femininity and gayness.

involves three components: 1) "aggressive behavior that entails unwanted negative actions," 2) a "pattern of behavior that is repeated over time," and 3) an "imbalance of power."[43] In other words, bullying is not a conflict between two individuals or groups for whom the playing field is equal. It is a form of victimization in which the perpetrator has *power over* the victim and uses this power to deliberately and repeatedly inflict emotional or physical harm. Bullying is a form of scapegoating violence, where an individual or group is the target of unmerited hostility. Bullying is not simply fighting. Nor is it just one misplaced comment to a friend or coworker. Bullying "involves a clear intention to humiliate a victim [or victims] as a stepping stone toward overall social dominance."[44] It is "conscious, willful, and deliberate hostile activity intended to harm, induce fear through the threat of further aggression, and create terror."[45]

Bullying can take many different forms. It can be physical (kicking, spitting, punching), verbal (threatening to harm, racist remarks, abusive language), or indirect (purposely and systematically ignoring, excluding, or isolating someone, spreading malicious rumors). Studies now show that relational aggression can continue long into adulthood.[46] Perhaps the most insidious form of bullying is cyberbullying. Cyberbullying is "bullying that takes place using electronic technology" such as cell phones, computers, and tablets as well as communication tools such as Facebook, Instagram, text messaging, and chat.[47] In the case of cyberbullying, humiliation is

---

43. Dan Olweus, "What is Bullying?," *Olweus Bullying Prevention Program*, http://www.olweus.org/public/bullying.page.

44. Stuart W. Twemlow and Frank C. Sacco, *Why School Antibullying Programs Don't Work* (Latham, MD: Jason Aronson, 2008), 56.

45. Coloroso, *Bully*, 13.

46. Personal communication with Laura M. Crothers, October 8, 2012. For examples, see Darla J. Twale, and Barbara M. De Luca, *Faculty Incivility: The Rise of the Academic Bully Culture and What to Do About It* (San Francisco: Jossey-Bass, 2008).

compounded by its reach and anonymity. Not only can the bully "hide behind online anonymity and attack around the clock, invading the privacy," but bystanders can extend into the thousands, multiplying the humiliation and shame victim-survivors experience.[48]

One of the most frustrating things about bullying is that most of the time, it happens in front of an audience. Psychologist Christina Salmivalli explains that most kids know that bullying is wrong and support the idea of being an "upstander."[49] But, when the situation arises, at least a third acknowledge that they laugh when they see others victimizing a peer in school.[50] Part of the problem, according Salmivalli, is that "bullies are often perceived as popular and powerful, it takes a lot to thwart their behavior. . . . Behaving aggressively (or at least not being friendly) towards the target of bullying becomes like a trend, a way of 'fitting in' and emphasizing one's belonging to the peer group."[51] Students learn at an early age that getting to the top and staying at the top involves the use of power as dominance, or at least not saying anything about those who do. Silence may temporarily protect bystanders from harm's way, but it can have lasting consequences.

Gay Bashing, Heteropatriarchy, and Bystander Complicity

On the morning of February 2, 1996, fourteen-year-old Barry Loukaitis dressed in the clothing he had laid out the night before: black pants,

47. "What is Cyberbullying?," http://www.stopbullying.gov/cyberbullying/index.html.
48. Cindy Long, "Silencing Cyberbullies," *NEA Today* 26, no. 8 (2008): 28, as quoted in Juliane E. Field, et. al in *Understanding Girl Bullying and What to Do About It: Strategies to Help Heal the Divide* (Thousand Oaks, CA: Corwin, 2009), 12.
49. Christina Salmivalli, "Bullying and the Peer Group: A Review," *Aggression and Violent Behavior* 15 (2010): 114.
50. Ibid., 115. For example in a recent Finnish study, approximately 20 percent of students defended the target. This is compared with 20–29 percent who assisted the bully and 26–30 percent who passively withdrew from the situation.
51. Ibid.

black shirt, black cowboy boots and cowboy hat, and a long black trench coat his mother had bought him. He strapped on a holster with two handguns, western style, and slung eighty rounds of ammunition across his body. Through a hole cut in the pocket of his coat, he carried his father's rifle. Barry then walked a mile and a half to Frontier Junior High School in Moses Lake Washington. He headed for his algebra class, entered, aimed his rifle at Manuel Vela Jr., and fired.[52]

Barry shot and killed two others that day. As Klein recounts, at his trial, students testified "that Barry had pledged to kill Manuel," whom he viewed as the primary instigator of the gay bashing he experienced at school.[53] An anonymous blogger, who grew up in Moses Lake, wrote on the tenth anniversary of the shooting,

> [Barry] was a screwed-up kid, to be sure, but not a psychopath. He knew right from wrong. He knew, for example, that bigger kids beating up and humiliating a smaller one is wrong. Barry was assaulted, called names, swirlied, wedgied and (so I've heard) even held down in the school locker room and urinated on. Combined with the troubles he had at home, he simply reached a point where he couldn't take any more, and he snapped in a huge way.[54]

The question raised by this anonymous blogger is the role of the larger community in bullying violence. Barry was sentenced to life in prison without the opportunity for parole. While some in town felt that his sentence offered a sense of "closure," in reality, little was done to address the role of bystander complicity in the bullying Barry endured.

Bullying tends to be portrayed as an act of interpersonal violence that occurs between individuals. Yet, it is difficult to analyze bullying without examining the ways in which social constructions of

---

52. As recounted by Jessie Klein in *Bully Society*, 81.
53. Ibid.
54. Anonymous Blogger, "Groundhogs, Bullies, and Lawyers: Part One," http://ontheotherfoot.blogspot.com/search?q=bullies lawyers. Quoted by Klein in *Bully Society*, 82.

masculinity disguise and hide violence. As Klein argues, "masculinity expectations in the form of heterosexism [continue to be] a crucial but under examined motivation for school shootings and school violence generally."[55] While gender norms may be more relaxed today, gay bashing continues to be one of the "most prevalent and devastating forms of school bullying."[56]

Gay bashing, as the term is used here, "includes abuse against people who identify themselves as gay; it can also involve any abuse that is based upon its victims' perceived lack of hypermasculine qualities."[57] Gay bashing is commonplace in American schools. As documented by national surveys conducted by the Gay, Lesbian and Straight Education Network (GLSEN) in 2011 and again in 2012, over 70 percent of students indicated that they heard homophobic slurs "often" or "frequently" in school.[58] The association between bullying and gay bashing is so strong that a number of Christian fundamentalist groups have refused to participate in anti-bullying programs for fear of promoting a "gay agenda."[59] In October 2012, schools around the country withdrew their participation in Mix It Up at Lunch Day due to pressure from the American Family Association, a Christian fundamentalist lobbying group. The program, initiated by the Southern Poverty Law Center in an effort to break up school cliques, encourages children to hang out with someone with whom they might not normally speak.[60] Mix It Up at Lunch Day does not explicitly address gender identity or sexual orientation. Yet the response of parents, fueled by fear of difference instead of factual

55. Klein, *Bully Society*, 82.
56. Ibid.
57. Ibid.
58. Koswic et al., "2011 School Climate Survey." It is worth noting that these numbers are down by approximately 10 percent since 2005.
59. Kim Severson, "Christian Group Finds Gay Agenda in Anti-Bullying Day," October 15, 2011, *New York Times*, A-15.
60. Ibid.

information, led to the program's cancellation. Such a response not only teaches children to fear difference, but suggests that they are entitled to do so. In this case, parents modeled blind obedience and mindless conformity, instead of informed decision making.

Gay bashing attests to the prevalence of homophobia as well as the ways in which heteropatriarchy continues to define human relationality within Western Christian contexts. As Klein contends, gay bashing is symptomatic of the acceptance of heteropatriarchy, wherein power and authority are often demonstrated by the dominance and denigration of that which is not masculine.[61] As Mary Hunt explains, "patriarchy expresses itself as sexism" and refers to ways in which the "entire social fabric is so imbued with the normativity of male experience that female experience is excluded."[62] In patriarchal contexts "schools, churches, businesses, governments, etc., are arranged according to male principles of competition, aggression, and production to the extent the female characteristics of cooperation, agreeability, and process are negated."[63] Power is understood to be unilateral, meaning it cannot be shared. Only one person can make it to the top. There is no value in second place. In heterosexist cultures, "normative value is given to heterosexual experience to the extent that legal and acceptable expression of homosexual experience is excluded."[64] The term *heteropatriarchal* points to the ways in which patriarchy and heterosexism are linked. Maleness is often performed in relation to femaleness, and this relationship is marked by male dominance of that which is feminine. Common examples would include locker room talk, whereby

61. Klein, *Bully Society*, 82–83.
62. Mary E. Hunt, "Lovingly Lesbian: Toward a Feminist Theology of Friendship," in *Sexuality and the Sacred: Sources for Theological Reflection*, 2nd ed., ed. Marvin M. Ellison and Kelly Brown Douglas (Louisville: WJK, 2010), 183.
63. Ibid.
64. Ibid.

manliness is demonstrated through a flamboyant heterosexuality (i.e., bragging about—or making up—sexual exploits, trash talking women, etc.). To be clear, as Hunt points out, the use of the terms *heterosexism* and *patriarchy* do not include the claim that there is something intrinsically wrong with heterosexual or male experience.[65] Rather, at issue is the ways in which these two realities have been used to define what it means to be human so as to discredit and exclude other ways of expressing one's gender or sexual identity.[66]

In US culture, hegemonic masculinity also intersects with class, race, ability, and ethnicity. For many young men, climbing the social ladder is often directly correlated with one's perceived ability to conform to hegemonic definitions of masculinity. Those who lack the body capital or social means to achieve "top dog" status feel pressure to find alternative ways to "achieve the power, income and influence expected of them."[67] As Klein argues, "Masculinity is effectively diminished to the extent that it is associated with anything other than being wealthy, white, heterosexual, and traditionally able-bodied."[68] Those who deviate from the dominant norm are forced to find alternative ways to publically prove their masculinity or else be belittled and degraded on a daily basis. Gay bashing offers one such mechanism for doing so. Uttering homophobic slurs and, in some cases, simulating rape affords the opportunity to publicly distance oneself from a homosexual orientation, while simultaneously demonstrating dominance over that which is considered feminine.[69]

---

65. Ibid.
66. Ibid., 184.
67. Klein, *Bully Society*, 52.
68. Ibid. Also see Jewelle Taylor Gibbs and Joseph R. Merighi, "Young Black Males: Marginality, Masculinity, and Criminality," in *Just Boys Doing Business? Men, Masculinities, and Crime*, ed. Tim Newburn and Elizabeth A. Stanko (New York: Routledge, 1994), 64–80.
69. Klein, *Bully Society*, 89. As Connell notes, there is a long history of linking gayness with femininity. See *Masculinities*, 78.

Moreover, as recounted by a male student Klein interviewed, girls also participated in gay bashing: "They would pretend that they liked me. But if I asked them out, they would say 'Hell no, get away from me, loser.'"[70]

Gay bashing does a great deal of emotional and physical harm to individuals and communities. Not only does the prevalence of gay bashing illustrate that it is still unsafe for LGBTQ persons to come out, but it is also a mechanism of social control, of gender policing. Bullying is an expression of the use of power in the form of dominance that functions to support social structures of privilege by sending a message about who stands on the inside and outside of the dominant group. For example, in the case of Barry Loukaitis or, even more recently, Tyler Clementi, the individuals were targeted because their behavior or appearance visibly contested reigning notions of heteronormativity and masculinity. Clearly, the bullying to which these individuals were subjected crushed their personal sense of dignity and worth; yet it also sent a message about the appropriate expression of gender identity and sexuality to the larger community.

Gay bashing must be understood as a collective phenomenon, dependent upon the passive complicity of onlookers. While our impetus may be to blame gay bashing on the actions of a hateful few, this is an inadequate explanation of what happens to victim-survivors and perpetrators because it fails to take serious account of the social construction of reality and the silent complicity of the larger community. Blaming the few bypasses the significance of collective behavior in upholding heterosexism. There were few Twitter posts contesting LGBTQ bullying at Rutgers prior to Clementi's death, and the school administration did not intervene to prevent the harassment of Loukaitis. While there can be legitimate

70. Klein, *Bully Society*, 94.

reasons for maintaining silence in violent contexts, the only way to put a stop to bullying is to change the culture in which such behavior flourishes. With respect to gay bashing, this means countering deeply seated heterosexism and gender bias. Moreover, given the links between gay bashing and violence, it is critical to name participation within these systems as sinful.

Slut Shaming and Violence against Women

On January 14, 2010, Phoebe Prince, a high school freshman in South Hadley, Massachusetts, committed suicide. As a new student, Phoebe drew the fury of a group of popular girls by dating a senior football player.[71] Court documents reveal a pattern of abusive taunts and threats, including "Irish slut" and "whore," on Twitter, Craigslist, and Facebook in the months preceding her death. While a closer analysis paints a much more complicated picture of Phoebe Prince's suicide, it doesn't change the fact that she was victim of slut shaming, also referred to as slut bashing.

Hegemonic masculinity is also performed through a misogynist and homophobic denigration of the feminine.[72] Compelled to demonstrate what Klein terms *flamboyant heterosexuality*, young men across college campuses can be heard "talking about their sexual exploits with girls, publicly commenting on girls [and women's] bodies" in an effort to "[differentiate] themselves from [those] who appear less conventionally masculine."[73] In other words, in environments where there is gay bashing, one also often finds slut bashing.

---

71. Helen Kennedy, "Phoebe Prince, South Hadley High's 'New Girl,' Driven to Suicide by Teenage Cyberbullies," *Daily News*, March 2010, 29, http://www.nydailynews.com/news/national/2010/03/29/2010-03-29_phoebe_prince_south_hadley_high_schools_new_girl_driven_to_suicide_by_teenage_cy.html#ixzz1CuSR5vNO.
72. Connell, *Masculinities*, 83.
73. Klein, *Bully Society*, 53.

Slut bashing or *slut shaming* is a form of sexual harassment that functions to humiliate and stigmatize the female in question. While slut shaming is a "classic illustration of the double-standard" for men and women in American society, it doesn't always have to do with sex.[74] As Leora Tanenbaum illustrates in *Slut! Growing Up Female with a Bad Reputation*, "Very often the label is a stand-in for something else: the extent to which a girl fails to conform to the idea of 'normal' appearance and behavior."[75] A girl's sexual status is often a metaphor for how well she fits into American ideals of femininity and beauty. As gay bashing is often directed at boys who don't measure up to standards of masculinity, slut shaming is more common among girls who are overweight or those who refuse to adhere to traditional feminine ideals. Furthermore, as Tanenbaum points out, the term *slut* has strong class associations.[76] To be called a slut is to be perceived as a girl without a future. It is to represent "soiled femininity."[77] It is also worth noting that slut shaming is not just a phenomenon between men and women. Young women also participate in slut shaming. As Klein explains, "Growing up in this climate both boys and girls are encouraged to be tough and independent rather than emotional, supportive and compassionate."[78] Slut shaming is a way for both girls and boys to demonstrate the virtues of hegemonic masculinity. Yet its effect is different for women than for men.

While slut shaming is increasingly commonplace in cyberspace, it is hardly a new phenomenon. Feminist scholars have long pointed to the double standard in place for women's and men's sexual conduct. Women deemed to have had too many sexual partners are

---

74. Leora Tanenbaum, *Slut! Growing Up Female with a Bad Reputation* (New York: Seven Stories, 1999) 13.
75. Ibid., 11.
76. Ibid., 12.
77. Ibid..
78. Klein, *Bully Society*, 105.

stigmatized (sluts, whores) and subject to personal attacks. In contrast, multiple sexual partners form the basis of bragging rights for their male counterparts. Regardless of a person's actual sexual history, repeatedly calling someone a slut "sends the message to all girls, no matter how 'pure' their reputations, that men and boys are free to express themselves sexually, but women and girls are not."[79] In effect, slut shaming is a form of gender policing that is rooted in the heteropatriarchal conviction that women are in need of male control. Fueling these stereotypes are traditional interpretations of the biblical character of Eve.

Within the history of Western Christian thought, Eve has come to signify the prototypical woman in that her "personality traits and behavior were understood to be characteristic of all women and to be instructive of how men should regard and treat women."[80] Normative interpretations of the narrative "featured Eve's derivation from Adam's body—'a sort of second human being'—her leadership in disobedience, and her condemnation to subordination and painful childbearing."[81] This heteropatriarchal interpretation of Genesis 2–3 continues to inform misogynist responses to sexual violence, offering religious justification for victim-blaming tactics with the operative assumption being that women are temptresses, unreliable, and responsible for the downfall of men.[82] As Tanenbaum points out, one of the more famous examples is the media description of Anita Hill as "a bit nutty and a bit slutty."[83] Two decades after Hill's testimony against Clarence Thomas, victim-survivors of sexual violence continue to be shamed into silence. Recently, media coverage

---

79. Ibid., 16.
80. Margaret R. Miles, *Carnal Knowing: Female Nakedness and Religious Meaning in the Christian West* (New York: Random House, 1989), 86.
81. Ibid., 87.
82. Traci C. West, *Wounds of the Spirit: Black Women, Violence, and Resistance Ethics* (New York: New York University Press, 1999), 125.
83. As quoted by Tanenbaum in *Slut!*, 19

surrounding the conviction of two Steubenville high school football players for rape focused exclusively on how the reputations of the young men were forever damaged.[84] The implication is that the young woman and her parents "ruined" the future careers of promising athletes. Religious communities are not immune to participating in such victim-blaming tactics. *Washington Post* columnist Melinda Henneberger pointed to a similar tactic used in sexual assault cases occurring on the University of Notre Dame's campus.[85] Slut shaming continues to play a major role in the dismissal of violence against women. It acts as a public deterrent for victim-survivors in terms of reporting and often follows a girl or woman for years.[86] While feminists have made strides in changing attitudes about women, in many cases, men continue to be rewarded (or at least not penalized) for sexual harassment.

The case of Phoebe Prince is more complicated than what meets the eye. While Prince's suicide can be linked to slut shaming, as Emily Bazelon, editor of *Slate* magazine, reports, Phoebe also had a history of illegal drug use and mental illness.[87] Bullying can exacerbate depression and other forms of mental illness. Bazelon characterizes Phoebe as "a troubled young woman trying to cope with depression and trying, like all teenage girls do, to fit in."[88]

---

84. See Meghan Clark," F*&k Patriarchy: What about the "Promising Future" of Rape Victims?," http://catholicmoraltheology.com/fk-patriarchy-what-about-the-promising-future-of-rape-victims/.

85. Melinda Henneberger, "Reported Sexual Assault at Notre Dame Campus Leaves More Questions than Answers," *National Catholic Reporter*, March 26, 2012, http://ncronline.org/news/accountability/reported-sexual-assault-notre-dame-campus-leaves-more-questions-answers. Also see Kat Stoeffell, "Notre Dame Finds Fake Dead Woman Easier to Talk about than Real Dead Woman," *NY Magazine*, http://nymag.com/thecut/2013/01/fake-woman-easier-to-talk-about-than-dead-woman.html.

86. According to statistics found on the Rape, Abuse, Incest National Network (RAINN), 54 percent of rape/sexual assaults are never reported to the police. For more information, http://www.rainn.org/get-information/legal-information.

87. Emily Bazelon, *Sticks and Stones: Defeating the Culture of Bullying and Rediscovering the Power of Character and Empathy* (New York: Random House, 2013), 90.

88. Ibid., 95.

Crossing one of the most popular girls in school was enough to turn the tide and to make it impossible for her to fit in.

> Phoebe wasn't entirely passive and she also wasn't *merely* a victim. She was a person who had social power on some days and none others, and who seems to have suffered from a terrible mental illness that left her especially vulnerable. It's complicated, and if we really want to understand what happened to her, and to really unpack bullying more generally, we need to make room for a more complicated set of dynamics.[89]

Bazelon is right: bullying is much more complicated than an altercation between an innocent victim and a guilty perpetrator. We tend to view bullying, and violence more generally, as black and white realities wherein one party is completely innocent and the other does all the harm. Not only does this fail to reflect the complex ways in which power is enacted, but it also creates a dynamic wherein undue attention is given to punitive justice. The conversation surrounding the charges that were filed by the district attorney against the so-called "Mean Six" at South Hadley High School is illustrative of this phenomenon. South Hadley's "Mean Six" sought to "punish" Phoebe by bullying her for transgressing social laws. In the wake of her death, the district attorney zeroed in on six students at South Hadley and pursued criminal charges.[90] While individuals and communities must be held accountable for their actions, the pursuit of criminal charges has done little to remedy the problem of bullying violence. In the aftermath of Phoebe's death, students and adults report that not much has changed. Many continue to view bullying a normal part of life.[91]

89. Ibid., 175–76.
90. Ibid., 177–90.
91. Ibid.

Analysis

Bullying is violence, yet it is not often recognized as such. This is partly a reflection of the increasingly anonymous nature of bullying behavior (for example, cyberbullying), but it is also tied to the narrow definition of violence operative in society at large. As Robert McAfee Brown points out in *Religion and Violence*, the word *violence* often invokes a mental picture of "*overt physical acts of destruction*: someone is roughed up, pushed around, hit, stabbed, raped, or in some way made the object of physical abuse."[92] While this definition has the advantage of making "instances of violence tangible and clear-cut,"[93] it fails to account for the full spectrum of ways that we are capable of harming one another. As the examples discussed in this chapter illustrate, not all violence involves overt physical assault. In the case of Phoebe Prince, violence can be psychologically destructive, creating and compounding emotional distress and mental illness. Covert violence can also become institutionalized, wherein the structures of society function so to "violate the personhood of society's members," treating them as objects rather than subjects.[94] In this chapter, we have discussed the ways in which heterosexism and patriarchy fuels gay bashing and slut shaming as well as the tactic acceptance of violence. For example, this happens when bullying is dismissed on the grounds that "boys will be boys."

Violence is that which violates personhood; it is that which denies the full humanity of another.[95] Violence transforms a person into a thing. Violence includes unethical passivity. Cheryl Kirk-Duggan explains, "Ignoring the rights of another person, desensitizing oneself by observing more violent acts, and the rationalization and

92. Robert McAfee Brown, *Religion and Violence*, 2nd ed. (Philadelphia: Westminster, 1987), 6.
93. Ibid.
94. Ibid., 9.
95. Ibid., 8.

justification of personal or systemic use of damaging thoughts, words, and deeds is violent activity. Some violence manifests as one intimidating others for the purpose of domination."[96] While bullying can span the gamut in terms of intensity, when institutionalized and coded in cultural mores and prejudices this abuse of power can become so subtle that is difficult to detect our own complicity in it. The violence incurred through bullying not only violates the personhood of those targeted, but it also "places everyone and everything in a survival mode."[97] Bullying lends toward and flourishes within cultures of relatedness that are shaped by fear and the use of power as domination. While this does not excuse the behavior of those who perpetrate such violence, it does point to the necessity of making a shift in the ways that we view power, privilege, and difference within sacred and secular spheres.

Bullying is a learned behavior that must be evaluated within a particular social context. To use an often-quoted feminist phrase, the personal is political. Interpersonal interactions cannot be separated from cultural mores and prejudices. Men are not intrinsically hardwired for aggression. Rather, the association between masculinity and violence is a learned behavior that is condoned by a culture that continues to grant sports heroes who have committed felonies multimillion dollar contracts, and whose military overlooked the sexual humiliation of prisoners of war.[98] In a parallel fashion, slut shaming must be understood in view of stereotypes that portray women as liars, temptresses, and the weaker sex. Slut shaming and gay bashing are related to larger societal issues: heterosexism,

---

96. Cheryl A. Kirk-Duggan, *Misbegotten Anguish: A Theology and Ethics of Violence* (St. Louis: Chalice, 2001), 21.

97. Ibid., 16.

98. For example, consider the sexual humiliation of prisoners at Abu Ghraib. Or, allegations of rape against Pittsburgh Steeler Ben Roethlisberger, wherein the victim-survivor, despite evidence, decided not to pursue criminal charges due to media pressure in 2010. For details of the incident visit, http://www.cnn.com/2010/CRIME/04/16/roethlisberger.incident/.

homophobia, and patriarchy. Gay bashing and slut shaming reveal that gender-based violence remains endemic to Western culture despite increased public tolerance of same-sex behavior. These forms of violence often remain invisible because of cultural conditioning predicated upon the normalcy of structural and social inequities that are protected by silence and passivity.

There are very few situations in which the human person is completely powerless, devoid of all agency. On the one hand, by definition, "conditions of oppression and violence seek to disempower those on the underside of social and personal power dynamics, resulting in an actual loss of power. The diminishment of our power in such situations is unavoidable to some degree."[99] Yet, as Kathleen Greider argues, even in situations marked by radical inequality, we have to be careful not to further compound oppression and violence by unnecessarily abandoning the resources we have for resistance.[100] This is not to suggest that victim-survivors are responsible for the damage done to them. Indeed, the conversation about power, violence, and passivity would look very different from the vantage point of victim-survivors of trauma.[101] Yet, from the perspective of a bystander, an analysis of unethical passivity, or what I will also term apathy, is critical. To be clear, in using the terms *unethical passivity* or *passive bystanding*, I am speaking of situations wherein passivity "does not affirm life in any way" and is "a failure to honor the *imago dei* in humanity."[102] This being said, there are instances in which relinquishing one's power can be life-affirming (for example, for the purpose of safety). I am not speaking of these

---

99. Kathleen J. Greider, *Reckoning with Aggression: Theology, Violence, and Vitality* (Louisville: WJK, 1997), 63.

100. Ibid., 64.

101. For examples, see Jennifer Beste's *God and the Victim: Traumatic Intrusions on Grace and Freedom* (New York: Oxford University Press, 2007) and Serene Jones, *Trauma and Grace: Theology in a Ruptured World* (Louisville: WJK, 2009).

102. Greider, *Reckoning with Aggression*, 63.

situations in this book. Rather, my aim is to critically examine the ways in which conflict-avoidant behavior and indifference to suffering participate in the maintenance of hegemonic forms of violence. As I will argue in the next chapter, passive bystanding is learned behavior that must be contextualized in view of the valuation of innocence purported through systems of social privilege and religious ideation surrounding divine perfection that suggests only God is good enough, powerful enough, and wise enough to offer the remedy. Such narratives reinforce the bystander phenomenon, suggesting that someone else will take care of the problem. This is a crucial concept for bystanders to violence that must be explicitly examined in view of the ways in which unethical passivity is compounded by social privilege.

A theology of redemption that acknowledges human complicity in sin and, at the same time, bespeaks of the power of human agency to cooperate with God in the transformation of the world is sorely needed. This is especially pertinent given the increasingly covert forms violence takes today. This is true in the context of interpersonal violence discussed in this chapter—gay bashing and slut shaming—and its connection to structural forms of violence. It is also the case for our own participation in structural forms of violence at the national and international levels. Unethical passivity in the face of coercive forms of power marks race and socioeconomic relations in the United States. Social privilege continues to render sins of omission invisible, even to well-intentioned individuals and communities. We have become so accustomed to obeying hegemonic ideals that we are trapped in them and are unable to recognize the crosses in our midst. We need the theological tools to start talking about the socialization of difference and the indifference to violent dehumanization that is precipitated by such socialization.

Unethical passivity is compounded by the invisibility of violence. The ability to name one's own position with respect to power and privilege is a critical first step in redemption. The ways we name the divine shapes praxis (action) and vision (what we imagine to be possible), individually and communally. On the one hand, traditional notions of sin and grace have stunted human agency in view of the problem of bystander passivity and the social construction of violence. Scholars from a cross section of theological disciplines have argued that individualized notions of sin play a role in obfuscating systemic violence and evil.[103] On the other hand, Christian tradition has inspired prophetic and courageous witnessing. Black liberation, feminist, and womanist theologies have emphasized the importance of human action, foregrounding the liberative aspects of Jesus' mission and identity—caring for the poor, inviting the marginalized to the table, and calling into question structures that are oppressive.[104] The legacies of Oscar Romero, Fannie Lou Hamer, Martin Luther King Jr., and Dorothy Day all proclaim that to be a Christian is to act with courage and conviction; it is to challenge the will to power, to engage in this worldly practice of empowering the least among us. Passive bystanders must uncover and take responsibility for the myths (religious and secular) that have enabled them to live deceitfully.

Conclusion

As the examples discussed in this chapter illustrate, sin and grace cannot always be easily parsed within lived experience. It is no accident that the weapon used by Adam Lanza in the December 2012 Newton, Connecticut shootings continues to be marketed with

---

103. For examples, see chapter 3.
104. For an overview of liberation theologies in North America, see Miguel A. De La Torre, ed. *Handbook of Theologies of Liberation* (St. Louis: Chalice, 2004). Early pioneers in the area of Christology include the work of Jon Sobrino, James Cone, Rosemary Radford Ruether, and Delores Williams.

the phrase "Consider your man card reissued."[105] Social expectations to prove one's manhood in the face of constant emasculating degradation is so strong that, in many cases, perpetrators of school violence like Barry Loukaitis, Eric Harris, or Dylan Klebold feel they have no other options.[106] As a student of mine once put it, we don't teach men how to be masculine, we teach them how not to become feminine or gay. It is tempting to point the finger at one individual or group. Yet it is rarely the case that the lines between good and evil are drawn so starkly. Gay bashing and slut shaming cannot be chalked up to the actions of a hateful few. Rather, these phenomena must be understood in view of the cultural systems that reward obedience to authority, competitiveness, indifference to suffering, and punish difference, compassion, and vulnerability. Such a framework fails to recognize our interdependence, purporting a false sense of innocence.

False narratives of innocence need to be challenged. As the author of Genesis 3 contends, there is no return to paradise. Perhaps the fundamental sin can be traced to our propensity to hide our vulnerability—from God and from one another.[107]

> But the Lord God called to the man, and said to him, "Where are you?" He said, "I heard the sound of you in the garden, and I was afraid, because I was naked; and I hid myself." He said, "Who told you that you were naked? Have you eaten from the tree of which I commanded you

---

105. Emma Gray makes this point in "Bushmaster Rifle Ad Reminds Us to Ask More about Masculinity and Gun Violence," *Huffington Post*, http://www.huffingtonpost.com/emma-gray/bushmaster-rifle-ad-masculinity-gun-violence-newtown-adam-lanza_b_2317924.html

106. Erick Harris and Dylan Klebold shot and killed twelve students and one teacher, and injured twenty-four students, on April 20, 1999 at Columbine High School in Columbine, CO. This incident is credited with drawing attention to the problem of school violence in the twentieth century in the United States.

107. In particular, I am talking about the hiding involved in indifference to suffering and escapism from social responsibility. The pressure to hide one's sexual orientation or racial identity would require a different analysis than what is offered here. For one such an analysis, see Cheng, *From Sin to Amazing Grace*, 84–89.

not to eat?" The man said, "The woman whom you gave to be with me, she gave me fruit from the tree, and I ate." (Gen. 3:9-12)

To confess the sin of hiding is to risk revealing oneself to the world. It is to stand exposed in your own insecurities and self-doubt. It is to occupy a place of vulnerability, of acknowledging weakness.[108] This is threatening on multiple fronts. Ours is a culture that does not look kindly on the public display of weakness. In punitive fashion, we tend to prey upon those who display vulnerability, seizing it as an opportunity for personal advancement. To confess the sin of hiding is risky on an internal level, for, while we have been escaping from ourselves, we haven't really learned to cope with our own shortcomings, talents, or desires.[109] It is much easier to immerse ourselves in the problems of others than to deal with our own. Yet, without doing so, we all lose.

Passive bystanding signifies a loss of relationality that extends far beyond issues of personal self-esteem. It marks our collective failure to engage in compassion, to suffer with those who are marginalized, dehumanized, and humiliated by interpersonal and systemic forms of violence. Passive bystanding points to ways in which we continue to engage in escapism—from our pain and the pain of others. This has profound theological consequences, especially for Christians. For at the very heart of the Christian narrative of redemption lies the violent crucifixion of Jesus of Nazareth. To be a Christian disciple, to claim this particular identity as one's own, is to reckon with violence and the suffering it causes. It involves finding a way to continue to witness to the healing work of Jesus in the midst of suffering and tragedy.[110] I do not suggest that we adopt a theology that glorifies

---

108. Nelson, "Sin of Hiding,"324.
109. Ibid., 325.
110. Rita Nakashima Brock makes a similar point in *Journeys by Heart: A Christology of Erotic Power* (New York: Crossroad, 1989), 100.

self-sacrificial suffering. Rather, we must find new ways of sitting with pain, of embracing vulnerability, if we are going to participate in the healing of the world. Such a task is fraught with a great deal of difficulty in the modern world given the ways in which violence, and the suffering it causes, remains invisible to those who occupy locations of social privilege.

2

Bypassing Redemption: White Racial Privilege and Christian Apathy

"America has a high tolerance for black suffering."[1] These words, uttered by Rev. Jesse Jackson in the aftermath of Hurricane Katrina, point to the problem of white racial indifference. In Katrina's wake, nonwhites were abandoned without electricity, food, or health care by public officials while the city's white residents were evacuated. As the country watched this death-dealing racial disparity unfold from the comfort of our homes (on television), few whites questioned it. While Katrina is but one example of racial injustice out of many, the question for white people becomes, in the context of racial injustice, on whose "side" are you? In other words, the distance between the egregious inaction of public officials in New Orleans and white Christians (like myself) who did little more than "feel sorry for those who were stranded" is not as far as most of us would like to believe. This is because both forms of unethical passivity, which I will also call privileged apathy, are tied to white racial privilege.

---

1. As quoted by Bryan N. Massingale in *Racial Justice and the Catholic Church* (Maryknoll, NY: Orbis, 2010), 32.

Permission to ignore persons and communities that occupy nondominant social sites is endemic to American culture and manifest through various forms of social privilege (e.g. racial, heterosexual, gender, economic, ethnic, and class). This chapter will take a closer look at white racial privilege and its role in the perpetuation of white racism in the United States. From socioeconomic policy to interpersonal relationships, we live in a world where events and relationships continue to be governed by the dynamic of whiteness. The premium placed on whiteness engenders a false sense of entitlement in white people while dehumanizing persons of color. In the United States, "'White' denotes a frame of reference that is *unquestioned*. It is unquestioned because it is *invisible* and *unnamed*. It is unquestioned and invisible because it is the *norm* by and against which all other frames of reference (that is, cultures) are measured."[2] The unquestioned and invisible nature of whiteness has pushed it to the edges of consciousness for many white people. For most white people, whiteness is perceived as "normal." Such a racial frame erroneously leads white people to ignore their own complicity in racial injustice. The white response to white racism can largely be characterized by dismissal, disregard, and outright denial of black suffering—in a word: apathy. As Dorothee Sölle has suggested, "the toleration of exploitation, oppression, and injustice points to a condition lying like a pall over the whole of society: it is apathy, an unconcern that is incapable of suffering."[3]

Privileged Apathy as a Form of Passive Bystanding

Apatheia is a Greek word whose root means nonsuffering. Those inflicted with the social condition of apathy do not "want to be

---

2. Massingale, *Racial Justice*, 22. Italics original.
3. Dorothee Sölle, *Suffering*, trans. Everett R. Kalin (Philadelphia: Fortress Press, 1975), 36.

touched, infected, defiled, drawn in."[4] In other words, we want to keep our distance from those who suffer. As Sölle suggests, this form of consciousness "bears the imprint of the middle-class."[5] In more contemporary language, one could say that apathy is prevalent among the systemically privileged. To be clear, I do not suggest that privileged people and privileged nations do not suffer. Rather, at issue is our approach to suffering. We not only lack awareness of our "own suffering and sensitivity for the suffering of others," but suffering does not move us.[6] It becomes something to tolerate, "to put up with."[7] Static suffering, or suffering that does not move us, is dangerous. It is the fuel for oppression. This happens as apathy isolates and blinds human beings.

Apathy isolates human beings, particularly in environs marked by the use of unilateral power. "Unilateral power is grounded in competing claims for power, in either/or choices and in the assumption that when someone gains power another has less."[8] Unilateral power inculcates competitiveness and rampant individualism. People are out for themselves. Actions tend to be fear driven (we fear being judged, of losing what we have, of being singled out), and success is marked by the absence of suffering. Such a worldview participates in the objectification of others. People are valued according to whether they enhance our claim to power or function as obstacles to it.

Apathy blinds human beings, muting their capacity to perceive reality.[9] Desensitized to *patheos*, "the person and his circumstance are accepted as natural, which even on the technological level signifies

---

4. Ibid., 39–40.
5. Ibid., 36.
6. Ibid., 37.
7. Ibid.
8. Rita Nakashima Brock, *Journeys by Heart: Christology of Erotic Power* (New York: Crossroad, 1989), 28.
9. Sölle, *Suffering*, 39.

nothing but blind worship of the status quo: no disruptions, no involvement, no sweat."[10] Such blindness, lack of passion, is often the predisposition of the privileged.[11] Only from the standpoint of satiation can one maintain the masquerade of indifference and say, "I wasn't there. I don't know. It's not my problem." Suffering is an unavoidable part of life that only defeats us when we try to avoid it. "Our pain defeats us, and we fear it . . . because we regard it as inevitable disaster falling upon us from *outside* us. As long as we try to escape it, we cannot resolve it."[12] Suppressing pain does not and cannot lead to its transformation. Pain can only be transformed when we are willing to face it.

Furthermore, this unwillingness "to bear passion" in "an active sense of power in relation" is culpable.[13] As Shawn Copeland argues, "Not difference, but indifference, egotism, and selfishness are the obstacles to solidarity."[14] In specific, Copeland is referring to the silent indifference of those who occupy social sites of dominance in society when faced with the suffering of those who are marginalized. Such silence "can be understood comprehensively as failures in authentic religious, intellectual, and moral living" and cannot be chalked up to "personal preference" or "accidental ignorance."[15] Rather, unethical passivity on the part of dominant elites bears the mark of arrogance: it is a "more or less conscious decision to refuse corrective insights or understandings, to persist in error."[16] Apathy reflects an interest in

---

10. Ibid.

11. Ibid., 40.

12. Ibid., 44. Here Sölle is citing Kazoh Kitamori, *Theology and the Pain of God* (Richmond, VA: John Knox, 1965), 80.

13. Carter Heyward, *Our Passion for Justice: Images of Power, Sexuality, and Liberation* (New York: Pilgrim, 1984), 206.

14. M. Shawn Copeland, "Toward a Critical Christian Feminist Theology of Solidarity," in *Women & Theology*, ed. Mary Ann Hinsdale and Phyllis H. Kaminski, Annual Publication of the College Theology Society 40 (Maryknoll, NY: Orbis, 1994), 24.

15. Ibid. In particular, Copeland is referring to Bernard Lonergan's notion of authenticity vs. *scotosis*.

16. Copeland, "Toward a Critical Christian," 24.

one's own triumph over the flourishing of the whole. In this sense, privileged apathy is a form of passive bystanding.

Unethical passivity is learned behavior that must be contextualized in view of the valuation of innocence and the silence surrounding such valuation purported through systems of privilege and religious ideation regarding divine suffering. In this chapter, I attend to the ways in which unethical passivity (apathy) is manifested by whites in the form of systemic unknowing, permission to escape, and ineffective guilt. I argue that white apathy is further compounded by interpretive tendencies within the classical Christian atonement tradition. In particular, the alignment of divinity with maleness, rationality, and whiteness not only functions to reinforce patterns of white dominance within contemporary American contexts, but also makes it difficult to love living bodies. In the classical Christian tradition, Jesus' body is only redemptive when it is dead, lifeless, passive, and submissive. In view of white indifference to black suffering, God-talk emphasizing "pain incurred through dispassionate invulnerability to relation"[17] further inculcates apathy within the white Christian moral imaginary as it offers religious justification for sacrificial scapegoating, a form of victim-blaming. Victim-blaming tactics create confusion about who is responsible for violence and are used by perpetrators and bystanders in order to minimize the consequences of their actions and to "preserve their sense of themselves as good."[18] In short, classical Christian atonement theory works to maintain false notions of white moral innocence.

17. Carter Heyward, *The Redemption of God: A Theology of Mutual Relation* (Washington, DC: University Press of America, 1982), 54.
18. Pamela Cooper-White, *The Cry of Tamar: Violence against Women and the Church's Response*, 2nd ed. (Minneapolis: Fortress Press, 2012), 18.

White Racism as Culturally Entrenched

Scholarship in whiteness studies and critical race theory illustrates that racism is culturally entrenched and transmitted through "tacit understandings" or unconscious socialization. Drawing upon the work of legal scholar Charles R. Lawrence, Bryan Massingale explains,

> Culture—including, for example, the media and an individual's parents, peers and authority figures, transmits certain beliefs and preferences. Because these beliefs are so much a part of the culture they are not experienced as explicit lessons. Instead, they seem part of the individual's rational ordering of her perceptions of the world. The individual is unaware, for example, that the ubiquitous presence of a cultural stereotype has influenced her perception that blacks are lazy or unintelligent [or more prone to violence]. . . . Even if a child is not told that blacks are inferior, he learns that lesson by observing the behavior of others.[19]

As culture shapes one's consciousness, conditioning the ways in which we perceive the world—our thoughts, values, and actions—so, too, does racism shape action and belief. Moreover, as white people rarely articulate or question these actions and beliefs, they often go undetected.[20] Contrary to popular belief, most white racism does not result from deliberate or blatant bigotry.[21] Rather, white racism appears in the form of unconscious bias, wherein white people rely

---

19. Massingale, *Racial Justice*, 27–28.
20. By using the term *white*, I am not referring to a "race" or skin color alone. Rather, I follow Bryan N. Massingale's definitions here. For Massingale, the term *white* signifies "the dominant cultural group in our country" (*Racial Justice*, 2). It refers to those who have "access to political, social, economic, or cultural advantages that people of color do not share" (ibid). This is because whiteness has been a fluid category through US history. The terms *people of color* or *nonwhites* are used to refer to those who do not share political, social, economic, or cultural advantage (ibid, 3).
21. Ibid., 13. Massingale refers to this as "commonsense" understanding of racism, which he describes as follows: "Person A (usually, but not always, white) consciously, deliberately, and intentionally does something negative to Person B (usually, but not always, black or Latino) because of the color of his or her skin."

upon latent racial bias (i.e., the association of dark skin color with criminality or laziness) in interpreting situations. Unconscious racial bias has the practical effect of generating "racially selective sympathy and indifference," which makes it easier to ignore certain lives and to attend to others, underscoring "a great deal of society's neglect of poor persons of color."[22]

As illustrated in Massingale's analysis of Hurricane Katrina, "the association of blacks with crime and criminality . . . fueled frenzied reports of lawlessness, mayhem, murder, and rape occurring at the Superdome, the Convention Center, and throughout the city."[23] These unverified reports had dire consequences, including the halt of rescue efforts and food drops and racially targeted policing. Unconscious racial bias evoked a climate of fear, which would not have been the case if white people were involved in similar circumstances.[24] Furthermore, racial bias "rendered intelligible" the neglect of poor persons of color. Public officials fled while failing to devise and put into place a comprehensive evacuation plan. White tourists were evacuated, while the city's black and poor residents were left without food, water, sanitation, or access to medical care.[25]

22. Ibid., 32.
23. Ibid., 31.
24. Ibid.
25. Ibid., 32.

Unethical Passivity within White Supremacy

White racism functions to maintain and justify white privilege.[26] Structural oppression disadvantages persons of color, women, the elderly, LGBTQ persons, and the differently abled, and it confers "status, profit, and other benefits" on the dominant group.[27] Oppression and dominance represent two sides of the same coin. Where one finds systemic oppression, such as culturally entrenched white racism, one also finds social advantage, or white privilege. Moreover, as Barbara Applebaum maintains, "Through practices of whiteness and by benefiting from white privilege, [white people] contribute to the maintenance of systemic racial injustice."[28] Similar to culturally entrenched white racism, white privilege is a systemic reality that confers unearned advantages and benefits to all white persons. As persons of color cannot step outside of white racism in the United States, whites cannot step outside of white privilege. In particular, white privilege confers upon white people the permission to escape—that is, to ignore race and nonwhite bodies in giving an account of history, in the making of social policy, and even, in naming the divine. White privilege has granted white people the permission to remain silent about black suffering and black triumph.[29]

26. As Jennifer Harvey, Karin A. Case, and Robin Hawley Gorsline suggest, white supremacy is helpful in naming the "integrated system of individual, institutional, societal and civilizational racism in which whiteness . . . is seen as normative and superior" (22). See "Introduction," in *Disrupting White Supremacy from Within: White People on What We Need to Do*, ed. Jennifer Harvey, Karin A. Case, and Robin Hawley Gorsline (Cleveland, OH: Pilgrim, 2004), 22. I use the terms *white privilege* and *racism* to refer to these realities, respectively. It is also important to note that a great deal of this analysis of white privilege is indebted to Barbara Applebaum's *Being White, Being Good: White Complicity, White Moral Responsibility, and Social Justice Pedagogy* (Lanham, MD: Lexington, 2011).

27. Mary Elizabeth Hobgood, *Dismantling Privilege: An Ethics of Accountability,* rev. and updated ed. (Cleveland: Pilgrim, 2009), 18.

28. Applebaum, *Being White,* 3.

29. Jon Nilson, *Hearing Past the Pain: Why White Catholic Theologians Need Black Theology* (Mahwah, NY: Paulist, 2007), 6.

To be white is to be unquestioned. To be white is to be presumed innocent, credible, and good. This is because whiteness is the norm through which things are interpreted. For example, as a white person, I can walk around campus off-hours dressed in shorts and T-shirt without anyone questioning whether "I am in the right place." I can go shopping without being followed by the watchful eye of sales associates or store security. I can purchase a home without wondering whether I will be welcome in the neighborhood. While most of the things that I have listed are things we would expect for everyone, they are what Peggy McIntosh calls unearned advantages.[30] Social privilege can also take the form of conferred dominance. Conferred dominance can be displayed as physical intimidation or aggression, yet most often manifests in a sense of entitlement that grants systemically privileged people the permission to ignore certain lives, certain types of violence, without ever questioning the status quo. The refusal of systemically privileged students to acknowledge the existence of systemic oppression itself illustrates this phenomenon. For example, in giving a presentation on racism to students in a course on multiculturalism, critical race philosopher George Yancy recounted an experience of racial profiling. Immediately after sharing the experience with the class, a white student declared that his story was "Bullshit!" In reflecting upon this teaching experience, Yancy explains that the white student's response erased his credibility and "functioned as a form of erasure of the experiences of Black men" who have experienced similar situations,[31] while maintaining a sense of her own moral innocence and goodness. That is, the white student

30. Peggy McIntosh, "White Privilege and Male Privilege: A Personal Account of Coming to See Correspondences through Work in Women's Studies," in *Critical White Studies: Looking Behind the Mirror*, ed. Richard Delgado and Jean Stefancic (Philadelphia: Temple University, 1997): 291–99.
31. George Yancy, *Black Bodies, White Gazes: The Continuing Significance of Race* (Lanham, MD: Rowman & Littlefield, 2008), 228.

was able to maintain control of the situation (as the authentic interpreter of experience), while denying complicity.

White Denial

White denial is a function of white privilege: "The mere fact that [whites] can question the existence of systemic oppression is a function of their privilege to choose to ignore discussions of systemic oppression or not."[32] Moreover, white denials of complicity are an example of conferred dominance because of their potential to render silent the voices of those who are marginalized, making those who have experienced oppression feel as if their own life experiences do not count. In the classroom, this silence is compounded by what Sandra Lee Bartky has described as "the relentlessly white and middle-class cultural style of the university as an institution [that] in effect marginalizes the speech and cultural style of non-white students."[33] Not only are most professors white, but students can graduate without ever having to confront white racism in their studies. White bodies, white minds, and white theorists have welded the power to define history. Being a part of the in-group means you have the power to define which stories are told and which ones are pushed underground.

Systemic Ignorance

In the *Racial Contract*, Charles W. Mills asks the question, "How [are white] people able to consistently do the wrong thing while thinking they [are] doing the right thing?"[34] Mills argues that a covert agreement or set of "meta-agreements" between white people

---

32. Applebaum, *Being White*, 107.
33. Sandra Lee Bartky, "Race, Complicity, and Culpable Ignorance," in *"Sympathy and Solidarity" and Other Essays* (Lanham, MD: Rowman & Littlefield, 2002), 152.
34. Charles W. Mills, *The Racial Contract* (Ithaca, NY: Cornell University, 1997), 94.

functions to secure the privileges of white citizens and the subordination of nonwhites.[35] In most cases, this contract is not overt nor a conspiracy. It is more akin to selective hearing and seeing based upon white socialization. As Mills further explains in an essay entitled "White Ignorance," individuals interpret the world (human interaction, history, culture) "with eyes and ears that have been socialized. Perception is in part also conception, the viewing of the world through a particular conceptual grid."[36] Family members, educators, mentors, and role models shape what we are taught to recognize as being important and to remember and pass on as a part of history. In a society where relations are structured in terms of domination and subordination, this conceptual grid is not neutral, but oriented toward maintaining the interests of the dominant group. Therefore, the conceptual grid through which white people in the United States interpret experience systematically ignores the interests, history, suffering, and questions of people of color.[37] "White ignorance is a type of knowledge that protects systemic racial injustice from challenge."[38] This selective attention is socially sanctioned and rewarded.

White ignorance, a product of white socialization, is culpable. It is complicit in racial injustice in the sense that white ignorance produces a type of knowing that "arrogantly parades as knowledge" itself.[39] It is "a particular way of everyday knowing or thinking that one knows how the social world works that is intimately related to what it means to be white."[40] So, for example, white theology parades as theology proper, with the idea that all knowledge of God, all

---

35. Ibid., 11.
36. Charles W. Mills, "White Ignorance," in *Race Epistemologies of Ignorance*, ed. Shannon Sullivan and Nancy Tuana (Albany: SUNY, 2007), 23–24.
37. As Mills notes, this conceptual grid can also inform the black knowing.
38. Applebaum, *Being White*, 37.
39. Ibid., 39.
40. Ibid.

naming of sin, grace, and evil, (or at least that which counts) can be encapsulated by white (usually male) theologians. The link between arrogance (I already know it all) and deliberate ignorance (I do not need to know anything else) is what makes white ignorance culpable. It is akin to being treated by a medical doctor who, despite having access to the latest research and treatment, has refused to read the material on the grounds that he or she already knows everything about medicine.[41] In this situation, the doctor who failed to apply the latest treatment would be liable for harm done to patients. White knowledge also makes white people more likely to dismiss the knowledge of that which challenges their worldview. In other words, white people have a vested interest in not knowing.[42] Not knowing functions to protect one's moral self-image (e.g., "I am a good, hard working person"), while maintaining the benefits and privileges one accrues. To be clear, "ignorance is not a simple lack, absence or emptiness, and it is not a passive state."[43] Ignorance is self-constructed myopic vision. Through white ignorance, white people fail to pay attention to anything other than white interests.

Returning to the classroom situation described by Yancy, while I am troubled by the white student's adamant denial of racism and white privilege, I am equally if not more troubled by the white students who sat there, eyes turned toward their desks, and said nothing at all. (This behavior is something that I frequently witness in my own classroom when discussing racism and white privilege.) In particular, I am troubled by the ways in which whites appropriate silence as a mechanism for distancing themselves from racism and white privilege and protecting white innocence. Silence is

---

41. This example belongs to Holly Smith, "Culpable Ignorance," *The Philosophical Review* 92 no. 4 (1983): 543–71, and is cited by Applebaum in *Being White*, 134.

42. Applebaum, *Being White*, 40.

43. Marilyn Frye, *Difference and The Politics of Reality: Essays in Feminist Theory* (Freedom, CA: Crossing, 1983), 118. As cited by Applebaum in *Being White*, 41.

performative. It shapes the stories we tell about ourselves, the divine, and others. Silence is also a form of white denial as it functions to create the perception of communal agreement.

Permission to Escape

This concept took on new meaning when I was a graduate student on an international experiential learning trip in Kenya, which brought together four white women from the United States with four Kenyan women scholars of religion.[44] While the experience was marked by "highs" and "lows" for all involved, throughout the entire trip I struggled with profound homesickness that was frustrated by knowledge that I couldn't easily pack up and leave. The problem wasn't simply that I missed the company of my friends and family and the comfort of my own bed. Rather, the issue was that I felt "lost in a land" not my own. I did not know the language or customs, and, as a white person, I stood out like a sore thumb. I could not escape my own whiteness, as whiteness was not the norm. For the first time in my life, I was poignantly aware of the way that whiteness colored everything that I do: from taking public transit to preparing meals. While this experience heightened my awareness of the ways in which "permission to escape"[45] inhabits my day–to–day living, the "homesickness" I experienced in Kenya was privileged in and of itself. For, at the end of the trip, I was going home, back to my own white "utopia." With the phrase *white "utopia"* I am not intending to suggest that America is a better place to live than Kenya. Rather, I am referring to my own desire to leave a geographical space that engendered racial discomfort. In the United States, I do not have to

44. For more on the experience, see Eunice Karanja Kaamara, Elisabeth Vasko, and Jeanine Viau, "Listening & Speaking as Two Sides of the Same Coin: Reflections on Intercultural Feminist Learning," *Journal of Feminist Studies in Religion* 28, no. 2 (2012): 49–67.
45. McIntosh, "White Privilege," 297.

contend with my own racial identity in the same way that I did in Kenya. By and large, I dealt with my "homesickness" through silence.

Silence is a double-sided coin. On the one hand, the silence that informs active listening is crucial to the work of solidarity. We live in a world that expects instant results—something that is often intensified when it comes to dealing with uncomfortable issues like racism, sexism, and imperialism. We want to be able to say "racism . . . we've dealt with that already, so let's move on." Part of the work of active listening involves acknowledging that there are no overnight fixes to structural issues that are deeply entrenched in our society. We need silence in order to be able to sit with this reality. Silence affords us the opportunity to take a step back from the conversation, to take a step back from imposing our own framework on another person's words. In effect, this silence respects the listening and speaking process. Not only does it provide both parties with the opportunity to let the words that have been spoken sink into our minds and our hearts, but also creates space for others to ask questions of clarification, to speak, and to listen once again. This is something that is critically important in a world that too often expects us to "get it" the first time around.

Silence can also signify white racial disengagement. It can be a form of hiding from that which makes us uncomfortable, of conflict avoidance marked by a failure to engage persons of color and the issues of racism and white supremacy, especially when engagement challenges our own sense of moral innocence. For example, in the context of higher education, this is the silence of optional reading lists, last-minute invitations, selective reading, and token representation on syllabi. It is also the silence of white discomfort and shame. It is the silence of being afraid to say the wrong thing, of having one's own version of reality critiqued, of knowing your own white identity participates in the suffering of nonwhites. Thandeka, author of *Learning to Be White: Money, Race, and God in America*, names this experience as white shame.[46] In her words, "The experience of shame is thus a negative self-exposure, a revelation of forbidden desires. The self exposed is incongruous with itself. It is seen as who it is not supposed to be. It feels what it is not supposed to feel. It is aware of what it is not supposed to know."[47] Thandeka describes this as white shame because the incongruity with the self is discovered within the framework of having a white racial identity. White shame refers to a feeling of "not being at home within one's own white community."[48]

Americans have lost the art of deep listening. We are constantly interrupted by things and people that need our attention. This constant interruption creates an environment where we have lost the capacity to sit still, to be quiet. This inability to "pause" translates into our conversations with others. Often when others are speaking, instead of listening to them, we are thinking of what to say next. To engage in the silence of solidarity means learning how to "pause," to create space for the voices of others and to internalize the meaning of what has been said. When we engage in the silence of solidarity, we acknowledge that we have heard what the other person has to say. This acknowledgment needs to be reflected in the concrete: through actions and words.

The time I spent in Kenya had a profound impact on my own racial consciousness. While I cannot speak for the other white participants, nor is it my intention to make universal claims about all white people, I do believe that my own experience is illuminative of the way in which white shame participates in white apathy. The trip, which was student initiated and university supported, was well-

---

46. Thandeka, *Learning to Be White: Money, Race, and God in America* (New York: Continuum, 2007), 12.
47. Ibid., 13.
48. Ibid.

intentioned and arose out of a sincere desire to be attentive to the dynamics of geography and race in shaping feminist listening. My own experiences of gender oppression had given me insight into feelings of "homelessness,"[49] as a misfit in male-dominated settings. The time I spent in Kenya engendered a feeling of white homesickness, of wanting to return to the familiarity of a world defined by whiteness. I choose to use the term *homesickness* as opposed to *homelessness* in order to represent that fact that I had a "home" to which I could easily return. In most academic and feminist settings, whiteness is normative. It colors events, actions, and relationships. In this way, *homesickness* speaks to privilege and advantage in a way that *homelessness* does not. Moreover, as someone who identifies as a feminist, acknowledging my own desire to return to a world defined by whiteness evoked feelings of profound shame, as it contrasted with feminist ideals of justice for all people. These feelings of homesickness, compounded by shame, led to my own withdrawal—in seminars and casual conversations. I kept my mouth shut, fearing I would not only "say the wrong thing" and offend someone, but that I (and my white Western identity) would be subject to a rightly deserved critique. I sat quietly in the background instead of putting myself out there.

Implicated in whiteness in America is a false sense of certainty or confidence about how the world works. As whiteness defines the norm, white people are not used to being questioned or critiqued. Yet, as George Yancy argues, the experience of being critiqued "should be regarded as valuable to growth, not a sign of defeat."[50] For in being critiqued, white people open themselves up to the possibility

49. Nelle Morton, feminist theologian, has applied the metaphor of "home" to the feminist journey in order to signify the way in which "hearing to speech" within a supportive community can create a place of welcome. This metaphor is the basis of her text *The Journey Is Home* (Boston: Beacon, 1985).

50. Yancy, *Black Bodies,* 240.

of transformation and growth. During the Kenya trip, I did do some listening. Yet, I did not achieve the mutuality or solidarity of which Ada María Isasi-Díaz speaks because of my own selective hearing and reading.[51] Through my own unethical silence, I missed out on the opportunity to cultivate deeper friendships with some fabulous women and limited the opportunity for my own growth. Moreover, doing so had the effect of pronouncing the words of my Kenyan colleagues as unworthy of serious consideration. The listening or efficacious silence to which Isasi-Díaz refers has to be a silence that responds to questioning.[52]

White Apathy and Christian Theology

White silence is also a problem for Christian theology. Sin and grace have not only been historically named from the vantage point of the dominant elite within Christian tradition, but the contributions of black scholars of theology have also been systematically ignored by white Christian theologians. James Cone names this problem as follows: "They engage Feminist, Latin American, and other White reflections on God. Why are they silent on Black theological reflections? If one read only White Catholic theologians, one would hardly know that Blacks exist in America or had the capacity for thought about God."[53] The silence of white theologians (Catholic and Protestant) speaks volumes. This silence implies that the contributions of black theologians and womanist theologians have nothing of value to say about who God is and what it means to be human.[54] To nonwhite Christians it says, "Your experiences of struggle, suffering and triumph and your Christian reflections on

---

51. The reference is to the quote in the introduction, page 12.
52. Isasi-Díaz, *Mujerista Theology*, 96.
53. James H. Cone, "Black Liberation Theology and Black Catholics: A Critical Conversation," *Theological Studies* 61 (2000): 737.
54. Nilson, *Hearing Past the Pain*, 6.

your experience do not count."[55] When taken within a social matrix that privileges whiteness, such silence functions to "regulate social arrangements to the immediate well-being of the dominant racial group and thereby despoils the common good."[56] Silence in the form of unethical passivity distorts the meaning of Jesus' mission and identity.

As related in the Christian Gospels, Jesus' ministry and healing work was motivated by compassion. Compassion, which in the original Greek connotes "a visceral response of profound feeling and strong emotion; it emanates from one's bowels or guts," is a response stirred within one's "deepest humanity when confronted with human agony or need."[57] Compassion differs from sympathy or pity that presumes social distance. Rather, compassion moves beyond emotion to include empathy (identification with the other) and social action. As articulated by Massingale, "genuine compassion manifests itself in action for the sake of another's dignity, respect, and social worth."[58] Compassion disrupts or crosses social and religious boundaries for the sake of another. We often see this in the parables and ministry of Jesus. The Samaritan comes to the aid of a sworn enemy because of compassion (Luke 10:25-37). In the parable of the Prodigal Son, the Father's compassion leads him to welcome his estranged son (Luke 15:11-32). Jesus raises a widow's dead son out of compassion (Luke 7:11-17).[59]

Unethical white passivity in the form of silence, ineffective guilt, and systemic ignorance signifies a loss of relationality: it fails "to feel deeply, suffer with, and reach out to others—and is therefore a

---

55. Ibid.
56. M. Shawn Copeland, *Enfleshing Freedom: Body, Race, and Being* (Minneapolis: Fortress Press, 2010), 14.
57. Massingale, *Racial Justice*, 114.
58. Ibid., 115.
59. Massingale gives these examples in *Racial Justice*, 114.

poignant failure to connect with God."[60] In short, unethical passivity is a failure of compassion, of Christian vocation. Yet this failure of compassion often goes unnoticed by white Christians.[61] The role of classical Christian atonement theory in justifying Christian indifference to and toleration of suffering through its appropriation of sacrificial scapegoating and retributive justice is of particular concern.

Within the Western world, the symbol of the cross has the power to redeem and to liberate those who are suffering. It also has the power to falsely convict the innocent, acquit the guilty, and to hide privileged participation in structural violence. As Kelly Brown Douglas argues, the cross has created a lot of trouble for Christians.[62] While the particularities of the experience of trouble depend upon the side of the power differential upon which one lies, all are impacted by the cross's propensity to collude with the interests of violent domination. In Douglas's own words,

> While the cross in and of itself may not precipitate deadly terror, the cross invested with power does. If nothing else, the cross, when empowered, makes it almost theologically irresistible for people not simply to inflict unwarranted suffering on others but also to sacrifice their very lives. The cross can easily spell the sacrifice of innocent, powerless people. The Christian cross and power thereby represent a deadly union. And so it is an almost predictable fate for Christians to be amongst the rowdy crowd cheering for the noontime lynching of Richard Coleman.[63]

Douglas maintains that the undue emphasis on Jesus' death as atonement for human sin has detrimentally shaped the moral

---

60. Kathleen Greider, *Reckoning with Aggression: Theology, Violence, and Vitality* (Louisville: WJK Press, 1997), 65.
61. There are certainly notable exceptions. See note 68 in the introduction.
62. Kelly Brown Douglas, *What's Faith Got to Do with It? Black Bodies/Christian Souls* (Maryknoll, NY: Orbis, 2005), 56.
63. Ibid., 69

imagination, and subsequent praxis, of privileged and oppressed groups alike. The challenge to white theologians, as raised by Douglas and others, is white silence in view of the crucifixion of black people—namely, how is it possible for white Christians to stand so easily at the foot of the lynching tree without murmuring a word of protest? In the remainder of this chapter, I examine how the scandal of the cross is not only overt participation in violence, it also indicts systemic ignorance and privileged escape. The words of James Cone are apt here: "White conservative Christianity's blatant endorsement of lynching as a part of its religion, and white liberal Christians' silence about lynching placed both of them outside Christian identity."[64]

While most white Christians openly condemn overt forms of racial violence, racism and white privilege continue to malform white Christian identity through unethical silence and privileged indifference to suffering. Christian theology, which is an essential component of discursive power, has played a role in fostering such indifference by providing "religious legitimation of inequitable social relationships."[65] In particular the classical Christian tradition, with its emphasis on divine omnipotence and radical transcendence, has paved the way for white apathy.

Drawing insight from the work of Delores S. Williams and Kelly Brown Douglas, I examine two tendencies of Christian atonement theory: sacrificial scapegoating and retributive suffering. Given the historical ways in which African Americans have been blamed for welfare, illiteracy, and the breakdown of the nuclear family, models of redemption in which justice is accomplished by penal substitution affirms patterns of relationality that undergird white racism in the

---

64. James H. Cone, *The Cross and the Lynching Tree* (Maryknoll, NY: Orbis, 2011), 132.
65. Douglas, *What's Faith*, 9. Here Douglas draws upon Michael Foucault's notion of discursive power.

United States today, erasing them from white consciousness and reaffirming the motif of white moral goodness.

To be clear, I am not arguing that Christian theology directly causes hegemonic violence. To claim this would be to erase the individual moral responsibility of Christians themselves. At the end of the day, individuals are responsible for their actions. Rather, at issue is the power of Christian discourse to shape the collective moral imaginary within violent contexts. Theological language is not neutral. The way in which Christians describe God and God's relationship to the created world plays a role in shaping Christian vision and Christian praxis.[66] God-talk mirrors back to the community the attitudes, behaviors, ways of knowing, and, even desires that are considered to be acceptable. It also plays a role in shaping personal and collective identity of Christians. I am arguing that Christian interpretations of redemption have participated in maintaining narratives of privileged (white) innocence in view of structural oppression (culturally entrenched racism).

White Apathy and Sacrificial Scapegoating: Protecting White Moral Innocence

Sacrificial scapegoating, a mechanism of social control, creates confusion about who is responsible for violence and who is responsible for putting an end to violence through victim-blaming tactics. Scapegoating involves the persecution of an innocent party for the sake of protecting the interests of the dominant group. While a number of scholars have rightly called into question René Girard's contention that mimetic desire is the root of all violence, his notion of surrogate victimage exposes the ways in which scapegoating "is often a vehicle for shaping social order and for stabilizing relational

---

66. Elizabeth Johnson, *She Who Is: The Mystery of God in Feminist Discourse* (New York: Crossroad, 1992), 4.

[power] differences" along hierarchical lines.[67] For Girard, violence is a by-product of human relationality. Mimesis leads toward human conflict as the subject imitates the model's desires. In an effort to put a stop to violent conflict, the group subconsciously looks for a scapegoat upon whom to project its aggression. As the one whom the community views as the source of evil, sickness, or unrest, the scapegoat detracts from the original conflict and becomes a new rival upon whom to focus. In death or expulsion, the surrogate victim becomes a means of unification, and conflict is temporarily dispersed within the community.[68]

Within a Girardian framework, scapegoats are those who are on the fringes of society by virtue of their social identity. They are persons who have been excluded from "establishing or sharing the social bonds of the community."[69] The marginal character of the surrogate victim is important for two reasons. First, the person's "otherness" functions as the rationale for his or her guilt. In the absence of a clearly defined and visible crime, the community seeks justification for expelling the victim by pointing to aspects of his or her personhood that holds the widest variance from the dominant norm. Second, the surrogate victim's marginal location allows the community to make an act of sacrifice without the risk of vengeance.[70] That is, the scapegoat's vulnerability lies in the fact that he or she lacks the social resources to fight back.

For a moment, let us return to the case of Richard Coleman in Maysville, Kentucky, mentioned in the above quote by Kelly Brown Douglas. In 1899, twenty-year-old Coleman was arrested

---

67. Cheryl A. Kirk-Duggan, *Misbegotten Anguish: A Theology and Ethics of Violence* (St. Louis: Chalice, 2001), 38.

68. René Girard, *Things Hidden Since the Foundation of the World*, trans. Stephen Bann and Michael Metteer (Stanford: Stanford University, 1987), 27.

69. René Girard, "Sacrifice as Sacral Violence and Substitution" in *The Girard Reader*, ed. James G. Williams (New York: Crossroad, 1996), 81.

70. Ibid., 82.

for allegedly murdering and raping his white employer's wife, Mrs. Lashbrook.[71] After his arrest, Coleman confessed to the crime, agreed to forego a trial, and asked to be executed swiftly in a nearby town. Authorities denied his request. When Coleman returned to Maysville for his trial, he was seized by a mob of white men and white women, beaten, mutilated, and slowly burned to death, while an enthusiastic crowd watched on the sidelines.[72] Vivid descriptions of Coleman's torture and the crowd's malicious response were captured by newspapers around the country.[73] By and large, the brutal treatment of Coleman was directly tied to white women's "fear" of "black male brutality."[74] This same fear is manifest in stereotypical depictions involving the rape of "innocent" white women by "violent" black men often found in the movies and television. Yet, as studies show, most rape does not take place in dark alleys among strangers. Statistically, most rape occurs among acquaintances, friends, or family members.[75] In the case of Coleman, the projection of white male and white female angst onto black male bodies created the illusion of safety in the community. Several white women testified after Coleman's execution that "they now feel as if they could walk the loneliest country road at midnight without being molested by a white or black man."[76] The execution of the scapegoat, Coleman, led to a false sense of peace in the community, veiling the root of the problem.

71. Crystal Nicole Feimster, *Southern Horrors: Women and the Politics of Rape and Lynching* (Cambridge: Harvard University, 2009), 149. At the turn of the twentieth century, black men accused (falsely or not) of raping white women did not stand a chance of exoneration. Coleman could not fight back.

72. George C. Wright, *Racial Violence in Kentucky, 1865–1940: Lynchings, Mob Rule, and "Legal Lynchings"* (Baton Rouge: Louisiana State University Press, 1990), 93–95.

73. Ibid.

74. Feimster, *Southern Horrors*, 149

75. According to RAINN (Rape Abuse Incest, National Network) Approximately two-thirds of rapes are committed by someone known to the victim-survivor. See http://www.rainn.org/get-information/statistics/sexual-assault-offenders.

76. As quoted in Feimster, *Southern Horrors*, 149.

Coleman's lynching and the cheering of the white bystanders points to the narrow continuum between passive bystanding (apathy) and being an active participant in torture. In the context of white supremacy, if white bystanders decide to act, are they more likely to join in the violence (e.g., stand at the foot of a lynching and cheer) or defend the victim? While this is a question that cannot be addressed here, it is an important one to consider in light of the dynamism of scapegoating and social privilege that continues to govern racial relations in the United States today.[77]

In her analysis of scapegoating and structural violence, Cheryl Kirk-Duggan explains that a person "who looks, acts, or thinks different, and is vulnerable, often ends up being the focus of a group's consolidated effort to define itself and those deemed other, by turning their own pursuit of power against those who cannot react. Thus, a group establishes itself by psychologically or physically eliminating or ousting the ones who are different."[78] At stake is the creation of unity and group identity through the establishment and reinforcement of a social hierarchy whereby the dominant group "[defines] itself and [creates] unity among its members by identifying a susceptible group as 'other' or 'outside.'"[79] In view of racial relations in the United States, persons of color have been blamed when things went wrong with white people's employment, health, and welfare. Williams reflects, "The media makes the black individual into the national symbol of everything wrong in this country—crime, overdependence on welfare, decaying urban neighborhoods, even the high national illiteracy rate."[80] Scapegoating has functioned as a mechanism for

---

77. I am grateful to Karen Teel for this insight.
78. Kirk-Duggan, *Misbegotten Anguish*, 35.
79. Ibid., 35.
80. Delores S. Williams, "Christian Scapegoating," *The Other Side* 29 (May–June 1993): 43. For example, consider the recent stalemate over raising the national debt ceiling. Republicans refused to budge on the grounds that we need to reduce US spending to national assistance programs, many of which support the livelihood of nonwhites. The rhetoric surrounding this

preserving white dominance, providing concrete material rewards for whites in the economic, political, ecological, and cultural sphere.[81] Sacrificial scapegoating blames victims, allowing those who are systemically privileged to maintain a sense of moral innocence without relinquishing social dominance and the benefits that they accrue. In the context of racial privilege (the focus of this chapter, but a similar analysis could be applied to heterosexual or male privilege), white denial—in its overt or covert manifestation—functions to preserve white dominance while denying white complicity in racial injustice. By projecting blame onto surrogate victims, oppressors preserve a sense of moral goodness "to maintain control while disguising the fact that they have it."[82] Pamela Cooper-White maintains, "If victims, were, in fact, co-responsible for their abuse, and perpetrators were to be understood as victims of abuse or victims of circumstance in their own right, then causality" rests with the victim's own dysfunction and "society would not be to blame."[83] Whites can reassure themselves that they would not do what nonwhites did to bring injury upon themselves (e.g., "settle for low paying jobs," "walk through gated communities wearing a hoodie at night"). Nor would they be as sick or evil as Klansmen or bigots.

Scapegoating also works to minimize the consequences of racial injustice through ignoring or blatant denial. Informed by the myth of meritocracy (the notion that one's assets result directly from one's skill or work), whites can write off the suffering of nonwhites as result of laziness, criminality, or lack of intelligence or skill. In so doing, whites protect themselves from confronting their own complicity in racial injustice while maintaining their own social status.

included the complaint that wealth should no longer be taken from hardworking families and given to those who are not deserving.

81. See Hobgood, *Dismantling Privilege*, 50.
82. Cooper-White, *The Cry of Tamar*, 18.
83. Ibid., 18.

While black lynching at the beginning of the twentieth century is an overt example of white scapegoating, today the practice is often more subtle. Consider the case of Fisher v. University of Texas at Austin, in which a group of white students sued on the grounds of "reverse discrimination." Since 1997, the University of Texas at Austin has admitted all in-state high school seniors who are in the top 10 percent of their class. Race plays a factor in the remainder of the open slots. In 2008, Abigail Fisher and another white student were denied admission to UT Austin. Neither student was in the top 10 percent of her high school class. Fisher and others sued, arguing that the university's use of race in admissions was a violation of the Fourteenth Amendment's Equal Protection Clause, which states that persons in similar situations be treated equally in accord with the law. The Supreme Court denied Fisher's appeal. In the aftermath, Fisher was made out to be a victim by conservative supporters. The narrative told was, "[Abigail] did everything right. She worked hard, received good grades, and rounded out her high school years with an array of extracurricular activities. But she was cheated, they say, her dream snatched away by a university that closed its doors to her because she had been born the wrong color: White."[84] Behind this narrative is the assumption that Abigail Fisher, as a white student whose scores were similar to those of other applicants, was more suited for a college education than students of color. Students of color were taking her "rightful" place at UT Austin, and were "cheating" her of her God-given opportunity. In a YouTube video, Fisher explains, "There were people in my class with lower grades who weren't in all the activities I was in, who were being accepted into UT, and the only other difference between us was the color of our

84. Nikole Hannah-Jones, "A Color Blind Constitution: What Abigail Fisher's Affirmative Action Case is Really About," *Pro Publica*, http://www.propublica.org/article/a-colorblind-constitution-what-abigail-fishers-affirmative-action-case-is-r/.

skin."[85] The problem with this analysis is that it fails to account for the ways in which racial bias permeates the American educational system itself, creating an unfair advantage for white students.

The role of unconscious bias in education is well-documented. Teacher expectations are lower for Hispanic and for black students than they are for white students.[86] Lower expectations can be traced to decreased teacher attention and lower test scores. Moreover, a recent study by the Department of Education's Office for Civil Rights illustrates racial disparities in the implementation of school discipline practices. Similar infractions resulted in detention for white students and suspension for those who are nonwhite.[87] This, along with radical disparities in funding (e.g., inner-city schools often lack the financial resources to attract the best teachers and learning tools), leaves minority students at a disadvantage when applying to college. While there may be individual cases where this can be contested, as a whole we can say that when white students and nonwhite students apply to college, the playing field is not neutral.

Scapegoating protects the moral innocence of the dominant group by shielding perpetrators and accomplices from attending to their own complicity in racial injustice.[88] "People who are different from us undermine our own cosmology or worldview: a destabilization of all we deem normative and true."[89] Encountering persons and

---

85. "Abigail Fisher v. University of Texas at Austin," YouTube, http://www.youtube.com/watch?v=sXSpx9PZZj4.

86. Linda van den Bergh et al., "Implicit Prejudiced Attitudes of Teachers: Relations to Teacher Expectations and the Ethnic Achievement Gap" *American Educational Research Journal* 47, no. 2 (June 2010): 497–527.

87. White students comprise 51 percent of those in school, but receive only 33 percent of expulsions. As reported by Stacy Teicher Khadaroo in "School Suspensions: Does Racial Bias Feed the School-to-Prison Pipeline?" *The Christian Science Monitor*, March 31, 2012, http://www.csmonitor.com/USA/Education/2013/0331/School-suspensions-Does-racial-bias-feed-the-school-to-prison-pipeline.

88. Cheryl A. Kirk-Duggan, *Refiner's Fire: A Religious Engagement with Violence* (Minneapolis: Fortress Press, 2001), 116.

89. Ibid., 117

communities who are different can create unease and anxiety. Instead of dealing with our unease, we degrade those who have challenged our worldview. Doing so allows us to feel better about ourselves and our own inadequacies, creating an emotional and psychological escape. We are given temporary peace (release) from facing our own pain. White scapegoating protects white apathy as it shields whites from having to face guilt and shame. The place of primacy of scapegoating in theological metaphors and models further compounds the issue of white apathy. The next section will take a closer look at the ways in which this plays out in two of the most common models for atonement (God's forgiveness of human sin): satisfaction tradition and moral exemplar theory.

Satisfaction Theory and the Justification of Social-Role Surrogacy

Throughout the ages, Christian thinkers have employed a variety of images in order to describe the process of human liberation from sin.[90] In particular, Anselm's notion of atonement as satisfaction continues to play a role in shaping the Christian understanding of the cross and its role in the processes of atoning for human sin. Scholarly debate surrounding the interpretation and appropriation of his work continues today.

In *Cur Deus Homo*, Anselm postulates that the reason for the incarnation was to redeem human sinfulness, or to "re-order the beauty of the universe."[91] Similar to patristic thinkers that had gone before him, Anselm argued that sin entered the world via human disobedience of divine commands.[92] In order to set things back on

90. Gustaf Aulén postulates three models for Christian atonement: Christus victor, moral influence, and satisfaction. See *Christus Victor: An Historical Study of the Three Main Types of the Idea of Atonement*, trans. A. G. Herbert (New York: MacMillan, 1969).

91. Anselm of Canterbury, "Why God Became Man," in *Anselm of Canterbury: The Major Works*, ed. Brian Davies and G. R. Evans (New York: Oxford University Press, 1998), 260–356, at 288.

track, restitution must be made. "To forgive a sin in this way [out of mercy alone] is nothing other than to refrain from inflicting punishment. And if no satisfaction is given, the way to regulate sin correctly is none other than to punish it. If, therefore, it is not punished, it is forgiven without being regulated. . . . It is not fitting for God to allow anything in his kingdom to slip by unregulated."[93] Therefore, Anselm concludes that all sin must be atoned for. One should note, for our discussion, that this assumption rests upon a particular image of the divine. Anselm's theory projects a divine being that is omnipotent (all-powerful) and omniscient (all-knowing) and exercises power scrupulously. The relationship between God and creation is likened to that of a Lord and servant in the medieval feudal system. Like the servant, who is indebted to his master for sustenance, human beings are indebted to God for their very being. The debt owed is great from the start, rendering payment of future infractions, while a necessity, impossible.[94] As a consequence Anselm posits the necessity of a divine-human surrogate to pay the price to restore God's honor. In Jesus' death on the cross, salvation is effected once and for all and Christian virtue is marked by self-sacrificial obedience unto death. "There can, moreover, be nothing that a man may suffer—voluntarily and without owing repayment of debt—more painful or more difficult than death. And there is no act of self-giving whereby a man may give himself to God greater than when he hands himself over to death for God's glory."[95]

While Anselm's constructive engagement of the imagery of his day is interesting, his satisfaction theory has rightly been critiqued

92. Ibid., 283.
93. Ibid., 284.
94. Ibid., 303. For further discussion of Anselm's application of the feudal imagery see Darby Kathleen Ray, "Anselm of Canterbury," in *Empire and the Christian Tradition: New Readings of Classical Theologians*, eds. Kwok Pui-lan, Don H. Compier, and Joerg Rieger (Minneapolis: Fortress Press, 2007), 123–38, 502–4.
95. Ibid., 331.

for its potential to malform the Christian moral imagination within violent contexts. In Anselm's satisfaction theory, the focus is not on righting wrongs but on punishing wrongs. Such a framework makes God appear a tyrant who cares more about divine control than human suffering. This imagery, which is informed by Anselm's appropriation of forensic categories of his day, is intended to foreground the difference between God and creation and risks reifying social relations of dominance and subservience found in the social order today.

For example, in *Sisters in the Wilderness: The Challenge of Womanist God-Talk*, Delores S. Williams argues that models of satisfaction atonement glorifies black women's experiences of oppression in the forms of coerced and voluntary surrogacy.[96] In the antebellum period, slave women were called upon to take the place of the slave owner's wife in the role of mammy or nurturer in the "big house," to carry a "man's load" in the fields, and "to stand in place of white women and provide sexual pleasure for white male slave owners."[97] Williams terms this *coerced surrogacy* because slave women could not refuse participation in these roles.

Postbellum, black women's surrogacy became "voluntary" in the sense that black women had the right to refuse. Yet, the "voluntary" nature of the situation could hardly be described as freedom, as many African American women continue to be pressured into a social-role surrogacy due to their economic situation. Poverty continues to force many into minimum-wage jobs as domestic servants, childcare workers, and day laborers. For example, "employment expectations

96. Delores S. Williams's *Sisters in the Wilderness: The Challenge of Womanist God-Talk* (Maryknoll, NY: Orbis, 1993), 162. For Williams, coerced surrogacy "was a condition [in the antebellum period] in which people and systems more powerful than black people forced black women to function in roles that would have ordinarily been filled by someone else" (ibid., 60).
97. Ibid., 67. As Williams explains, this last practice was largely tied to Victorian ideals of white womanhood, wherein sexual relations between free men and women were only to be maintained for the purpose of procreation.

such as welfare-to-work programs have sent the messages that poor black women are more valuable—or less dangerous?—to society in minimum-wage jobs than at home with their children (labor surrogacy)."[98] As argued by Jacquelyn Grant, social-role surrogacy continues to be rooted in and sustained by stereotypes regarding white superiority and black inferiority. "The stereotype that Blacks were more suited for service work reflects the fact that even after slavery and to some extent today, the term 'chattels personal' can still be used to describe the way Blacks are treated, especially in the area of domestic service."[99] White American women needed servants in order to save them from "the dirt, monotony, and drudgery of their own homes."[100] Moreover, it is worth pointing out that social-role surrogacy is not (and never has been) a black and white issue. Today, it is a global phenomenon that extends beyond our national borders to include undocumented and migrant workers. Social-role surrogacy has exacted (and continues to exact) an enormous economic, physical, and psychic toll on women of color and their families.

For scholars like Williams and Grant, Christian atonement theory (regardless of the author's original intent) can be seen as glorifying black women's oppression. "Jesus represents the ultimate surrogate figure; he stands in the place of someone else: sinful humankind. Surrogacy, attached to this divine personage, thus takes on an aura of the sacred."[101] To suggest that salvation rests upon the surrogacy of Jesus, whether "coerced (willed by the Father)" or "voluntary (chosen by the Son)," divinizes the exploitation of black women.[102] "If black

---

98. Teel, *Racism and the Image of God*, 80.
99. Jacquelyn Grant, "The Sin of Servanthood: And the Deliverance of Discipleship," in *A Troubling in My Soul: Womanist Perspectives on Evil and Suffering*, ed. Emilie M. Townes (Maryknoll, NY: Orbis, 1993), 208.
100. Ibid.
101. Williams, *Sisters in the Wilderness*, 162.
102. Ibid.

women accept this idea of redemption, can they not also passively accept the exploitation that surrogacy brings?"[103] Ultimately, for Williams, Jesus' life, not his death, is salvific. The cross symbolizes the sin of human desecration. It reminds us "of how humans have tried throughout history to destroy visions of righting relationships that involve transformation of tradition and transformation of social arrangements sanctioned by the *status quo*."[104] To glorify the cross is to glorify human defilement; it is to glorify sin.[105] Instead, Williams proposes a theology of survival that emphasizes Jesus' healing ministerial vision. Jesus came to live and to give life. Redemption "had to do with God, through Jesus, giving humankind a new vision to see the resources for positive, abundant relational life."[106] As such, Williams counsels black women to emulate Christ's life, not the cross.

Though not all womanist theologians agree with Williams, Kelly Brown Douglas takes up her critique in order to discuss the implications of classical atonement theology for white complicity.[107] She writes,

> If one follows the theological logic of Christianity's classical atonement tradition, then the Christian God is one who in some way accepts human sacrifice. A crowd that lynches, therefore, would not immediately repulse such a God. A God that sanctions a human sacrifice as brutal as crucifixion can serve as a divine ally for those who make such a sacrifice—even a sacrifice as horrific as lynching.[108]

At stake is the potential for theological language and symbolism to shape the Christian moral imagination in ways that domesticate death and human suffering, rendering it as acceptable—and even

103. Ibid.
104. Delores S. Williams, "Surrogacy and Redemption," *Witness* (March 1995): 30.
105. Williams, *Sisters in the Wilderness*, 167.
106. Ibid., 165.
107. Joanne Marie Terrell argues for a critical retrieval of the cross for African American women in *Power in the Blood? The Cross in the African American Experience* (Maryknoll, NY: Orbis, 1998).
108. Douglas, *What's Faith*, 72.

praiseworthy—behavior. Given the history of white scapegoating of black bodies in this country (recall the lynching of Richard Coleman and Abigail Fisher's case against UT Austin), models of salvation whereby atonement is accomplished via penal substitution fail to contest the sin of racism in a contemporary American context. Rather, the satisfaction tradition, in and through its appropriation of a divine scapegoat, normalizes and sanctifies patterns of relationship that undergird white racism. In the United States, whiteness is marked by the presumption of dominance and entitlement.[109] Such a dynamism not only lends toward the scapegoating of nonwhite people, but when paired with Christian imagery of Christ as Divine Scapegoat, it can contribute to the false notion that somehow the suffering of black people is "merited" or "redemptive." In such a framework, white racism no longer appears to be a sin—that is, incompatible with the gospel message of love and redemption.

Scapegoating is a form of collective violence. Highly competitive societies produce the need for people to define themselves against one another and, in so doing, encourage scapegoating practices. Given the ways in which the satisfaction theory mimics sacrificial scapegoating through the surrogate victimage of Jesus, it is difficult to maintain this tendency within Christian tradition as a resource for contesting such patterns of relationality operative in US history and the present. Scholars like Girard have maintained that the surrogate victimage was the work of Jesus alone, never intended to be emulated by humanity; yet this is far from being the case in Christian religious practice.[110] From the practices of asceticism within the monastic period to the inscription of obedience and submission upon the bodies of women in the context of intimate partner violence,

---

109. Massingale, *Racial Justice*, 23.
110. See René Girard, "A Non-Sacrificial Reading of the Gospel Text," in *Things Hidden Since the Foundation of the World*, trans. Stephen Bann and Michael Metteer (Stanford: Stanford University Press, 1987), esp. 205–15.

theological imagery surrounding Christ's suffering has had tremendous practical effect.[111] Moreover, at issue with respect to a Girardian typology is also the notion that while the cross may make the violence of scapegoating visible, it is difficult (and problematic) to substantiate his claim that the violent scapegoating of an innocent individual begets lasting peace. While a more detailed discussion of Girard's work is beyond the scope of this book, it is worth noting that his claim that Christ's sacrifice puts an end to all scapegoating gives an unwarranted primacy to Christian tradition in view of other religions and fails to attend to the social construction of violence itself.[112] As Christine Gudorf explains, "If social violence is not a disease but a symptom of a number of related diseases, then the sacrifice of a surrogate victim serves only to relieve the symptom. The sacrifice is not at all a cure. It does not make the social diseases that produce violence any less dangerous. It only lowers the fever for a minute, an hour, maybe a day."[113] Structural violence cannot be quelled by the sacrifice of one individual or group, no matter how holy or innocent. The violence of white racism and white privilege are structural problems requiring social transformation.

Satisfaction theory also lends credibility to notions of retributive (also termed punitive) suffering. It suggests that wrongs are not to be righted as much as they are to be punished. In early Christianity, this resulted in Christian persecution of Jews, whose suffering was interpreted as "a divinely imposed consequence for the rejection of

---

111. Historian Margaret R. Miles discusses the significance of the suffering Christ in ascetical practice in *Practicing Christianity: Critical Perspectives for an Embodied Spirituality* (New York: Crossroad, 1988), 165–75. In the context of sexual violence, see see Rita Nakashima Brock and Rebecca Ann Parker, *Proverbs of Ashes: Violence, Redemptive Suffering, and the Search for What Saves Us* (Boston: Beacon, 2002).

112. For further reading on the issue of the significance of Girard for violence in other religions, see the essays in *Violence and the Sacred in the Modern World*, ed. Mark Juergensmeyer (London: Frank Cass, 1991).

113. Christine E. Gudorf, *Victimization: Examining Christian Complicity* (Philadelphia: Trinity International Press, 1992), 14–15.

the Christian God."[114] In this way, the symbol of the cross became a theological excuse for imperially sanctioned persecution, a practice than cannot be separated from the history of Christian participation in lynching and social-role surrogacy in the United States.

Patrick Cheng makes a parallel claim with respect to religious-based persecution of LGBTQ persons. In *From Sin to Amazing Grace: Discovering the Queer Christ*, Cheng argues that theological ideation surrounding penal substitution underscores Christian homophobia, as gender-variant behavior and same-sex acts have been construed as a crime against God in Western Christian tradition. Natural disasters, military conquest, and the bubonic plague have all been interpreted as the result of collective divine punishment for gender-variant behavior and same-sex acts.[115] The theological criminalization of LGBTQ persons and behavior has been used to authorize their physical torture and execution throughout history.

In sum, juridical notions of sin and atonement do little to challenge social structures of dominance operative in Western Christianity. Not only have these models been appropriated in pastoral and liturgical contexts in order to encourage those on the underside of history to accept abuse, but they also play a role in the normalization, and in some cases divinization, of victim-blaming tactics, protecting privileged elites from facing their own complicity in violence. Punitive notions of suffering encourage escapism and denial, not responsibility, as human beings seek to avoid being implicated in violence in an effort to avoid punishment. This kind of religious ideation engenders a fear-driven scrupulosity, where following the

---

114. Douglas, *What's Faith*, 48.
115. Cheng, drawing upon Peter Coleman's *Gay Christians: A Moral Dilemma* (London: SCM, 1989), cites the decrees of Christian emperor Justinian in the sixth century, wherein prohibitions about same-sex acts and gender-variant behavior followed natural disasters and military conquest. See *From Sin to Amazing Grace*, 46.

"rules" becomes more important than developing spiritual maturity and social responsibility.

Moral Exemplar Theory and White Guilt

Aside from satisfaction atonement theory, Christian tradition has interpreted human suffering as God's way of drawing near to us in order to win us over and train us in the Christian life. This heuristic frame for interpreting human tragedy is particularly evident within what has been referred to as the moral influence theory of atonement.

A generation after Anselm's treatise, Peter Abelard developed the moral influence theory.[116] Similar to Anselm, Abelard rejected the patristic idea of Jesus' death as ransom paid to the devil. He also rejected the notion that Jesus' death paid a debt to God. For Abelard, the question was not how to change God's attitude toward sinners (via retributive suffering or surrogate victimage), but how to bring about a change in the subjective consciousness of sinners. From Abelard's point of view, the cross was not a sign of God's wrath or judgment of humanity. Rather, the cross pointed toward God's compassionate love for human beings. As demonstrated to us on the cross and in the Gospels, Christ's love compels human beings to act in kind. In particular, the moral influence theory rests upon the notion that "an innocent, suffering victim and only an innocent, suffering victim for whose suffering we are in some way responsible has the power to confront us with our guilt and move us to new decision."[117] Contemplation of Christ's love for God, submission to God's will, concern for others, and death on the cross (which Abelard describes

---

116. Peter Abelard, "Exposition of the Epistle to the Romans," reprinted in *Readings in the History of Christian Theology*, ed. William C. Placher, vol. 1 (Louisville: WJK, 1988), 150–1.

117. Joanne Carlson Brown and Rebecca Parker, "For God So Loved the World?" in *Christianity, Patriarchy, and Abuse: A Feminist Critique*, ed. Joanne Carlson Brown and Carole R. Bohn (New York: Pilgrim, 1989), 12.

as an act of perfect love) will inspire human beings to turn from sin and toward God, effecting their redemption.

In such a framework, wherein Christ assumes the role of Divine Victim, Christian discipleship is signified in and through suffering itself instead of active resistance to suffering. In the context of feminist theology, Joanne Carlson Brown and Rebecca Parker explain this phenomenon:

> The central image of Christ on the cross as savior of the world communicates the message that suffering is redemptive. If the best person who ever lived gave his life for others, then, to be of value we should likewise sacrifice ourselves. . . . The message is complicated further by the theology that says Christ suffered in obedience to his father's will. Divine child abuse is paraded as salvific and the child who suffers 'without even raising a voice' is lauded as the hope of the world.[118]

At issue is the equation of Christian discipleship with the virtues of self-sacrifice and suffering obedience without attending to the particularities of social context. Certainly, self-sacrifice is an important virtue at times. However, self-sacrifice does not always lead to a greater good, especially in situations marked by radical inequality. In the context of abusive social and sexual relationships, assertions about the salvific character of suffering act to reinforce cycles of violence. Drawing upon her work with battered women, Sarah Bentley points out that many women "will persist in returning to increasingly dangerous relationships citing this very model of Christian love as 'turning the other cheek' or 'following Jesus' example.'"[119] Furthermore, given the effect of gender and racial

---

118. Ibid., 2.
119. Sarah Bentley, "Bringing Justice Home: The Christian Challenge of the Battered Women's Movement for Christian Social Ethics," in *Violence against Women and Children: A Christian Theological Sourcebook*, ed. Carol J. Adams and Marie M. Fortune (New York: Continuum, 1995), 155.

socialization, claiming that Christ's suffering and death is the outgrowth of Jesus' obedience to the Father's will does not make the situation any better. At issue is the identification of innocence and victimhood as well as the presupposition that emotional and psychological manipulation are appropriate tools for Christian edification.

In the context of white racism, the moral exemplar model within Christian atonement tradition would suggest that white people's contemplation of Christ's self-sacrificial love on the cross would lead to a contrition of heart. Not only does such a model of redemption render the repentance of the oppressor more important than the liberation and healing of those who have suffered injustice, but not all oppressors recognize much less feel badly about their own complicity in violence. Further, in view of the emotionally laden nature of white responses to white racism, the moral exemplar model has the potential to exacerbate white paralysis surrounding racial injustice.[120] For many whites, confronting complicity in white racism surfaces a number of emotions: fear (of being blamed or misunderstood), frustration, anger, shame, and even guilt over our own ties to a history and present marked by suffering and degradation. These affective responses can leave people frozen, unsure of what to do. When teaching about racism and white privilege, I have seen students become so emotionally overwhelmed that they shut down.[121] While repentance and lament (described in chapter 3) are, indeed, appropriate in view of white complicity in racial violence, guilt is not. The problem with white guilt, as well as declarations of white guilt, is that its function is all too often one of alleviating white anxiety surrounding the loss of the sense of oneself as morally good.[122]

---

120. Massingale, *Racial Justice*, xiii.

121. For more, see Anna Floerke Scheid and Elisabeth T. Vasko, "Teaching Race: Pedagogical Challenges in Predominantly White Undergraduate Theology Classrooms," *Teaching Theology and Religion* 16, no. 1 (2014): 27–45.

Often white guilt depends upon the fear or stigmatization of being called a racist instead of the moral impetus to acknowledge harm done, make reparations, and work toward structural change.

Guilt is an ineffective tool for engendering social responsibility. At its best, guilt provokes moral scrupulosity, or an obsession with defining "right" or "wrong" behaviors, not mature reflection on social patterns and systems. When we feel guilty, we feel badly for a particular behavior committed in the past or for not living up to a given standard. While guilt may signal that we need to change our actions in a particular context, it does not necessarily draw our attention to the fact that something may be wrong at the meta-level. The assumption is that the background conditions "are morally acceptable, if not ideal."[123] The bad action, sinful deed, or poor posture is viewed as a discrete and bounded event—a diversion from the norm. Participation in structural injustice is often habitual and unconscious. Most white people participate in racial injustice because we follow "the accepted norms and rules and conventions of the communities and institutions in which we act."[124] Therefore, the harm done *is* in accepting the background conditions themselves as morally good, just, or appropriate.

Guilt does not help us to attend well to the sufferings of others. Rather, guilt is a narcissistic emotion, which despite good intentions, drives the search for a quick fix in an effort to alleviate cognitive dissonance. In the words of Audre Lorde, "All too often, guilt is just another name for impotence, for defensiveness destructive of communication; it becomes a device to protect ignorance and the

122. Sara Ahmed, "Declarations of Whiteness: The Non-Performativity of Anti-Racism," *Borderlands* 3, no. 2 (2004), http://www.borderlands.net.au/vol3no2_2004/ahmed_declarations.htm.
123. Iris Marion Young, "Responsibility, Social Connection, Labor Justice," in *Global Challenges: War, Self-Determination and Responsibility for Justice* (Malden MA: Polity, 2007), 176.
124. Ibid., 177

continuation of things the way they are, the ultimate protection for changelessness."[125] In principle, the moral influence theory supports the manipulation of innocent suffering for the sake of redeeming the guilty. There is little here that encourages concrete social analysis of sin or responsibility. As such, "we fail to see the suffering that is built into social structures in which we all participate and our responsibility for the transformation of such structures."[126]

Divine *Apatheia* and White Apathy

In this chapter, we have been examining the ways in which unethical passivity is manifest in and compounded by social privilege. In particular, we have been looking at the way in which privileged apathy is inculcated through white supremacy within the United States. Drawing upon the critical work of womanist, feminist, and black liberation theologians, I have argued that dominant strands of classical Christian atonement theory are, at best, ineffective theological paradigms for engendering social responsibility among privileged persons. Rather, satisfaction and moral influence models of atonement function to normalize patterns of sacrificial scapegoating already operative within American society, offering privileged elites a theological "escape" from having to address their own complicity in systemic injustice. Punitive models of sin and redemption encourage denial through victim-blaming tactics. They do not encourage mature responsibility. This is not to state that Anselm and his followers, or those who have taken up Abelard's notions of moral influence theory, are to blame for privileged indifference to nonwhite suffering. Nor is it to suggest that Anselm, Abelard, and those who

---

125. Audre Lorde, "The Uses of Anger: Women Responding to Racism," reprinted in *Sister Outsider: Essays and Speeches* (Berkeley, CA: Crossing, 2007), 130.

126. Rita Nakashima Brock, *Journeys by Heart: A Christology of Erotic Power* (New York: Crossroad, 1988), 57.

adopt similar theological perspectives deliberately intend(ed) to instill paradigms of social dominance or to privilege unknowing that supports systemic injustice. Rather, the issue at stake for both Abelard and Anselm was one of interpreting Chalcedon's claim of "one person, two natures" in a way that maintained divine omnipotence and immutability.[127]

While the emphasis on divine transcendence (i.e., the notion that God is beyond human ideas of knowledge, power, and goodness) reflects the desire of Christian writers to engender in the faithful a sense of "radical dependence upon God," imagining God in this way divinizes a unilateral conception of power and the experience of the powerful.[128] Feminist and womanist scholars have noted that ideas of transcendent power are rooted in cosmic dualisms, which produce a number of binaries: transcendence/immanence, rationality/sensibility, independence/dependence, God/nature, man/woman, white/black, and so forth. These binaries have been used to justify social and religious stratification wherein whiteness and maleness are divinized, and blackness and femaleness are sexualized and demonized.[129] The association of transcendence with separation and independence mirrors the ideals of white masculinist culture wherein subjectivity entails overcoming and controlling the material constraints of the body, the distractions of the affections, and the unpredictable effects of others on oneself. Within this ideal, being

---

127. It is worth noting that this challenge was perhaps greater for Abelard than Anselm, as Abelard was concerned with the way in which Anselm's theory reflected a change in God's perception of human beings after the cross of Christ. Yet, in *Cur Deus Homo*, Anselm denies that God is mutable.

128. Feminist scholars have long noted the intersection between notions of power as controlling and distant and images of divine transcendence. For example, Elizabeth Johnson makes this critique in *She Who Is: The Mystery of God in Feminist Theological Discourse* (New York: Crossroad, 1992), chapters 10 and 11.

129. Kelly Brown Douglas points to the way in which platonized Christian tradition has sexualized and demonized those deemed inferior within this dualistic framework. See *What's Faith*, 50–52.

(in the metaphysical sense) remains unaffected, unchanged, and unmoved by others.

The ideals of white masculinist metaphysics have been transposed onto Christian conceptions of God despite their incongruence with biblical imagery. The notion that God is a spiritual, immortal, infinite being who remains untouched by suffering contradicts Gospel imagery that depicts Christ suffering "hunger and thirst, exhaustion and beatings, pain, being forsaken by God and death."[130] While questions surrounding the nature of divine suffering continue to remain unsettled, Christian orthodoxy has tended to land on the side of divine apathy. This is echoed in mainline Protestantism and Catholicism. The writings of Martin Luther, John Calvin, and Karl Barth depict God as Wholly Other. In Roman Catholicism, this is clearly manifest through magisterial condemnations of those who have attempted to suggest otherwise: Roger Haight, Jon Sobrino, and most recently, Elizabeth Johnson.[131] In the face of radical human

---

130. Sölle, *Suffering*, 42. For example, see Jesus wept (John 11:35), slept (Mark 4:35), hungered and thirsted (John 4:6-7).

131. Consider for example the CDF's recent condemnation of the work of Jon Sobrino as articulated in *Jesus the Liberator: A Historical-Theological Reading of Jesus of Nazareth* (Maryknoll, NY: Orbis, 1993) and *Christ the Liberator: A View from the Victims* (Maryknoll, NY: Orbis, 2001). See Congregation of the Doctrine of Faith, "Notification on the works of Father Jon Sobrino, SJ," October 13, 2006, http://www.vatican.va/roman_curia/congregations/cfaith/documents/rc_con_cfaith_doc_20061126_notification-sobrino_en.html. The basis of the CDF's criticism centers on Sobrino's construction of the divinity of Jesus, as well as his theological methodology. According to the authors of the document, "he fails to affirm Jesus' divinity with sufficient clarity. This reticence gives credence to the suspicion that the historical development of dogma, which Sobrino describes as ambiguous, has arrived at the formulation of Jesus' divinity without a clear continuity with the New Testament." While the document critiques Sobrino's christological constructions on a number of points, the biggest issue seems to be his theological methodology, which begins with the experiences and questions of the poor in Latin America. In 2004, Roger Haight's *Jesus Symbol of God* (Maryknoll, NY: Orbis, 1999) was critiqued on similar grounds by the CDF. According to the CDF, Haight has failed to properly affirm the divinity of Jesus. See http://www.vatican.va/roman_curia/congregations/cfaith/documents/rc_con_cfaith_doc_20041213_notification-fr-haight_en.html. He has since been ordered to stop teaching and publishing on theology. Finally, the CDF issued a notification on Elizabeth Johnson's *Quest for the Living God: Mapping Frontiers in the Theology of God* (New York: Continuum, 2007), citing her critique of radical transcendence. See http://www.usccb.org/about/doctrine/publications/upload/statement-quest-for-the-living-

suffering, the emphasis on divine omnipotence and impassibility renders God a divine spectator to human pain. God has the power to stop human suffering, but chooses not to do so in order to punish, train, or test. These ideals are far from being limited to the purview of the "ivory tower," as they commonly shape pastoral practice and liturgical prayer. Within the Catholic mass, the laity responds, "Lord, I am not worthy that you should enter under my roof, but only say the word and my soul shall be healed."

Elizabeth Johnson has maintained that "such a God is morally intolerable," falling short of "the modicum of decency expected even at the human level."[132] One has to wonder, given the problem of unethical passivity as discussed here, whether such a God is all too tolerable and not challenging enough. Namely, does this kind of divine imaging, especially within a soteriological context, function to reify human apathy? For privileged elites, I believe it does.

Models that support divine transcendence tend to render the task of salvation as something outside ourselves. Salvation is an otherworldly affair, distinct from human concern and human effort. This kind of "hoping" from without engenders a flight from pain—whether it is our own or the pain of others. Such theological models not only minimize the soteriological significance of human suffering in the present, but they also work to diffuse responsibility for shaping a new future, for bringing about the reign of God here on earth. Only God is perfect enough, good enough, and powerful enough to effect healing; human action and agency are ancillary to the work of divine grace. God is rendered a divine hero who has the power to swoop in and save the day, but, for the sake of a greater good (be it moral edification or retributive justice), chooses not to do so.

god-2011-03-24.pdf. While radical Christological transcendence was one issue among several in the CDF's reprise, it is a common theme among all three notifications.

132. Johnson, *She Who Is*, 249.

Humanity, weak and vulnerable, awaits salvation from earthly mire. The identification of Christ as Superhero reaches far into popular imagination, as superheroes often have Christlike features.[133] For instance, Warner Brothers played off this link in its marketing of *Man of Steel*, wherein Superman, at age thirty-three, is trying to save the planet from its own evil.[134] While superheroes and superheroines make great fodder for movies, they are best left out of Christian theology, as they tend to engender passive bystanding in the face of divine paternalism—inadequate Christian responses to white hegemony.

In reflecting upon the legacy of Christian atonement tradition and Christian complicity in violence, Rebecca Ann Parker states that we have "to stop sleeping by the fire."[135] Drawing insights from the experiences of a parishioner who was a POW during the Korean War, she explains that while it may have been warmer to sleep by the fire at night during the war, doing so lowers your resistance to illness. In parallel fashion, theologies of atonement that mystify violence through the glorification of suffering or sanctification of scapegoating "offer dangerously false comfort,"[136] masking the violence that surrounds us and teaching us to endure it. Such is the way that traditional atonement theologies have participated in white tolerance of nonwhite suffering. In the white moral imaginary, the satisfaction tradition has contributed to the normalization and sanctification of patterns of surrogate victimage and retributive

---

133. For a full analysis, see Susie Paulik Babka "Arius, Superman, and the *Tertium Quid*: When Popular Culture Meets Christology" *Irish Theological Quarterly* 73 (2008): 113–32. Her work will be discussed further in chapter 5.

134. In an interview with John Burnett aired on NPR, June 21, 2013, producer Craig Detweiler explains that the latest Superman movie was directly marketed to Christian audiences. John Burnett, "Superman Takes A Deliberate Christ-Like Turn In New Film," National Public Radio, http://www.npr.org/templates/story/story.php?storyId=194330396.

135. Brock and Parker, *Proverbs of Ashes*, 48.

136. Ibid., 49.

suffering, which continue to mark the racial landscape of the United States today. Privileged folks (whether by race, class, gender, orientation or ethnicity) need a new soteriological vision, one wherein redemption is not predicated upon the sacrifice of an innocent victim, but is found in the power of the collective whole seeking the full flourishing of all creation.

Conclusion

Privileged apathy bypasses the redemptive power of divine love. At its root, Christianity is an incarnational religion. Christians believe that God is incarnate, in the flesh, among us, in between us, alive and active in history. This core Christian belief is attested to by the Gospels and early councils of the church. Jesus Christ is one person, two natures. Fully divine, fully human. One cannot live an embodied (incarnate) life apart from an engagement of pain—whether one's own or the pain of others. As Carter Heyward states, "There is no way to avoid pain. There is only the choice between pain steeped in passion and pain incurred through dispassionate invulnerability to relation."[137]

Apathy is contrary to Christian identity. "The root meaning of passion or suffering—*passio*—is to bear, to withstand, to hold up. [Christians] are called, collectively to bear up God in the world."[138] Yet such a vocation involves vulnerability to pain, as one cannot live with an open heart to oneself and one's neighbor without witnessing pain. For those who are systemically privileged, this means leaving behind false notions of innocence and coming face to face with our own complicity in injustice. Such a task is painful, as it comes with a personal cost. In other words, serious attempts on the part of the

137. Heyward, *Redemption of God*, 54.
138. Heyward, *Passion for Justice*, 206.

privileged to dismantle hegemony cannot be drawn from sympathy or benevolent paternalism. They must involve deliberate attempts to relinquish power and privilege.

Privileged pain is not the same as the pain of those who have suffered at the hands of injustice, but these two realities are related. Understanding this relation is what helps us to begin the work of naming redemption anew. The first stop on this journey is to take a closer look at sin. The language of sin is used to describe the wrong of the world. Sin-talk is what allows us to adequately describe and critique violence, terrorism, economic and racial inequality, and sexual exploitation. The metaphors we use to describe sin not only help us to the name the ways in which we have been harmed, but they are also important in diagnosing our participation in the suffering of others.

3

Lament from "the Other Side": Sin-Talk for Bystanders

"I am also responsible for the house which I did not build but in which I live."
Dorothee Sölle

Sin alienates us from God, other human beings, and creation.[1] Sin is an important category for theological reflection, providing Christians with the tools to describe and critique the state of the world. The categories of *sin* and *evil* allow us to name actions and structures that generate brokenness and suffering in the world.[2] The usefulness of these terms "is predicated on the conviction that once named, sin and evil lose the power of mystification and become phenomena to which people of faith may respond in fitting ways."[3] In Christian tradition, to speak of sin is to avoid fatalism. Rather, speaking of sin rightly opens the potential for healing.

Emilie M. Townes captures the essence of this reality when she speaks about the difference between pain and suffering. Drawing

---

1. The phrase lament from "the other side" is Denise M. Ackermann's. See *After the Locusts: Letters from a Landscape of Faith* (Grand Rapids, MI: Eerdmans, 2003), 117.
2. Darby Kathleen Ray, ch. ed., "Sin and Evil," in *Constructive Theology: A Contemporary Approach to Classical Themes*, ed. Serene Jones and Paul Lakeland (Minneapolis: Fortress Press, 2005), 118.
3. Ibid.

insight from poet and writer Audre Lorde, Townes points to the importance of naming brokenness for the in-breaking of resurrection. "Suffering is unscrutinized and unmetabolized pain…. It is a static process which usually ends in oppression."[4] Suffering is akin to reliving an experience of brokenness over and over again, hidden in silence, whereas "pain is an experience that is recognized, named, and then used for transformation."[5] The naming of pain is "a dynamic process pointing toward transformation."[6] Pain, not suffering, "allows the person to critique her individual circumstance and that of her community partnership."[7] As the distinction by Townes shows, when it comes to brokenness, naming makes an important difference. The very act of naming violence resists the isolation incurred by violence itself. Naming fosters a communion, a sense that one is not alone and that healing may indeed be a possibility. In this way, the accurate and appropriate naming of pain points toward resurrection.

I do not suggest that all sin-talk is equally useful in every context. To use a medical analogy, if a doctor misdiagnoses a patient's symptoms, "the medicine prescribed according to that diagnosis will not be effective and the patient's health can be in jeopardy."[8] As the wrong medication can further mask the originating illness, a description of the world that fails to capture the essence of the problem may also do more harm than good. This is of particular concern given the ways in which sin-talk (contemporary and historical) has been used to mask human participation in evil.

4. Emilie M. Townes, "Living in the New Jerusalem: Rhetoric and Movement of Liberation in the House of Evil," in *A Troubling in My Soul: Womanist Perspectives on Evil & Suffering*, ed. Emilie M. Townes (Maryknoll, NY: Orbis, 1993), 84.

5. Ibid.

6. Ibid.

7. Ibid., 86.

8. Andrew Sung Park and Susan L. Nelson, "Introduction," in *The Other Side of Sin: Woundedness from the Perspective of the Sinned-Against*, ed. Andrew Sung Park and Susan L. Nelson (Albany: SUNY, 2001), 1.

Within much of Western Christian tradition, the vantage point for reflecting upon brokenness "has been through the eyes of the sinner," whereby "reflection on happenings that entail moral culpability (sin) has been a backward glance from the event of evil to the interiority of the culpable sinner."[9] Presuming this framework, Christian writers have typically interpreted sin as an act of the will gone awry, resulting from malintentioned individuals. While such an approach may be helpful for holding individuals responsible, it is not particularly useful for naming group complicity in structural violence such as racism, heterosexism, white privilege, and heterosexual privilege. This is for two reasons. First, as discussed in the last chapter, most participation in structural forms of violence (e.g., racial injustice) is not the result of a conscious decision to harm groups or individuals. By and large, participation in structural forms of violence goes unnoticed and unnamed by privileged persons. Traditional individualized formulations of sin fail to capture the ways in which brokenness and alienation embed themselves within the structures of society. Second, inordinate attention to actual sins has contributed to patterns of shaming those who fail to fit into cultural norms for behavior.[10] In such a framework, sin-talk often degenerates into a laundry list of "dos" and "don'ts," many of which pertain to matters of sexual morality. As Patrick Cheng points out, the obsession with defining "right" or "wrong" behavior has been used to denigrate women and LGBTQ persons, muting their sense of self-dignity and worth.[11] As

9. Ray et al, "Sin and Evil," 119.
10. The category of sin has been used to sanctify violence against those who defied gender and sexual norms throughout history. One prominent example is the persecution of witches during the medieval period. See Lyndal Roper, *Oedipus and the Devil: Witchcraft, Sexuality, and Religion in Early Modern Europe* (New York: Routledge, 1994), chapter 2. In a contemporary context, sin-talk is used to justify the persecution of LGBTQ persons. For more on this see, Patrick S. Cheng, *From Sin to Amazing Grace: Discovering the Queer Christ* (New York: Seabury, 2012), chapter 1.
11. Cheng, *From Sin to Amazing Grace*, 48.

such, traditional sin-talk has been largely malappropriated to evoke a rhetoric of blame, not responsibility.

While sin reflects the use of our own free will, the term also refers to the ways in which we are "thrust into a 'world of evil,' of which [we] had no hand in the making."[12] To speak about sin in this sense is not only to shift the primary locus for theological reflection to that of the sinned against, but it is also to acknowledge the phenomenon of collective guilt. We are born into conditions that we did not create. As we live and have our being within these conditions, we "live in sin."[13] As the quote by Dorothee Sölle, at the beginning of this chapter, relays, though we may not be liable for the creation of structural injustice, we are responsible for its attenuation.[14] Within this framework, the language of sin evokes the language of lament. Here, the focus is not so much on blame, but on examining collective responsibility in view of structural violence and its effect on the sinned against.

In this chapter, I argue that sin-talk for bystanders must be filtered through the language of lament instead of blame or disobedience. In the Hebrew Scriptures, lament is "a cry of utter anguish and passionate protest at the state of this world and its brokenness."[15] Lament holds together both loss and hope, oppression and resistance, in a form of honest reckoning that recenters the plight of those who

---

12. Ray et al., "Sin and Evil," 119.

13. Dorothee Sölle, *Thinking About God: An Introduction to Theology*, trans. John Bowden (New York/London, SCM, 1990), 54–55. Christian tradition has used the concept of original sin, most fully developed by Augustine, to name this reality. Yet the category of original sin has been subject to a great deal of misinterpretation. Given this history and the limited capacity of the term to capture the dynamism between individual culpability and collective participation in structural violence, I choose not to use it here. This, however, is not to suggest the category of original sin is irrelevant for a modern Western context. For examples, see Marjorie Hewitt Suchocki, *The Fall to Violence: Original Sin in Relational Theology* (New York: Continuum, 1995) and Tatha Wiley, *Original Sin: Origins, Developments, Contemporary Meanings* (New York: Paulist, 2002).

14. Sölle, *Thinking About God*, 55.

15. Byran N. Massingale, *Racial Justice and the Catholic Church* (Maryknoll, NY: Orbis, 2010), 105.

have suffered injustice. The lament of the oppressed is revelatory, as it "unveils social truths" to others—namely, that "social injustice is more rampant and virulent than one has been led to believe."[16] In particular, the lament of those who have suffered injustice "is what enables the privileged to engage in lament as well," to name sin in ways that acknowledge the harm done to others as well as one's complicity in social injustice.[17]

The chapter will conclude by offering a critical reconstruction of sin for bystanders to violence that draws insight from the contributions of feminist, womanist, black liberation, and queer theologies.

- *Starting with the relational self*—the point of departure from which we name sin, and the corollary of redeeming grace, is grounded in a radical notion of the interconnected nature of the human person. Adopting such a view of the human person forfeits any notion that innocence exists.

- *Sin as hiding*—a critical tool in naming the ways that harm has been done by escapism and unethical passivity.

- *Structural dimensions of sin*—as related to and distinguished from personal (or individual) interpretations of sin.

- *Ambiguity in naming sin and grace*—given the reality of structural sin, we often make a choice for good within the context of knowing evil.

Why Not Just Talk about Evil?

Given its troubled history, why continue to talk about sin? Is not evil a more powerful category through which to analyze structural

16. Ibid. 111.
17. Ibid.

injustice? The answer to this question is yes and no. Sin and evil are mutually reinforcing concepts. In her often quoted essay, "Evil, Sin and the Violation of the Vulnerable," Mary Potter Engel describes the relationship of these two terms as follows. Sin refers to "those free, discrete acts of responsible individuals that create or reinforce these structures of oppression."[18] By way of contrast, evil signifies "structures of oppression, patterns larger than individuals and groups, that tempt us toward injustice and impiety. It is social, political, and economic arrangements that distort our perceptions or restrain our abilities to such an extent that we find it difficult to choose or do good."[19] What Engel describes as evil is also often referred to as structural or social sin. As such, when I speak of social sin, I also speak of evil. Structures and systems of discrimination and oppression are evil.

From the vantage point of privileged bystanders (the primary audience for this text), one must acknowledge that individual choices flow from structural arrangements. Yet, for the purposes of this book, I give preference to the language of sin because I find it helpful in resisting the "common tendency of perpetrators [and accomplices] to externalize evil to such an extent that each individual is exempt from all responsibility and accountability for it."[20] In the context of passive bystanding, we jump too quickly to the conclusion that the violation occurring is "none of our business" and "if it were, there would be little we could do anyway" as the source of structural injustice extends beyond our reach. To the extent that the externalization of evil is invoked in order to rationalize passive bystanding, I give the term *sin* priority here.

18. Mary Potter Engel, "Evil, Sin, and Violation of the Vulnerable," in *Lift Every Voice: Constructing Christian Theologies from the Underside*, ed. Susan Brooks Thistlethwaite and Mary Potter Engel, rev. ed. (Maryknoll, NY: Orbis, 1998), 162.
19. Ibid.
20. Ibid.

Sin-Talk and the Rhetoric of Blame: A Critique of the Adamic Myth

In assessing the human situation, Christian theologians have identified distinguishing patterns for human sinfulness. Most common among these is the characterization of sin as prideful disobedience of God's law. Historians have largely credited Augustine of Hippo with shaping this trajectory in the Christian West, yet many others followed.[21]

Augustine's anthropology pivots around an interpretation of the Genesis story, wherein Adam fails to acknowledge that his existence depended upon God. Prior to the Fall (Genesis 2–3), human beings had the capacity to choose the Good (God). Yet, Adam's desire to take the place of God (to exercise the will to power) gets in the way. His indiscretion has consequences for all of humankind. Concupiscence hereafter marks human existence. Humanity, in a postlapsarian state (after the Fall), cannot rightly order its desires. Human beings curve inwardly toward themselves instead of outwardly toward God and neighbor. Therefore, in this model, pride becomes the fundamental moral sin.

For Augustine, the doctrine of sin underscores the need for salvation and the absolute dependency of human beings on God's grace. His discussion of the Fall is not so much prompted by a desire to examine the cause of humanity's demise as it is by the need to emphasize the gratuitous nature of divine grace and our complete dependence upon God.[22] Echoing Paul, Christ as the second Adam

---

21. Augustine's influence is widespread, ranging through Protestant and Catholic thinkers alike. For more see Allan D. Fitzgerald, ed., *Augustine through the Ages: An Encyclopedia* (Grand Rapids: Eerdmans, 1999); Arnoud S. Q. Visser, *Reading Augustine in the Reformation: The Flexibility of Intellectual Authority in Europe, 1500–1620* (New York: Oxford University Press, 2011); and Aidan Nichols, OP, *The Thought of Pope Benedict XVI: An Introduction to the Theology of Joseph Ratzinger* (New York: Burns & Oates, 2007), chapter 2.

22. Roger Haight makes this point in the *Experience and Language of Grace* (Mahwah, NJ: Paulist, 1979), 37–38.

acts as a mediator restoring our relationship with God.[23] "And what greater example of obedience could be given to us, us who had been ruined by disobedience, than God the Son obeying God the Father *even to death on the cross* (Phil. 2:8)?"[24] Human beings, held captive by the prideful disobedience of Adam, now could be freed through the humble obedience of Jesus Christ. This reversal, a common motif throughout Western Christian thought, illustrates the dialectical relationship between sin and redemption. The classical Christian tradition has extolled obedience, innocence, and self-sacrificial love idealized by Christ's death on the cross as the antidote to human sinfulness. The remedy for our own pride is humble obedience.

Much can be said about naming sin to capture the ways in which we become so caught up in our own desires that we cannot look at the pain of others. Darby Kathleen Ray, Sallie McFague, and Carter Heyward have made the case that in view of the phenomenon of global capitalism, for those who reside in the so-called First World, it is, indeed, more appropriate to name sin as self-absorption.[25]

> Capitalism depends upon and actively cultivates misdirected desire. . . . To spend, purchase, and consume is not in and of itself evil, but when we do these things inordinately, beyond all need and reason and to the detriment of those in need around us—when we "swell greedily for outward things" and so ignore higher goods such as love of God and neighbor—then we participate in and are responsible for evil.[26]

---

23. The motif of Christ as a second Adam can also be found in the work of Augustine's predecessors. See Irenaeus of Lyon, *Against Heresies*, 5.21. http://www.newadvent.org/fathers/0103.htm.

24. Augustine of Hippo, *The Trinity*, trans. Edmund Hill, OP (New York: New City, 1991), 361.

25. Darby Kathleen Ray, "Tracking the Tragic: Augustine, Global Capitalism, and A Theology of Struggle," in *Constructive Theology: A Contemporary Approach to Classical Themes*, ed. Serene Jones and Paul Lakeland (Minneapolis: Fortress Press, 2005), 135–39, 141–43. Carter Heyward makes a similar point in *Saving Jesus from Those Who Are Right: Rethinking What It Means to Be Christian* (Minneapolis: Fortress Press, 1999), 82–88. Also see Sallie McFague, *The Body of God: An Ecological Theology* (Minneapolis: Fortress Press, 1993), 115–29.

26. Ray, "Tracking the Tragic," 138.

Yet, these scholars also identify the universal application of Augustine's explanation for the root of human misery as problematic. Context matters. Certainly, human misery can be attributed to inordinate pride. Yet, as Andrew Sung Park and Susan Nelson point out, this description of sin "can also be used to disguise and obfuscate human evil," teaching those on the underside of history to "shackle themselves in the name of righteousness."[27] Where one sits in relation to power and powerlessness within a given social context makes a difference in naming sin and evil. In certain contexts, rebellion, pride, and hardening one's heart are destructive. Yet, within other contexts, these same qualities can be lifesaving.[28]

Where we are makes a difference. This is an important distinction when thinking about sin from the vantage point of bystanders to violence. As discussed previously, many bystanders simultaneously occupy sites of power and vulnerability. In some contexts, bystanders are vulnerable insofar as they risk being the next target and cannot safely intervene. Yet vulnerability does not and cannot excuse participation in the abuse of power. Nor can vulnerability be a reason for declaring innocence.[29] There are also instances where we do have the ability to resist harm done to others and to stand in solidarity with those who are suffering, but fall prey to apathy and indifference, convincing ourselves that "it is not my problem," "it's really not that bad," or "the person got what he or she deserved." At other times, we fail to intervene because of the social costs. We don't want to look bad; we don't want to be associated with "those" people, and

---

27. Park and Nelson, "Introduction,"6.

28. Rita Nakashima Brock has argued that this framework is problematic for victim-survivors of violence insofar as innocence can become a prerequisite for justice. For example, if it can be proven that a victimized person or group lacks innocence, the implication may well be that they no longer deserve justice. See Rita Nakashima Brock, "Ending Innocence and Nurturing Willfulness," in *Violence Against Women and Children: A Christian Theological Sourcebook*, ed. Carol J. Adams and Marie M. Fortune (New York: Continuum, 1995), 80.

29. Ibid.

so on. We feign ignorance in order to protect our social status. While vulnerability and power often go together, it is the latter category that I am concerned about in this book. As argued in the previous chapter, bystander passivity is operative at the institutional and systemic level. Social privilege compounds bystander participation in hegemony by rendering violence invisible and granting permission for privileged persons to escape or ignore their complicity in human suffering.

Given the ways in which privileged apathy supports structural and interpersonal forms of violence, sin as prideful disobedience "misleads" when used as a theological metaphor,[30] because it works to justify the status quo instead of signaling the need for social transformation. Drawing insight from the work of Theodore Jennings Jr., I will briefly discuss how three tendencies, often accompanying pastoral and theological appropriation of the Adamic myth, work in tandem to further compound the problem of unethical passivity for privileged bystanders: verticalizing, individualizing, and criminalizing.[31]

Verticalizing

Jennings argues that descriptions of sin as pride and disobedience have been extracted from liberative discourse through verticalizing tendencies within Christian theology. In the Gospels, Jesus' appropriation of the Decalogue (Ten Commandments) places the moral imperative on our relationship with one another.[32] One of the best known examples is found in the Gospel of Matthew, where

---

30. Reference is to Heyward's *Saving Jesus*, 81. Similar to her statement "obedience misleads as a metaphor," one can also say that sin as prideful disobedience misleads as a metaphor.

31. These categories are Theodore W. Jennings Jr.'s in "Reconstructing the Doctrine of Sin," in *The Other Side of Sin: Woundedness from the Perspective of the Sinned-Against*, ed. Andrew Sung Park and Susan L. Nelson (Albany, NY: SUNY, 2001), 105–22.

32. Ibid., 111.

Jesus draws a parallel between our relationship with God and our relationship to the poor, disenfranchised, and oppressed.[33] To love God is to love one's neighbor and vice versa:

> For I was hungry and you gave me food, I was thirsty and you gave me something to drink, I was a stranger and you welcomed me, I was naked and you gave me clothing, I was sick and you took care of me, I was in prison and you visited me . . . just as you did it to one of the least of these who are members of my family, you did it to me. (Matt. 25:35-36, 40)

While Christian writers, preachers, and ministers have used the first part of this passage to extol the virtues of Christian charity and justice, they often bypass the second half of the parable.

> "I was a stranger and you did not welcome me, naked and you did not give me clothing, sick and in prison and you did not visit me." Then they also will answer, "Lord, when was it that we saw you hungry or thirsty or a stranger or naked or sick or in prison, and did not take care of you?" Then he will answer them, "Truly I tell you, just as you did not do it to one of the least of these, you did not do it to me." (Matt. 25:43-45)

As noted in the passage above, separation from God "consists in what is done to the neighbor; it refers to the affliction and humiliation of the most vulnerable in our midst."[34] Yet, despite the "horizontalizing" tendencies found in the Christian Gospels, dominant strands of Christian theological tradition have stressed violation of the individual's relationship with God in constructions of sin. Here, sin signifies "failure to comply with religious responsibilities in a narrowly defined religious sphere."[35] One prominent example can be found in *Cur Deus Homo*, introduced in the previous chapter,

33. Ibid., 112.
34. Ibid.
35. Ibid.

125

wherein Anselm frames sin as a debt of obedience owed to God.[36] As Jennings states, "Far more is at stake than a mere fetishizing of religiosity. For what transpires here is that the injustice perpetrated against the neighbor, the stranger, the other, comes to be seen as a matter of less consequence than, and as separate from, the question of one's appropriate attitude toward God."[37] In this context, one need not seek forgiveness from the person violated. The sinner must only seek God's forgiveness. Such an understanding of sin has supported practices that allow for the "atonement" of sins apart from "the inconvenience of dealing directly with those one has wronged."[38] For example, in the Roman Catholic tradition, one can participate in the sacrament of reconciliation without ever having to face the violated person or group.[39]

In the context of bystander passivity, verticalizing tendencies work to diffuse responsibility by diverting attention away from human violation, offering theological justification for apathy in the face of profound human suffering. Such a perspective holds that God's suffering on the cross for the sake of our redemption is what is important, not the suffering of the neighbor. In environments marked by white racism and heterosexism, such tendencies contribute to the unquestioning acceptance of racial disparities and heteronormativity by many Christians. In particular, it is this mentality that allows white Christians and heterosexual Christians to see themselves as "good Christians" apart from serious consideration of their own participation in the hierarchical stratification of gender, racial, or economic privilege. Verticalizing tendencies have also

36. See Anselm of Canterbury, "Why God Became Man," in *Anselm of Canterbury: Major Works*, ed. Brian Davies and G. R. Evans (New York: Oxford University Press, 1998), 260–357.
37. Jennings, "Reconstructing the Doctrine of Sin," 112.
38. Ibid.
39. An egregious but not entirely foreign example would be a priest assigning a penance of Mass attendance and individual prayer after the confession of sexual abuse. At the backdrop of this is the preservation of the sanctity of marriage at all costs.

supported the public/private and secular/sacred divide that implies as long as you are in church on Sunday, what you and others do outside the confines of the sanctuary is your own business.

Individualizing

Verticalizing tendencies have accompanied a focus on the individual in Western Christian articulations of sin. The prophetic view of sin "as the deviation of society and its elites from the divine will for justice" has shifted to an understanding of sin as "unrighteous acts or attitude of individuals."[40] On the one hand, the tendency to personalize sin can be helpful in stressing individual accountability and responsibility. Indeed, in view of systemic violence, retaining the moral agency of individuals and particular communities remains critical. (As I have already suggested, sometimes language about evil can allow us to distance ourselves from the problem at hand.) The issue, though, in view of bystander passivity, is how to retain a sense of personal accountability while having the language to evaluate social systems and structures. By itself, individualized notions of sin leave us wanting in terms of the theological language to evaluate cultural mores that normalize the dehumanization and marginalization of entire communities of people. The diversion of attention away from systemic injustices, as well as the invisibility of evil itself, remains critical. Cultural mores that support hierarchal notions of human relationality (e.g., the trivialization of aggression of males with the phrase "boys will be boys" discussed in chapter 1) mask violent aggression and dehumanization. For bystanders to resist violence, they have to be able to recognize that harm is afoot. The work of transforming privileged apathy requires the adoption of

---

40. Jennings, "Reconstructing the Doctrine of Sin," 113.

a paradigm for sin-talk that explicitly acknowledges the social and structural dimensions of sin.

Criminalizing

In addition to verticalizing and individualizing tendencies, the Adamic mythic is often accompanied by an interpretive focus where sin is equated to disobedience of the divine law. As Jennings notes, the notion of sin as disobedience can be found in the scriptures. Yet, in early Christianity, this focus was mitigated by the social location of the historical person of Jesus of Nazareth.[41] The memory of Jesus, as recalled by his disciples within the early Christian community, was that of one who "refused to comply with the notions of legality in normative Judaism and as one who was executed as a criminal by Roman authorities."[42] The alignment of Christianity with the Roman Empire accompanied a shift in the rhetoric of sin-talk. Post-Constantine, descriptions of sin as disobedience of divine law were appropriated in order to legitimate systems of the law.[43] Violation of the legal code of the day came to signify not only rebellion against God, but also a violation of sociopolitical authorities.[44] In this framework, "righteousness comes to be compliance with the laws that articulate the existing social structure."[45] When radical inequality marks the existing structure, such a framework can easily encourage or legitimize passivity in view of social injustice. This certainly applies in a number of contemporary contexts. For example, Engel argues that the construct of sin as disobedience has contributed to the entrapment of women and children in situations of domestic abuse.[46]

---

41. Ibid., 114.
42. Ibid.
43. Ibid.
44. See Joerg Rieger, *Christ & Empire: From Paul to Postcolonial Times* (Minneapolis: Fortress Press, 2007), 78 and 128.
45. Jennings, "Reconstructing the Doctrine of Sin," 114.

Children learn early that obedience of external authority figures is rewarded and disobedience punished. In contexts marked by violent abuse, the ascription of sin as disobedience further compounds the difficulties many encounter in resisting the violating actions of their parents or other authority figures. Rebellion is appropriate in the face of hegemony.

In other words, the other side of the coin is that "obedience [as a theological virtue] is [also] a misleading metaphor."[47] As a theological construct, it reinforces hierarchal authoritarianism and immaturity, failing to encourage theo-ethical maturity and interdependence. As Carter Heyward suggests, while obedience "may be the simplest way to teach children (of any age) right from wrong, it also guarantees that children will not develop the capacities for inner-discernment and moral-reasoning that accompany mature life in the Spirit."[48] It encourages children (and adults) to base moral decisions out of fear of punishment instead of the flourishing of all. It is harder to learn how to think and act ethically than to do simply what one is told. Adopting a paradigm in which sin is identified as disobedience and righteousness as obedience only further encourages passive bystanding in contexts where action is warranted.

Furthermore, as Heyward argues, obedience as a theo-ethical paradigm suggests that "God is a power over us more than a Spirit with us."[49] Obedience does not encourage creative partnership with God in the redemption of the world. It suggests that God has all the answers and human beings have none. As she suggests, perhaps "the root of evil of Jesus' situation was not primarily, if at all, wicked individuals set upon destroying anything."[50] The source of evil may

46. Engel, "Sin and the Violation of the Vulnerable," 164.
47. Heyward, *Saving Jesus*, 81.
48. Ibid.
49. Ibid.
50. Ibid., 91.

have been the inability of bystanders to realize their own capacity to effect social change. "The people around Jesus, like most of us much of the time, assumed that they were powerless to do much about anything except perhaps in small ways to take care of themselves and their own."[51]

Self-deception is a multifaceted reality, particularly for those of us who benefit more from social privilege than we suffer oppression. No one is innocent. We are all deeply implicated in sin. "To be 'innocent' would be to be *un*created, *un*involved, totally *dis*connected. If we are at all, we are implicated in both the presence and the brokenness of our bonds with one another."[52] By imagining that we are powerless to change the situation, or through believing that we need to control everything, we betray our common humanity. Unethical passivity and dominance manifest the entitlement of abuse. Both constitute an abuse of power. While the ascription of sin as pride can offer a helpful tool in critiquing power as dominance, the verticalizing and individualizing tendencies often accompanying this particular form of sin-talk restrain its use. Pride has come to signify an individual's attitude toward God rather than serving as a tool for critiquing the relationship of elites to those who are disenfranchised by structural inequalities.

Moreover, the metaphor of sin as disobedience does not adequately capture the very real ways that unethical passivity and dominance intertwine through the dynamics of social power and privilege. Social privilege not only points to the use of coercive power by elites in order to secure unearned advantage and entitlements, but it also supports the tacit acceptance of violence through the luxury of obliviousness. Privilege grants those in positions of power the ability to decide who to tolerate, who to ignore, and who to help. White

51. Ibid.
52. Ibid., 105. Italics original.

people can go about their day-to-day activities without having to consider their own racial identity. Cisgender and heterosexual individuals rarely have to think twice about posting pictures of their loved ones on Facebook or in the office. Privilege distorts privileged persons' view of reality. It tricks us into believing that we are innocent and the suffering that befalls those on the underside of history is the result of their own inadequacies.

Privileged elites fall prey to such tactics because we live segregated lives. By and large, isolation maintains privilege. Those who occupy spaces of privilege have the power to "opt out." As a white middle-class person, I can choose to opt out of participation in the lives of individuals who are different from me. I can purchase a home in an affluent part of town with good schools. I can choose to isolate myself and my family from individuals of different racial, economic, and ethnic backgrounds than me. I make these choices through purchasing power or economic wealth. Social isolation in homogenous environments inculcates ignorance, blinding us to the consequences of our actions. "In systems of power as dominance, those who are powerful have the least access to seeing the whole, and, therefore, have the most distorted picture of reality."[53]

This distortion has theological import. Given the ways in which social constructs like whiteness and heteronormativity are embedded within privileged subjectivity and privileged discourse itself,[54] it is difficult for privileged people to accurately recognize sin. As James Cone explains, "Sin is a community concept . . . there can be no knowledge of the sinful condition except in the movement of an oppressed community claiming its freedom. This means that whites, despite their self-proclaimed righteousness, are rendered incapable

---

53. Brock, *Journeys by Heart: A Christology of Erotic Power* (New York: Continuum, 1988), 26–27.
54. Jennifer Harvey, *Whiteness and Morality: Pursuing Racial Justice through Reparations and Sovereignty* (New York: Palgrave MacMillan, 2007), 37.

of making valid judgments on the character of sin. . . . In white theology, sin is a theoretical idea, not a concrete reality."[55] Therefore, sin-talk for privileged bystanders must begin by listening to the lament of those who have been sinned against.

Sin-Talk and the Language of Lament: Listening to the Sinned Against

In the Hebrew Scriptures, lamentation—with its vivid imagery and bold statements—is harsh, strident, and at times, even incoherent. As Walter Brueggemann explains, such speech is not civil, polite, or even politically correct. It is in the arena of "terror, raggedness, and hurt."[56] Through lamentation, voice is given to pain. By foregrounding the anguish and passionate protest of those who have suffered injustice, the failures of God and the human community are viscerally brought to attention. Such speech is risky because it demands that we "acknowledge and embrace" immutability—both human and divine.[57] Lament not only calls for justice, but it "pushes the boundaries of our relationship with one another and God beyond the limits of acceptability."[58]

According to Brueggemann, the linguistic function of such speech-acts "is to evoke reality for someone who has engaged in self-deception and still imagines and pretends life is well-ordered."[59] And it is precisely the harsh and abrasive nature of lamentation that is able to "penetrate" this "deception" and say, "No, this is how life really is."[60] It is in the sense, that for white people, lamentation holds

---

55. James H. Cone, *A Black Theology of Liberation*, 40th anniv. ed. (Maryknoll, NY: Orbis, 2010), 113.

56. Walter Brueggemann, *Message of the Psalms: A Theological Commentary* (Minneapolis: Augsburg Press, 1984), 53.

57. Ibid. 52.

58. Ackermann, *After the Locusts,* 111.

59. Brueggemann, *Message of the Psalms*, 53.

60. Ibid.

the potential to serve a theological language of "dis-ease" and "discomfort."[61]

Lamentation keeps "the justice questions visible."[62] In the words of Massingale, the lament of those who have suffered injustice resists the silencing of evil and "makes visible the masked injustice hidden beneath the deep rationalizations of social life."[63] In the context of racial injustice, lament has the power to disrupt the "apparent normalcy" of white superiority and nonwhite oppression.[64] Lament calls out the socially privileged's tendency to gloss over pain and to hide from God, one another, and ourselves in our own vulnerability. Therefore, it is no surprise that the language of lament has all but disappeared from our liturgical and sacramental life.[65] Yet, such avoidance comes with a great cost. For in muting the language of lament, we have muted our ability to hear pain—to reckon with sin and evil.[66]

Privileged people have inhabited religious worlds marked by escapism and denial. While I am hardly advocating a return to the immobilizing guilt of my parents' experience of Catholicism, I do think that in an era marked by feel-good escapism, it is time for us to learn how to embrace immutability—failure—that of our own, that of those who have gone before us, and that of God. In other words, we have to lose our innocence. In order to do so, we need to cultivate a new kind of spiritual listening, one that is attuned to the cry of lament. The listening of which I speak is an interior praxis, rooted in

---

61. Karen Teel uses these terms in "What Jesus Wouldn't Do," in *Christology and Whiteness: What Would Jesus Do?* (New York/London: Routledge, 2012), 30.
62. Walter Brueggemann, *The Psalms and the Life of Faith*, ed. Patrick D. Miller (Minneapolis: Fortress Press, 1995), 106.
63. Massingale, *Racial Justice*, 110.
64. Ibid.
65. Brueggemann, *Message of the Psalms*, 53.
66. John Swinton makes this point in *Raging with Compassion: Pastoral Responses to the Problem of Evil* (Grand Rapids, MI: Eerdmans, 2007), 115–16.

a public communal commitment. For example, as a white person, I can lament my own complicity in racial injustice and the ways with which white supremacy continues to leave racial relations undone in the United States. Yet, my own lament is nonsensical apart from a first hearing of nonwhite anguish. Moreover, a process of coming to awareness is necessary before the privileged can lament. Denise Ackermann describes this process as inclusive of "accountability, memory, repentance, receiving forgiveness, and the making of reparations."[67] It is in this sense that it becomes possible to "lament from 'the other side.'"[68] Namely, "lament from 'the other side'" requires a transformation of heart and relationships expressed through concrete actions: relinquishing economic and racial advantage, including the arrogant presumption of white primacy in naming God and the human condition. Similarly, in the context of heteropatriarchy, "lament from 'the other side'" means relinquishing heterosexual and gender advantage, in secular and religious contexts. Moreover, privileged lament must take place within the space of waiting for forgiveness. This is because waiting for forgiveness, according to Ackermann, "is an exercise in a state of dependence, an acceptance of a kind of unfreedom. Forgiveness denied is always a possibility."[69] It is in this space of "unfreedom"—of uncertainty—in this space of waiting—that privileged people enter into the conversation about sin.

We cannot continue to talk about sin in ways that render us comfortable in the face of rampant injustice. If sin-talk is to open up the potential for healing in the context of privileged apathy, it must disrupt the status quo and make a claim to our attention. Namely,

---

67. Denise Ackermann, "Lamenting Tragedy from 'the Other Side'," in *Sameness and Difference: Problems and Potentials in South African Civil Society,* ed. James R. Cochran and Bastienne Klein (Washington DC: Council for Research, 2000), 220.
68. Ackermann, *After the Locusts,* 117.
69. Ibid.

it must engage us viscerally. The lamentations of those who have suffered at hands of injustice bring to the fore the ways in which sin is embodied through the violence of poverty, war, colonization, and racial and gendered stigmatization. In attending to the cries, anguish, and anger of the sinned against, privileged Christians are called to acknowledge that "life and relationships have gone terribly wrong" and to join in protesting the violent state of the world, including their own participation in it.[70] In this way, sin-talk becomes a wake-up call, challenging us to arise from the "sleep of our inhumanity to a reality of humanity."[71]

Power, Privilege, and a Loss of Innocence: Sin-Talk for Bystanders

In view of passive bystanding, we need a hamartiology (theology of sin) that helps name the depths of participation in self-deception, as well as the harm that self-deception does to ourselves and others. Yet such a hamartiology must not fall prey to fatalism and anthropological pessimism that contends that human beings cannot effect change. Rather, the function of sin-talk is to point pathways toward healing, resurrection, and future hope. Sin-talk, in view of unethical passivity, outwardly contests fatalism and calls us to tap into the depth of shared power.

Drawing insight from the constructions of those who have occupied the "underside" of history, I identify and develop four critical markers of sin-talk for bystanders to violence: 1) relational anthropology, 2) sin as hiding, 3) the structural dimension of sin, and 4) ambiguity in naming good and evil. The model does not supplant existing models of sin-talk, but stands alongside them, helping us to

---

70. Massingale, *Racial Justice*, 106.
71. Jon Sobrino, *The Principle of Mercy: Taking the Crucified People from the Cross* (Maryknoll, NY: Orbis, 1994), 11.

reckon, in a deeper sense, with the unethical relinquishment of shared power and the inadequacy of apathy in the face of violence.

Starting with the Relational Self

All sin-talk points to a theological anthropology, whether explicitly or not. In the context of unethical passivity, the starting point for sin-talk must issue forth from a relational anthropology wherein the person is understood as a person-in-relation. While hardly a new concept, it is one worth reiterating, given the prominence of individualizing tendencies in shaping the Western ethos, secular and religious.[72] In the context of Western capitalism, the self is understood as an autonomous self through the narrative of hard work, which assumes that one's social station in life directly correlates with one's work ethic and intelligence. This thinking undergirds the stereotype that the poor are lazy and that the assets attained by the upper echelon of society directly result from their own efforts and ingenuity. Individualizing tendencies can also be found within the classical Christian tradition, wherein the status of one's salvation directly reflects on one's individual character.

As Mary Elizabeth Hobgood rightly notes, "The inordinate stress on the person as an autonomous self within the Christian West not only fosters a disproportionate focus on self-interest in decision-making and the individual and social level, but it also ignores the dynamics of power and privilege operative in society."[73] Individual rights are an important aspect of society. Yet, persons who tend to

---

72. Examples of those who have adopted such a view include many of the authors already discussed—especially in the areas of black liberation theology, eco-theology and feminist theology. Other prominent examples include Ivone Gebara, *Longing for Running Water: Ecofeminism and Liberation* (Minneapolis: Fortress Press, 1999), Catherine Keller, *From a Broken Web: Separation, Sexism, and Self* (Boston: Beacon, 1988), and Sallie McFague, *The Body of God: An Ecological Theology* (Minneapolis: Fortress Press, 1993).

73. Mary Elizabeth Hobgood, *Dismantling Privilege: An Ethics of Accountability*, rev. and updated ed. (Cleveland: Pilgrim, 2009), 28.

benefit most from these "rights" are white, able-bodied, heterosexual men. Moreover, "privileged groups are hardly autonomous as they are buttressed by an invisible foundation of subordinated 'others.'"[74] The wealth of white individuals has been purchased off the backs of nonwhite men and women in the United States.

Therefore, I reaffirm theological anthropologies wherein the self is understood as a self-in-relation that foregrounds the interdependence of all creation. The idea of the self-in-relation goes beyond the simple assertion that our actions—for better or for worse—impact the livelihood of others, and holds that our well-being intimately connects to the well-being of all creation. Creation is fluid and ever changing. We constantly engage in processes that define and redefine one another. One such proponent of this world view is Ivone Gebara.

Gebara's reflections on personhood and sin can be placed within the context of Brazil's ecological degradation and its economic import on the livelihood of Brazilian women. As an ecofeminist theologian, her theological reflections underscore the interdependence and interconnection of all living things. As such, she adopts the term *relatedness* in order to highlight the collective dimension of personhood.[75] Our being is part of a larger cosmic story and cosmic memory. We do not and cannot exist apart from being in communion with other human beings and the natural world. Our relationship with other creatures and persons is not only a necessary condition for life but constitutes our very being. To affirm relatedness "as a primordial and foundational reality requires us to eliminate dualisms and other forms of separation."[76] Relatedness calls forth a more holistic understanding of rationality, ethics, and religious experience.

74. Ibid.
75. Gebara, *Longing for Running Water,* 83.
76. Ibid., 88

Relatedness is vital to the naming of sin. In such a model, the root of suffering is interpreted as the idolatry of the individual, resulting in an imbalance of social goods, power, and resources. The imbalance or disequilibrium created by sin must be contextualized.[77] For some, sin bears the mark of a loss of self. It is experienced as the subordination and dehumanization that accompanies oppression. For others, disequilibrium manifests itself in the form of cultural narcissism and excess. "If we lean too far in the direction of self-love we easily slip into all kinds of narcissistic behavior, which has as a result the destruction of others or, at the very least, deafness to their cries."[78] On the other hand, we can move into "an excess of self-giving, an excessive obedience, excessive humility, silence on matters of social outrage, self-effacement."[79] The model of sin set forth by Gebara helps in view of passive bystanding because it makes clear the relationship between privilege and oppression. The excess of egotism connects to what those on the margins lack. In such a relational model, "there are no spaces of innocence."[80] Further, while we all may be complicit in sin and responsible for healing, the nature of one's responsibility and complicity is contingent upon one's social location.

While interdependence may not be compatible with individualism, it does not erase individuality. Part of the challenge in addressing bystander passivity concerns pluralistic ignorance—the ways in which we look to others in interpreting ambiguous violent situations.[81] Pluralistic ignorance results from the tendency "to rely

---

77. Ivone Gebara, *Out of the Depths: Women's Experience of Evil and Salvation*, trans. Anne Patrick Ware (Minneapolis: Fortress Press, 2002), 139.

78. Ibid., 141.

79. Ibid.

80. Ibid., 171.

81. Peter Fischer et al., "The Bystander-Effect: A Meta-Analytic Review on Bystander Intervention in Dangerous and Non-Dangerous Emergencies," *Psychological Bulletin* 137, no. 4 (2011): 517. See Bibb Latané and John M. Darley, *The Unresponsive Bystander: Why Doesn't He Help?* (Englewood Cliffs, NJ: Prentice-Hall, 1970).

on the overt reactions of others" in determining whether a situation is violent.[82] If everyone around us ignores the violence at hand, we are more likely to do so as well. This is especially true in situations where violence is covert or perceived as ambiguous. Reading social cues is a vital social skill. While conformity can be used to effect positive social change,[83] peer pressure can also be a negative force, quelling individuality and personal responsibility. In view of passive bystanding, too many privileged people have chosen to ignore violence. Practices of social exclusion, coercion, and intimidation continue to undergird human relationality within personal, social, and institutional spheres. These practices, which often go unnamed, have been so successfully normalized that we fail to notice violent activity within our midst. A relational anthropology challenges us to move beyond a posture of apathy toward that of solidarity and mutuality (two concepts that will be further developed in chapter 5).

When we speak of the problem of bystander passivity, the goal is not simply to challenge one person to intervene one time. The disruption of hegemonic forms of violence calls for more than this. Case in point: I can "justify my need at times to be altruistic to others who sometimes need my 'help' and are deserving of my self-sacrifice, but never warrant a mutual or reciprocal relationship with me."[84] Interdependence does not equate with acts of charity. Rather, it is much more risky than this. Interdependence requires lasting commitment and analysis of the social and personal dimensions of sin that is informed by a discernment of our place within the social hierarchy that continues to define race, class, and gender relations

---

82. Ibid.

83. Social movements have successfully capitalized on peer pressure in order to effect positive social change. For example, consider the role of the media in shaping the participation of the millennial generation in the 2008 presidential election, the March on Wall Street, or the It Gets Better campaign against bullying.

84. Hobgood, *Dismantling Privilege*, 30.

today. Relatedness calls for genuine listening and the development of compassionate relationships informed by a new use of freedom. As James Cone reminds us, freedom is a community concept that means "taking sides in a crisis situation, when a society is divided into oppressed and oppressors."[85] Relatedness helps us to understand that *"no one is free until all are free."*[86]

Sin as Hiding: Contesting Escapism and Mindless Conformity

Certainly, aspects of the human situation revolve around the inordinate use of power as domination, or pride. Yet, given the tendency of many to become the "chameleon-like" creatures of which Valerie Saiving once spoke, there also needs to be a concerted effort to examine the ways in which "self-aggrandizing tendencies" manifest themselves through passivity and escapism.[87] In other words, passive bystanding calls for a greater attention to the ways in which our hiding—from ourselves, others, and the divine—fractures relationship. Yet, such an analysis of sin cannot only be situated in an individual framework. It must also attend to the collective dimensions of hiding, a concept consonant with Cheng's description of sin as apathy and mindless conformity.[88]

Valerie Saiving was one of the first to critique the identification of sin with pride from the vantage point of women's lived experience. In her 1960 essay, "The Human Situation: A Feminine View," Saiving suggests that due to gender socialization, "the temptations of woman" are best described in terms of "triviality, distractibility, and diffuseness; lack of an organizing center or focus; dependence on others for one's own self-definition; tolerance at the experience of

---

85. Cone, *Black Theology of Liberation*, 100.
86. Ibid., 93. Italics original
87. Valerie Saiving Goldstein, "The Human Situation: A Feminine View," *The Journal of Religion* 40, no. 2 (1960): 100–12, quote is from p. 111.
88. Cheng, *From Sin to Amazing Grace*, 94–95 and 104–5, respectively.

standards of excellence; . . . in short, underdevelopment or negation of the self."[89] Moreover, such a framework also breeds a sense of powerlessness among those already marginalized, especially those trapped by domestic violence and child abuse.[90] The emphasis on self-sacrifice and obedience "has worked to the advantage of ruling elites, abusive parents, partners, and elders," encouraging the vulnerable to remain passive and compliant, as opposed to willfully resisting violence.[91] When taken to the extreme, the Adamic myth encourages mindless obedience to the status quo, leaving behind a society full of "chameleon-like creature[s] who [respond] to others but [have] no personal identity of [their] own."[92] Therefore, Saiving and her feminist contemporaries named sin as hiding, or a loss of self. Susan Nelson expresses the problem best when she states, "As she has been afraid to dream a dream for herself as well as for others, and as she has trained herself to live a submerged existence, she has hidden from her full humanity."[93] In hiding, we "center so completely on our continuity with others, and on maintaining that continuity by pleasing others, that [we] become emptied of ourselves and forget that to be human, to be free, is to have a center of agency from which to interpret the world, from which to name ourselves, from which to take responsibility for our lives."[94]

---

89. Saiving, "The Human Situation," 109. Saiving's critique was the first of many in feminist theological circles. Others include Susan Nelson Dunfee, "The Sin of Hiding: A Feminist Critique," *Soundings* 65, no. 3 (Fall 1982): 316–27, and Judith Plaskow, *Sex, Sin and Grace: Women's Experience and the Theologies of Reinhold Neibuhr and Paul Tillich* (Washington, DC: University Press of America, 1980).

90. See Rita Nakashima Brock and Rebecca Ann Parker, *Proverbs of Ashes: Violence, Redemptive Suffering, and the Search for What Saves Us* (Boston: Beacon, 2001); Traci C. West, *Wounds of the Spirit: Black Women and Resistance Ethics* (New York: New York University Press, 1999); and Marie M. Fortune, *Sexual Violence: The Sin Revisited* (Cleveland: Pilgrim, 2005).

91. Darby Kathleen Ray, *Deceiving the Devil: Atonement, Abuse and Ransom* (Cleveland: Pilgrim, 1998), 24–25.

92. Saiving, "The Human Situation," 111.

93. Nelson, "Sin of Hiding," 322.

94. Susan Nelson Dunfee, *Beyond Servanthood: Christianity and the Liberation of Women* (New York: University Press of America, 1989), 13.

While Saiving's original construction has rightly been critiqued on the grounds that it universalizes women's experience, when viewed in the context of unethical passivity, the sin of hiding points to the death-dealing ways in which we unnecessarily relinquish our own power, talents, and God-given gifts. Naming sin as the failure to self-actualize to such an extent that one fails to take responsibility for one's own life is helpful in pointing to a lack of maturity, collective and individual.[95] When we hide from ourselves and others, we live a "submerged" and "alienated" existence.[96] Shielded by fear and insecurity, our relationships betray our true selves—and our capacity for erotic power. Relationships with others, the divine, and ourselves are then based upon false pretense instead of genuine love.

Hiding takes many forms. Hiding can and does issue forth from a lack of self-esteem, or self-love. To the degree that women and minorities[97] have been taught to fear their own power, this remains true. Institutionalized violence usurps power by inculcating self-hate through cultural processes that teach women to see their place in the world as men's subordinates and teach nonwhites to see themselves as inferior to whites. To the extent that these norms continue to shape our day-to-day practices, hiding needs to be contextualized in view of gender, racial, and class socialization.

Hiding also manifests itself through mindless conformity and apathy, particularly when we rely too heavily upon external sources of authority in defining reality. At an early age, children are taught to fear difference. Such enculturation teaches us to hide our own uniqueness, reinforcing mindless conformity. In this sense, the relinquishment of personal power, talents, and gifts links to the social

95. This concept will be developed in chapter 5.
96. Nelson, "Sin of Hiding," 323.
97. For a discussion of the significance of sin as a loss of self in light of the marginalization of Latinos/as, see Miguel A. De La Torre, "Mad Men, Competitive Women, and Invisible Hispanics," *Journal of Feminist Studies in Religion* 28, no. 1 (2012): 121–26.

stratification of power. Social hierarchies diminish and humiliate the vulnerable. People who don't fit into cultural norms are cast out. Hiding, while it may protect us for a time, has a much greater cost in the long term, shaping one's engagement in the world in terms of passivity and conflict avoidance. This is particularly so given the human propensity toward immaturity during times of fear and uncertainty, wherein we lose sight of the importance of finding God within.

Drawing insight from the work of Robert Goss, Marcella Althaus-Reid, and Justin Tanis, Patrick Cheng suggests that to be Christlike is to transgress false binaries, to call into question hegemony.[98] Within this framework, sin is named as apathy and mindless conformity with the status quo. It is "the reluctance to be inclusive because of issues of expediency or convenience."[99] For example, Cheng highlights the participation of bystanders in the scapegoating of marginalized persons and communities as illustrative of the sin of mindless conformity. This includes those heterosexual bystanders who have failed to speak up or act on behalf of LGBTQ persons in the context of homophobic violence as well as LGBTQ persons who ignore racism and socioeconomic injustice.[100]

Hiding from God, one another, and ourselves, we conform to violence. Hiding is not only about a lack of self-assertion, it is also about segregation. Locking our doors, building fences, clutching our purses—we hide from the real possibility of relationship with others. Our hiding participates in the ongoing creation of separate and unequal worlds. Privilege creates myopic vision wherein the periphery is hidden from view. It encourages a culture of escapism where time and attention are diverted from the suffering of others to

98. Cheng, *From Sin to Amazing Grace*, 103–4.
99. Ibid., 95.
100. Ibid., 105 and 95 respectively.

the trivial. Through such forms of escapism, we conform to violence by denying that it exists at all.

Structural Dimension of Sin

Given the increasingly covert form violence takes, naming sin as hiding helps unpack the harm done through escapism and separatism. Yet our attention to the sin of hiding must be contextualized in view of the social dimensions of sin. Over the past several years, I have become convinced that one of the reasons bystanders fail to appear in public discourse on violence is directly related to the narrow definition of violence operative in society at large. When one understands violence as an act between two individuals or groups, it pushes bystander participation out of view and deems it irrelevant to the situation at hand. A parallel observation holds for discussions of sin within the Christian religious imagination. Inasmuch as sin is a descriptive category that helps us to name human participation in suffering and tragedy, attention to the social dimension of sin becomes a critical vantage point in naming sin for bystanders to violence.

In the 1960s, Latin American liberation theologies issued forth a new consciousness regarding sin and redemption. Thinkers like Gustavo Gutiérrez, Leonardo Boff, Jon Sobrino, and Ignacio Ellacuría challenged Christians in the West to speak of sin in terms of socioeconomic oppression, foregrounding its structural dimension.[101]

---

101. Gustavo Gutiérrez, *A Theology of Liberation*, trans. and ed. Sister Caridad Inda and John Eagleson, 15th anniv. ed. (Maryknoll, NY: Orbis, 1988), Jon Sobrino, *Christology at the Crossroads* (Maryknoll, NY: Orbis, 1978), and Leonardo Boff, *Jesus Christ Liberator: A Critical Christology for Our Times* (Maryknoll, NY: Orbis, 1978). For more on the history of Latin American liberation theologies, see Robert McAfee Brown, *Gustavo Gutiérrez: An Introduction to Liberation Theology* (Maryknoll, NY: Orbis, 1990). Black liberation theologians have also named sin in a communal or social sense. James Cone has argued that racism is America's original sin, as it is "institutionalized at all levels of society," it is "our most persistent and intractable evil." James H. Cone, "Theology's Greatest Sin," *Soul Work: Anti-Racist Theologies*

Arguing that the starting point for theological reflection must be the questions and concerns of the poor in Latin America, liberation theology put forth a radical critique of the verticalizing and individualizing tendencies found in Eurocentric Christian theology.[102] The promise of the reign of God is not a private reality. God's eschatological promise implies a historical liberation, calling out for the elimination of "misery and exploitation."[103] Therefore, any sin-talk must issue forth a serious consideration of socioeconomic oppression. Poverty creates a situation of alienation. To be poor is to be exploited and to be treated as a nonperson.[104] Sin is "regarded as a social, historical fact, the absence of fellowship and love in relationships among persons, the breach of friendship with God and with other persons."[105] Sin is found in the unjust and oppressive structures in society.

The category of structural sin allows us to name the harm institutions do. Often this type of harm relates to isms—racism, sexism, heterosexism, or classism. Social institutions play a necessary and important role in the organization of society. They are meant to enhance human freedom and to maintain social stability. Yet history provides many examples where this is not the case. Institutions can limit human freedom by privileging some groups and oppressing others. As illustrated in the previous chapter, African Americans, immigrants, and people of color have been systematically subjected to various forms of dehumanization and denied access to basic resources. Moreover, structural sin does not restrict itself to the secular sphere. Racism, sexism, classism, and heterosexism can also be found within

in Dialogue, ed. Marjorie Bowens-Wheatley and Nancy Palmer Jones (Boston: Skinner, 2002), 3. Also see Cone's *Black Theology of Liberation*, 114–15.

102. Gutiérrez, *A Theology of Liberation*, xxxiii.

103. Ibid., 97.

104. Ibid., 164.

105. Ibid., 102–03

religious organizations.[106] Churches have denied women participation in leadership roles. Christian religious groups have publicly denounced same-sex unions and gender-variant identities. Religious communions continue to be segregated along racial lines. As Jamie T. Phelps poignantly reminds us, "The perpetuation of these social systems has required the complicity of many."[107] In other words, structural sin is the result of inaction as much as it is the result of conscious decision.

Finally, structural sin cannot be separated from personal sin. The institutions we inhabit inform the decisions we make (or fail to make) as individuals. The cultural contexts in which we live and have our being shape what and whom we value, desire, or reject. Our use of freedom also plays a role in shaping institutional power. Who we vote for and the programs and communities that we support with our time, money, and energy help shape the direction of society. Sin is both structural and personal. This can make it difficult to discern the extent of our participation in evil. The ambiguous nature of good and evil further complicates the task of Christian discernment. In life, few circumstances allow for either/or moral decision making, whereby one rejects evil in favor of the good. Often, for bystanders, the moral choice calls us to choose the good in the context of knowing evil.[108]

106. A number of scholars have made this argument. For a discussion of the existence of racism within Roman Catholicism, see Bryan Massingale, *Racial Justice*, chapter 2. Rosemary Radford Ruether has long critiqued the existence of sexism within the Roman Catholic Church. See *Catholic≠The Vatican: A Vision for Progressive Catholicism* (New York: New Press, 2008). Kelly Brown Douglas has examined the presence of heterosexism and sexism in the Black Church. See *Sexuality and the Black Church: A Womanist Perspective* (Maryknoll, NY: Orbis, 1999). These are just a few examples.

107. Jamie T. Phelps, "Joy Came in the Morning Risking Death for Resurrection: Confronting the Evil of Social Sin and Socially Sinful Structures," in *A Troubling in My Soul: Womanist Perspectives on Evil & Suffering*, ed. Emilie M. Townes (Maryknoll, NY: Orbis, 1993), 57.

108. Ivone Gebara, *Out of the Depths*, chapter 1.

Ambiguity in Naming Sin and Grace

Good and evil intermingle in our day-to-day living. Access to healthcare, affordable housing, and meaningful work are all goods, or graces.[109] Yet, given the inequitable dynamisms of global capitalism, the attainment of these goods is often tied with conditions that produce great evils—poverty, unsafe working conditions, homelessness. For many who live in the United States, opting out of Western capitalism is not a viable choice. Therefore, we end up choosing goods—important things for the survival and well-being of our families—with the knowledge that our choices may support the dehumanization and degradation of others.[110] This does not justify unrestrained spending and the abuse of the world's resources, but rather names the ambiguous nature of sin and grace within daily life. Such a theological statement suggests that there are few spaces of innocence (if any) and few spaces completely deprived of grace. Tremendous grace can come out of suffering and evil, especially when people come together to work toward the transformation of society. Most activism, and the social change that it engenders, arises out situations of great injustice, of suffering. To be clear, I am not arguing that suffering is salvific or that God intended humans to suffer so that we would have the opportunity to participate in grace. Rather, foregrounding the ambiguity of sin and grace allows for an acknowledgement of our socially situated interdependence.

The concept of ambiguity breaks down dualisms, which have been used to maintain structures and practices to justify the subordination of those on the underside of history and the ideologies that support

---

109. My use of the term *goods* is taken from Ivone Gebara, who articulates a vision of saving grace rooted in the survival resources of day-to-day living. See *Out of the Depths*, 124. "Salvation seems to be a movement toward redemption in the midst of the trials of existence, one moment of peace and tenderness in the midst of daily violence, beautiful music that calms our spirit, a novel that keeps us company, a glass of beer or a cup of coffee shared with another" (ibid.).
110. Ray makes this point in "Tracking the Tragic," 141.

these structures and practices. The ascription of women, nonwhites, nature, and the body to evil (or lesser goods) and maleness, the divine, whites, and rationality to good has supported the degradation of the former and the privileging of the latter.[111] In view of privileged apathy, dualistic frameworks are problematic for another reason. They trick us into thinking that the realm of human agency is an either/or reality. This is not only in the sense of eschatological constructions wherein salvation is a "once and for all" reality accomplished by God (apart from human agency), but it also remains true in our day-to-day living and gives shape to what we believe to be possible. Theological models that stress radical divine transcendence hold the potential to reinforce passive bystanding. These models support the concept that what happens in this life matters little in comparison to what happens in the heavenly realm and that human beings have little effect in salvific matters. "God will take care of it, so what can I do?" Or, more commonly, "God has a reason for everything, so why get involved?" Such frameworks issue forth an anthropological pessimism where the impetus for change is rooted exclusively in radical divine intervention. In light of the problem of unethical passivity, we need to view salvation as an ongoing reality that requires human cooperation with divine grace. Such a model is risky, as the direction for action is less clear and we may not avoid mistakes. Yet it is also necessary because violence calls us to dare to have creativity. Compassionate witnessing does not have to be an either/or reality wherein we sacrifice our own safety or do nothing at all. It is within our reach. The starting point for such creativity can be found in the power of naming.

---

111. This point was discussed in chapter 2. For more on the influence of the dualistic frameworks of Platonism and Neoplatonism in Christendom, see Kelly Brown Douglas, *What's Faith*, 23–29.

Conclusion

As Dorothee Sölle suggests, social transformation begins with the power of language.[112] Standing under the burden of violence, we become more and more isolated. Those who suffer unjustly can feel abandoned by God and the human community. Those who watch from the sidelines may feel overwhelmed by the violence that transpires in our day-to-day living and powerless to effect change. Violence silences as it isolates. And, "without the capacity to communicate with others there can be no change."[113]

Naming provides a particularly important strategy of resistance in view of social privilege. As Allan G. Johnson explains, "Most cultures of privilege mask the reality of oppression by denying its existence, trivializing it, calling it something else, blaming it on those most victimized by it, or diverting attention from it."[114] The continued existence of privilege rests upon its invisibility. Therefore, sustained awareness of the dynamism of oppression and privilege, as well as a personal understanding of our own social location within these systems, is critical to their transformation. Dominant elites have to start paying attention. For those of a Christian disposition, part of paying attention is going to entail changing the way we think about sin and grace.

Through the practice of naming, connection is fostered through language. When we speak about the unspeakable (racism, heterosexism, privileged complicity, self-hate, hatred of others, etc.), we open ourselves to the possibility of fostering a living communion. Yet such naming must be predicated upon a valuation of openness and learning itself. That is, ideation surrounding self-sufficiency and

---

112. Dorothee Sölle, *Suffering*, trans. Everett R. Kalin (Philadelphia: Fortress Press, 1975), 76.
113. Ibid., 76
114. Allan G. Johnson, *Power, Privilege, and Difference*, 2nd ed. (New York: McGraw Hill, 2006), 137.

invulnerability (whether theological or secular) resists responsibility and growth.

For privileged bystanders, the journey to redemption begins by listening to the lament of those who have suffered injustice. In doing so, we begin to acknowledge the depths of our damage and the harm that we have caused others. In listening to the lament of those who are oppressed and in turn lamenting ourselves, we come face to face with some hard questions. For example, "To what degree am I/are we responsible for racial injustice?" "To what degree does the religious communion to which I/we belong adopt a theology that encourages gay bashing and slut shaming?" "To what degree do I/we isolate myself/ourselves from those who are considered 'untouchable'?" "What, if anything, am I/are we doing about structural violence?" To lament is to wrestle with the hard questions, including questions about the nature and identity of God. As Jacob wrestles with God (Gen. 32:22-32), we too must wrestle with the ways in which our theologies have "fudge[d] on truth-telling in order to protect our mannered sensibilities" and "to protect the character and reputation of God."[115]

Such a process is uncomfortable. No one likes to be confronted with the ways in which they have contributed (intentional or not) to the harm of others. Guilt often tempts us to take pathways of least resistance, denial, apathy, or segregation. To truly listen to the other means staying in the conversation, hearing the person out, and taking responsibility for our action and inaction. To listen and then to lament of our own accord is a crucial first step in bringing about the reign of God as justice for all. In and through the language of lament, we begin to make small movements toward healing, disrupting the

115. Walter Brueggemann, *Disruptive Grace: Reflections on God, Scripture, and the Church*, ed. Carolyn J. Sharp (Minneapolis: Fortress Press, 2011), 199.

silence that engulfs the participation of dominant elites in systems of privilege and oppression in the United States.

4

The Syro-Phoenician Woman: Disrupting Christological Complacency

From there he set out and went away to the region of Tyre. He entered a house and did not want anyone to know he was there. Yet he could not escape notice, but a woman whose little daughter had an unclean spirit immediately heard about him, and she came and bowed down at his feet. Now the woman was a Gentile, of Syrophoenician origin. She begged him to cast the demon out of her daughter. He said to her, "Let the children be fed first, for it is not fair to take the children's food and throw it to the dogs." But she answered him, "Sir, even the dogs under the table eat the children's crumbs." Then he said to her, "For saying that, you may go—the demon has left your daughter." So she went home, found the child lying on the bed, and the demon gone. (Mark 7:24-30)

In theory and practice, Christians privileged by class, race, gender, and imperial power have assumed that Jesus was on their side.[1] In the words of Jacquelyn Grant, "The central christological problem rests in the fact that Jesus Christ historically has been and remains

---

1. Karen Teel and Jennifer Harvey make this point in their essays "What Jesus Wouldn't Do: A White Theologian Engages Whiteness" and "What Would Zacchaeus Do? The Case for Disidentifying with Jesus," in *Christology and Whiteness: What Would Jesus Do?*, ed. George Yancy (New York: Routledge, 2012), 19–35 and 84–100, respectively.

imprisoned by the socio-political interests of those who have historically been the keepers of principalities and powers. This Jesus has been a primary tool for undergirding oppressive structures."[2] In religious imagery and in Christian theology, Christ has essentially become white through the dominant culture's near-exclusive portrayal of Jesus as a white man. Similarly, despite being a poor carpenter, Jesus largely has been exempted from the ways in which these categories would have functioned for him. The dominant Christian tradition has made Christ escape the realities of economic deprivation and political irrelevance.[3] For all practical intents and purposes, Western Christian theology has made Jesus out to be a privileged person.[4] Such christological imagery not only has a detrimental effect on the spiritual and physical lives of those who are marginalized, justifying the dominance of elites by identifying patterns of "patriarchal headship" and whiteness as Christlike,[5] but it also mutes the spirituality of the privileged.

In relying on the classical Christian tradition, privileged Christians have created a "comfortable Jesus."[6] This is the Jesus to whom we pray for help in times of personal strife and trouble, but never the kind of Jesus who challenges our core conceptions of what it means to be a follower of Christ in the world today. Christological understandings that stress divine omnipotence reinforce the Western tendency to "triumphalism and self-sufficiency."[7] As I have argued, such frameworks support holiness as submission and obedience to

---

2. Jacquelyn Grant, "Womanist Jesus and the Mutual Struggle for Liberation," *Journal of the Interdenominational Theological Center* 30, nos. 1–2 (Fall/Spring 2003–2004), 8.

3. Ibid., 18.

4. Ibid.

5. Elizabeth A. Johnson, *She Who Is: The Mystery of God in Feminist Theological Discourse* (New York: Crossroad, 1992), 38.

6. Grant, "Womanist Jesus," 19.

7. Walter Brueggemann, *Disruptive Grace: Reflections on God, Scripture and the Church*, ed. and intro. Carolyn J. Sharp (Minneapolis: Fortress Press, 2011), 180.

power as domination, leaving little room for lament of injustices, and downplays the significance of social transformation.

In contexts marked by radical inequality and violence, privileged Christians need a soteriological vision that resists comfortable assurance and generates affective "dis-ease" and "dis-comfort."[8] We need this in order to be "awakened from the sleep of inhumanity."[9] It is only when we are "[awakened] to the reality of an oppressed and subjugated world" and our own Christian complicity in this oppression and subjugation that we can begin to tap possibilities for transformation.[10] Such an understanding of salvation invites a new mode of encounter with God's Word that seeks to disrupt privileged ignorance and to engender social responsibility. This vision of redemption begins with the assumption that systems of power and privilege are linked in ways that support social injustice. Within such systems, there are no spaces of innocence, no places of self-sufficiency. We only find spaces of vulnerability and interdependence. Such a theology resists ideas of perfection, divine and human. Instead, one can find transformative grace in moments of vulnerability and solidarity.

The story of the Syro-Phoenician woman (Mark 7: 24-30) speaks to a soteriology of "dis-ease" and "dis-comfort." The narrative is one that resists a "comfortable Jesus," challenging privileged Christians to take a closer look at the ways in which we, as individuals and as members of Christian communities, are complicit in hegemonic violence. Drawing insight from postcolonial and feminist biblical scholarship on the Markan account and its Matthean parallel (15:21-28), I argue that the narrative authorizes a heterogeneous reading of salvation, otherwise submerged by monolithic

---

8. Teel, "What Jesus Wouldn't Do," 28–30.

9. Jon Sobrino, *The Principle of Mercy: Taking the Crucified People from the Cross* (Maryknoll, NY: Orbis, 1994), 1.

10. Ibid.

christological politics of privileged indifference.[11] In this biblical account, Jesus is "seen as engaging in an argument that discloses religious prejudice and exclusivist identity."[12] The Syro-Phoenician woman's response, when read through a critical feminist and postcolonial lens, effects a powerful reversal, contesting "Jesus' word in the name of his own iterated values."[13] Her response throws a mirror up to Jesus, challenging his own compliance with hegemony. As such, the text opens up the "discourse of Jesus to the possibility of the word of salvation issuing from an other who is 'not Christ,'" disrupting his word "from a subject position not his."[14] The soteriology issuing forth from such a Christology works to recenter the words of the oppressed as revelatory of God's *basileia*.

11. Texts informing my engagement of the pericope include Musa W. Dube, *Postcolonial Feminist Interpretation of the Bible* (St. Louis: Chalice, 2000); Hisako Kinukawa, *Women and Jesus in Mark: A Japanese Feminist Perspective* (Maryknoll, NY: Orbis, 1994) and "Decolonizing Ourselves as Readers: The Story of the Syro-Phoenician Woman as a Text," in *Distant Voices Drawing Near: Essays in Honor of Antoinette Clark Wire*, ed. Holly E. Hearon, Marvin L. Chaney, and Antoinette Clark Wire (Collegeville, MN: Liturgical, 2004): 131–44; Gail R. O'Day, "Surprised by Faith: Jesus and the Canaanite Woman," in *A Feminist Companion to Matthew*, ed. Amy-Jill Levine with Marianne Blickenstaff (Sheffield: Sheffield Academic, 2001): 114–25; Jim Perkinson, "A Canaanitic Word in the Logos of Christ: Or the Difference the Syrophoenician Woman Makes to Jesus," *Semeia* 75 (1996):61–84; Elisabeth Schüssler Fiorenza, *But She Said: Feminist Practices of Biblical Interpretation* (Boston: Beacon, 1992); Kwok Pui-lan, *Discovering the Bible in the Non-Biblical World* (Maryknoll, NY: Orbis, 1995); Sharon H. Ringe, "A Gentile Woman's Story, Revisited: Rereading Mark 7:24-31A," in *A Feminist Companion to Mark*, ed. Amy-Jill Levine with Marianne Blickenstaff (Sheffield, UK: Sheffield Academic, 2001), 79–100; and Leticia A. Guardiola-Sáenz, "Borderless Women and Borderless Texts: A Cultural Reading of Matthew 15:21-28," *Semeia* 78 (1997): 69–81.
12. Schüssler Fiorenza, *But She Said,* 11–12.
13. Perkinson, "A Canaanitic Word," 75.
14. Ibid., 61 and 82 respectively. Perkinson is responding to Robert Allen Warrior's call to put contemporary Canaanites at the center of christological reflection in "Canaanites, Cowboys, and Indians: Deliverance, Conquest, and Liberation Theology Today," *Christianity and Crisis* 49 (1989): 261–65. Drawing upon postcolonial studies, Perkinson reads the pericopes in Mark and Matthew's Gospel as opening up this avenue of reflection. This chapter is inspired by Perkinson's reading.

Reading for Liberation: A Word on Method

Catholic and mainline Protestant Christian traditions understand the Bible to be a living word wherein revelation about who God is and what it means to be a disciple is not restricted to the pages of the text. Revelation is found in one's faith-filled encounter with the biblical text.[15] The challenge, though, is that in acknowledging the living character of the Word of God, Christian writers have not always honored the socially situated nature of the readers themselves. Christians do not read from a neutral place. Our cultural, ethnic, racial, gender, sexual, and economic locations informs our readings. As Fernando Segovia explains, the "flesh-and-blood" reader is "always positioned and interested; socially and historically conditioned and unable to transcend such conditions—to attain a sort of asocial and ahistorical nirvana—not only with respect to socioeconomic class but also with regard to the many other factors that make up human identity."[16] Therefore, in addition to attending to (for example) the patriarchal nature of life in early Palestine and the ways in which the interests of biblical writers often coincided with imperialism, we must also attend to our own histories and social situatedness when approaching a biblical text. The issue, at hand, has to do with what Kwok Pui-lan terms "the politics of truth."[17] While the goal of attaining an impartial and objective reading of biblical texts may be "praiseworthy," it is also "naïve and dangerous."[18] Segovia writes, "It was naïve because it thought that it could really avoid or neutralize" the effects of social location on reading and

---

15. For example, in the Catholic tradition, this principle forms the basis of the ancient practice of reading (*lectio divina*) and Ignatian contemplation.
16. Fernando F. Segovia, "'And They Began to Speak in Other Tongues': Competing Modes of Discourse in Contemporary Biblical Criticism," in *Reading From this Place*, vol. 1, ed. Fernando F. Segovia and Mary Ann Tolbert (Minneapolis: Fortress Press, 1995), 28–29.
17. Kwok, *Discovering the Bible*, 9–19.
18. Segovia, "And They Began to Speak in Other Tongues," 29.

interpretation. "It was dangerous because in the end what were in effect highly personal and social constructions regarding texts and history were advanced as scholarly retrievals and reconstructions, scientifically secured and hence not only methodologically unassailable but also ideologically neutral."[19] Within the context of Christian theology, church leaders passed these interpretations on as doctrinal [T]ruth. Given that most interpretations came from a Eurocentric context and advanced a Eurocentric agenda, the voices of those who occupied non-Western, nonwhite, uneducated, and female positions were submerged. Patriarchal and colonial reading strategies have had a tremendous cost to those occupying marginal sites, as kyriocentric (master-centered) interpretations of the Bible have been and continue to be used to justify social and religious patterns of oppression.[20] Yet, privileged interpreters also bear a cost. In assuming that nonelites had nothing to add to the conversation, important aspects of Christian revelation are lost. Therefore, critical scholarship on the part of those who occupy nondominant social sites is vital for an engagement of the Word of God that is truly communal in scope.

Arguing that biblical texts can no longer be presumed to provide a window to historical reality, postcolonial and feminist reading strategies engage questions of power in interpreting texts and traditions: "How is meaning constructed? Whose interests are served? What kind of worlds are envisioned? What roles, duties, and values are advocated? Which social-political practices are legitimated?"[21] In attending to the power dynamics within the text and the history

19. Ibid.
20. Kwok Pui-lan describes the ways in which this passage has been used as a tool for gaining the humble submission of colonized peoples in Asia. See *Discovering the Bible*, 77. Elisabeth Schüssler Fiorenza points to the ways in which this text continues to be used to encourage women's silent submission. See *But She Said*, 161.
21. Elisabeth Schüssler Fiorenza, "The Ethics of Biblical Interpretation: Decentering Biblical Scholarship," *JBL* 107 (1988): 14.

of its interpretation, postcolonial and feminist biblical interpretations "make visible the ruptures within the text that undermine the closure of meaning, interrupting, shaking illusions of absolute coherence, completeness, and finality."[22] In so doing, these reading strategies "[magnify] the volume of otherwise weak voices barely recorded."[23]

After situating the pericope within the larger framework of Markan Christology and examining its geopolitical context, I discuss the scholarly contributions of women from the Western world and the Global South on Mark 7:24-30 in order to draw out the ethical consequences and political functions of the narrative in view of privileged apathy. In particular, what might this passage have to say to bystanders about christological identity and praxis? How might the passage inform liberative praxis within violent contexts? While the focus of this chapter is on Mark's account, research on the Matthean parallel (15:21-28) provides important points of intersection that illuminate the text.

Unearthing Power and Privilege in the Story of the Syro-Phoenician Woman: The Geopolitical Context of Mark 7:24-30

The Gospel of Mark is commonly understood as an account of Jesus dying for others' sins or as a presentation of Jesus as the Messiah, the Son of God.[24] Yet, as Richard A. Horsley has argued, such readings have obscured the sociopolitical character of Mark's Gospel.[25] Likely

---

22. Mayra Rivera, "Incarnate Words: Images of God and Reading Practices," in *They Were All Together in One Place? Toward Minority Biblical Criticism*, ed. Randall C. Bailey, Tat-siong Benny Liew, and Fernando F. Segovia (Atlanta: SBL, 2009), 320.

23. Ibid.

24. See, for example, Frank J. Matera, *New Testament Christology* (Louisville: WJK 1999), 24–26, although it is important to note that Matera emphasizes that there are multiple christologies within each Gospel.

25. Richard A. Horsley, *Hearing the Whole Story: The Politics of Plot in Mark's Gospel* (Louisville: WJK, 2001), 28–29. Horsley is not the only one to espouse this perspective. Latin American liberation theology and black liberation theology have adopted a similar interpretation of Jesus'

written to Gentile Christians under Roman rule in 66–70 CE, Horsley argues that Mark's Gospel is a story about the renewal of Israel and resistance to an ancient imperial order. Harkening the memory of "Israel's deliverance from oppressive foreign rule under the Egyptian Pharaoh," the Markan author presents Jesus' actions as the fulfillment of a once-subjugated people.[26] Jesus' mission and identity is centered on the liberation of Israel from the strain of imperial power. In doing so, Jesus threatened the powers that be, and as a consequence, he is executed by the Roman procurator in Judea.[27] Such a representation of the cross is a far cry from more common Christian interpretations of Jesus' death as atonement for the sins of humanity.[28] In Mark's Gospel, Jesus dies a martyr for a political cause.

Mark's Gospel ends in conflict and death, with the women at the tomb fleeing in "terror and amazement," telling nothing to anyone out of fear (Mark 16:8). The ending does not offer consolation to those suffering in times of uncertainty and persecution. Rather, as Rita Nakashima Brock points out, Mark's Gospel presents Jesus' death as "a disappointing conclusion to those who experienced a triumphant messiah and who could not see in his anger a mirror of their own passionate commitment to liberation and wholeness."[29] In this sense, the Gospel inculcates a sense of urgency and angst in the reader, as there is no happy ending to this narrative. There are no easy fixes to hegemony and no divine heroes. There is only a glimmer of hope that Christ's message of liberation will be carried out by those who follow him. Moreover, given the Gospel writer's

---

life and death. For example, see Jon Sobrino, *Jesus the Liberator: A Historical-Theological View* (Maryknoll, NY: Orbis, 1993).

26. Horsley, *Hearing the Whole Story*, 43–44.

27. Ibid., 42.

28. For further discussion of this point and its implications in view structural injustice, refer to chapter 2 of this book.

29. Rita Nakashima Brock, *Journeys by Heart: Christology of Erotic Power* (New York: Crossroad Publishing, 1989), 94.

negative portrayal of the disciples (they are increasingly portrayed as not understanding and, in the end, as deserting Jesus), it is likely that an outsider will be the one to carry out the message of God's *basileia*.[30] In Mark, "those who are farthest from power as dominance—slaves, children, and women—become the paradigms of true discipleship."[31] It is in this context that Jesus' encounter with the Syro-Phoenician woman must be interpreted.

In attempting to understand who this woman is and the nature of her dialogue with Jesus, one must also note the placement of the story within the larger schema of the Gospel. In both the Matthean and Markan accounts, pericopes focusing on purity or cleanliness precede the story of the Syro-Phoenician/Canaanite woman. In Matt. 15:1-9, Jesus, the scribes, and the Pharisees debate the nature of defilement in view of purity laws. In Mark 7:1-13, the Pharisees and some scribes are concerned that Jesus and his disciples eat with unclean hands, and in Mark 7:17-23, Jesus provides his disciples with additional teachings on personal defilement. As Gail O'Day notes (in reference of the Matthean account), "The geography of this sequence is more than happenstance. Jesus' rebuke of the Pharisees and scribes is intensified by his movements since he leaves the land and people who are 'clean,' to enter a land that is 'unclean.'"[32] Jesus' movement into the region of Tyre puts to the test the question of the source of defilement that is raised in the surrounding pericopes; namely, it raises the issue of who embodies God's *basileia* vision.[33]

---

30. Schüssler Fiorenza, *In Memory of Her*, 319–21.
31. Brock, *Journeys by Heart*, 71. Brock is drawing upon Schüssler Fiorenza, *In Memory of Her*, 318–23.
32. O'Day, "Surprised by Faith," 115.
33. There is significant debate as to whether Jesus traveled to the land of Tyre. Whereas it appears that Jesus crosses geographical and geopolitical boundaries in Mark's version of the story, many scholars believe that the woman meets Jesus on his own turf. Amy-Jill Levine argues that in the Matthean version the woman would likely have come to Jesus in order to be consistent with the narrator's rhetoric stressing Israel's temporal priority. In doing so, she is symbolically acknowledging the temporal priority of the Jews. See *Social and Ethnic Dimensions of Matthean*

Up to this point in Mark's Gospel, Jesus' ministry takes places in northern Galilee, part of the Jewish homeland.[34] In Mark 7:24-30, we see Jesus venture out from the "center (Jerusalem) of the national religion defining his area of mission."[35] The region of Tyre is located on the Mediterranean Sea in modern-day Lebanon. The region included the leading city of Phoenicia, from which it took its name, during the first millennium BCE. The port city of Tyre was important for both trade and politics and relied on the farms near the Galilee border to feed its population.[36]

The borderlands between Tyre and Galilee were fraught with tension. Gerd Theissen explains, "Economic dependence, political expansionism, and cultural distance provided a fertile soil for aggressive prejudices on both sides" of the border.[37] Jews and Gentiles resided in close proximity to one another, resulting in ethnic and religious tension. Textual evidence from the period indicates that the Tyrians were especially hostile to Jews, seizing property and enslaving Jewish people.[38] The economy of the region further compounded ethnic and religious prejudices. When food was scarce, wealthy urban dwellers in Tyre had the upper hand and were able to purchase grain, taking food out of the mouths of the rural dwellers

---

Salvation History (Lewiston, NY: Edwin Mellen, 1988), 137–38. Sharon Ringe follows Levine in interpreting the Markan version and argues that both Gospel accounts imply that the woman crossed into Jesus' space in order to attain healing. See "A Gentile Woman's Story, Revisited," 85n10. In contrast, Musa Dube suggests the primacy of empire would make it unlikely that the woman crossed the border. She posits that in the Matthean account it is Jesus' privileged status that allows him (unlike the Canaanite woman) to "leave his own geographical boundaries, travel to another land, and return at his own will." Dube, Postcolonial Feminist Interpretation, 146. Regardless of whether Jesus actually crossed the border, his geographical location is symbolic in both the Markan and Matthean accounts.

34. Ringe, "A Gentile Woman's Story, Revisited," 84. The location of his ministry in the Jewish homeland has often been interpreted as underlining the centrality of Jesus' mission to the Jews.
35. Perkinson, "A Canaanitic Word,"66.
36. Ibid.
37. Gerd Theissen, The Gospels in Context: Social and Political History in the Synoptic Tradition, trans. Linda M. Mahoney (Minneapolis: Fortress Press, 1991), 77.
38. Ibid.

who farmed the land.[39] While commerce was one means of securing the city's agricultural supply, the other was territorial expansion into Galilean lands. Roman occupation of Galilee frustrated Tyre's policy "of seeking as far as possible to exercise control of the territory that supplied its agricultural products."[40] Furthermore, religious differences surrounding cultic purity reinforced ethnic conflict and prejudice. Although Tyre was declared autonomous, Emperor Augustus "had consciously promoted the establishment of a large, contiguous Jewish territory in the area."[41] In those contiguous Jewish territories the Gentile residents of Tyre were viewed as unclean. Ironically, we see Jesus entering a region fraught with tension, trying to "escape notice," perhaps, in an effort to avoid further confrontations himself with the Pharisees and the scribes.[42]

In Mark's Gospel, the encounter begins when a "Gentile, of Syrophoenician origin" approaches Jesus sympathetically, "bowing down at his feet" (Mark 7:25), begging for her daughter's healing. Her designation as a Gentile signifies her non-Jewishness, yet we are told little else about her particular religious orientation and practice. Her nationality is Phoenician from Syria.[43] The woman's Syro-Phoenician origin accentuates ethnic and religious differences between her and Jesus. The Matthean account, with her identification as a Canaanite (15:22), further stresses these differences. With this label the author presents her not only as a foreigner, but as an enemy of Jesus.[44] For Matthew's likely Jewish audience, the term would evoke imagery in the Old Testament of "polytheism, sacred prostitution, and ethnicity beyond the pale."[45] Moreover, Musa

39. Ibid., 73.
40. Ibid., 76.
41. Ibid., 77.
42. James Perkinson makes a similar point in "A Canaanitic Word," 65–66.
43. The prophetic literature of the Hebrew Scriptures considered Tyre and Sidon to be Israel's dangerous enemies. See Isa. 23, Ezekiel 26–28, Joel 3:4.
44. O'Day, "Surprised by Faith," 115.

Dube argues, given Israel's history of colonizing Canaanite land as a part of the promised-land foundation myth, *Canaanite* marks her as a "one who must be invaded, conquered, annihilated."[46] However, the attribution of Greek status to the woman in the Markan account makes it more difficult to delineate her social status. The NRSV translates *hellenis* as "Gentile," when the word literally means "Greek."[47] Therefore, mention of her identity as Greek might mark her as one of the urban dwellers separated from Jesus by religion, ethnicity, and economic status. While Greek culture did influence the lower classes, it had a much greater impact on urban centers and those of higher social status.[48] Therefore, Theissen conjectures that the woman held a relatively high economic status compared to Galilean peasants.

Yet feminist and postcolonial analysis largely concurs that it would be highly unlikely for a woman without male relatives to occupy a position of high social status.[49] Hisako Kinukawa suggests that use of *hellenis* may simply be indicative of her foreign, non-Jewish status and argues that it is more likely that the Syro-Phoenician woman was a single mother who resided in the Tryian hinterland.[50] She bases this claim on the woman's persistence in the face of insult: "She is not knocked down by Jesus' harsh words" because "she does not identify herself with those to whom Jesus' bitter words are thrown."[51] Rather, she more likely resides in the rural area outlying the city and identifies more closely with the Galilean peasants for "she insists that Jesus'

45. Perkinson, "A Canaanitic Word," 64.
46. Dube, *Postcolonial Feminist Interpretation*, 147.
47. Bonnie Bowman Thurston, *Preaching Mark* (Minneapolis: Fortress Press, 2002), 87.
48. Theiseen, *Gospels in Context*, 70–71.
49. Sharon Ringe makes this point in "A Gentile Woman's Story, Revisited," 91n26. As Ringe states, the absence of mention of a male family member does not always mean impoverishment, though often it did. For a discussion on the status of women who were widowed or single mothers in the ancient world, see Schüssler Fiorenza, *In Memory of Her*, 160–84.
50. Hisako Kinukawa, "Decolonizing Ourselves as Readers," 138.
51. Ibid., 140.

harsh words do not apply to her and her child . . . for they are also suffering."[52]

What we can say is that this woman, who occupies a social site outside of Jesus' concern and experience, is marginalized by her gender, race, and non-Jewish status. "She is a 'born loser' on three counts: she is a woman in a man's world (and a single mother), the wrong religion, and the wrong race, since Syrophoenician was an unsavory racial term."[53] Not only "unclean by birth, a foreigner and a female," the woman is also "'untouchable' because of her daughter who is possessed by an unclean spirit."[54] In the ancient world, "demons were associated with that which threatened 'the new status quo,' from basic systems of organization to that of the social order itself."[55] The woman is triply polluted. Even in her approach to Jesus, she risks defiling him. In the Markan account, the question of her class and affluence remains ambiguous. One has to leave open the possibility of her benefiting from Tyrian practices that subjugated Galilean peasants.

Jesus occupies a social location between the margin and the center. While Jesus lived under the Roman Empire, he was a traveler whose race and gender endowed him with privilege and authority.[56] Musa Dube argues that not only was Jesus free to come and go as he pleased, but he also was free to ignore and to reject the requests of those who stood before him. Privilege affords one the power to escape when faced with controversy. In the wake of controversy with Pharisees and scribes, and intensifying pressure by those in power, Jesus exits Galilee seeking anonymity (Mark 7:24). As James

---

52. Ibid., 142.
53. Thurston, *Preaching Mark*, 87.
54. Kinukawa, *Women and Jesus in Mark*, 55.
55. Elaine Wainwright, "Not Without my Daughter: Gender and Demon Possession in Matthew 15.21-28," in Levine and Blickenstaff, *A Feminist Companion to Matthew*, 131. Citing Roger Baker, *Blinding the Devil: Exorcism Past and Present* (New York: Hawthorn Books, 1974), 21.
56. Ibid., 146.

Perkinson has suggested, while he may have been on retreat, "in view of the intensity of the opposition he has evoked (plots on his life begin in Mark as early as chapter 3), we might better think of his status as perhaps, 'underground.'"[57] Jesus may have been marginalized, but he had resources available to escape. Moreover, he was in a position to make the Syro-Phoenician woman beg, and she, having no other recourse, could not afford to be rude.

In the narrative, Jesus' initial response is that of silent disinterest. The Matthean account further stresses Jesus' silence by the request of his disciples: "Send her away, for she keeps shouting after us" (Matt. 15:23). In light of her pleas, one might expect that Jesus' heart will be softened and that he will come to her aid, as he has done countless other times (e.g., healing of the Gerasene Demoniac in Mark 5:1-20 and the hemorrhaging woman in Mark 5:25-34). Instead, he offers these harsh words: "Let the children be fed first, for it is not fair to take the children's food and throw it to the dogs" (Mark 7:27). Citing a well-known Jewish saying, scholars have often read Jesus' response as a referencing the exclusion of Gentiles from the household of God.[58] Read allegorically, the Jews are the children, welcome to partake of the Word of God, and the Gentiles are the dogs, excluded from the household of God.[59] Yet, as Theissen explains, in light of the strained economic relationships among Jews and Gentiles in the region, one can plausibly interpret Jesus' response as a reference to the exploitative behavior of Tyrian residents. One could interpret it as "First let the poor people in the Jewish rural areas be satisfied. For it is not good to take poor people's food and throw it to the rich Gentiles in the cities."[60] Such a reading would be consistent with Jesus' commitment to feed the poor found elsewhere in the Gospel.

57. Perkinson, "A Canaanitic Word," 66.
58. Schüssler Fiorenza, *But She Said*, 161.
59. Kwok, *Discovering the Bible*, 75.
60. Theissen, *Gospels in Context*, 75.

This interpretation would indeed make sense if the narrative stopped there.[61]

Yet, the woman's reply throws the reader for another loop. When one expects the woman to give up, hang her head in shame in the face of rejection, she responds, "Sir, even the dogs under the table eat the children's crumbs" (Mark 7:28). Sharon Ringe argues that this response "turns the story into a double *chreia*, with the punch line in the second half."[62] In turn, Jesus commends her: "For saying that, you may go" (Mark 7:29), and sends the woman home to find her daughter "lying on the bed, and the demon gone" (Mark 7:30). The result is puzzling. Not only is Jesus, "the character whose point of view Mark endorses throughout the gospel," portrayed in a negative light (i.e., via his engagement in name-calling tactics), but he appears to change his mind.

In interpreting this passage, commentators have sought to minimize the derogatory nature of Jesus' response. Elisabeth Schüssler Fiorenza characterizes this history of interpretation as follows: "Exegetes either declare this 'Jesus saying' historically unauthentic or they seek to explain away its religious-ethnic prejudice and exclusivity by resorting to features of the Matthean version or to anti-Jewish or folkloristic considerations."[63] Attributing the deprecating words to a "test of faith," some have argued that Jesus did not intend to insult the woman. Rather, his response was designed to test the woman's loyalty and persistence.[64] Others have suggested that Jesus

---

61. Ringe, "A Gentile Woman's Story, Revisited," 90.
62. Ibid. As Ringe explains, a *chreia* is a saying that conveys an example of wit and wisdom of a philosopher or another famous person. It was a common form in Greek rhetoric and often used as a pedagogical device.
63. Schüssler Fiorenza, *But She Said*, 161.
64. Patristic writers Augustine, Jerome, and the Venerable Bede all espoused this perspective. For a discussion of the history of interpretation of Mark 7:24-30, see Pablo Alonso, *The Woman Who Changed Jesus: Crossing Boundaries in Mk 7, 24–30* (Leuven: Peeters, 2011), 2–35. Kwok also makes this point in *Discovering the Bible*, 76.

was simply being playful with her, citing that the use of the diminutive in Greek often carries with it a note of endearment.[65] Some translations attempt to capture this nuance by rendering the diminutive as "little pup," or "puppy." Yet, as T. A. Burkill points out, "And, as in English, so in other languages, to call a woman 'a little bitch' is no less abusive than to call her 'a bitch' without qualification."[66] In the parable, the dogs are not truly members of the household. They are under the table and not at the table, left to consume the crumbs.

In addition to being problematic on historical grounds, these approaches work to reinscribe marginalizing tendencies already in the text by denying the harm that was done. Jewish literature contemporary to the passage largely described dogs as "scavengers, mangy parasites on the land."[67] Dogs were seen as unclean animals, banned from the kitchen and the house.[68] Given this context, Jesus' words are far from neutral. They aggravate, instead of ameliorate, the abuse, reminding the woman of her inferiority as she is infantilized along with her daughter. Jesus erases her particularity as he dismisses her along with all others who are outside the realm of his concern.

Arguments aimed toward muting the exclusivist and prejudicial character of Jesus' response also fail to critically evaluate the negative ways in which this text has shaped Christian identity. For many the issue is the protection of divine perfection and *apatheia*.[69] The idea

---

65. For example, Vincent Taylor, *The Gospel according to St. Mark* (New York: St. Martin's, 1966), 350ff.

66. T. A. Burkill, "The Historical Development of the Story of the Syrophoenician Woman (Mark vii: 24-31)," *Novum Testamentum* 9 (1967): 173.

67. Alan Cadwallader, *Beyond the Word of a Woman: Recovering the Bodies of the Syrophoenician Woman* (Adelaide: ATF, 2011), 23.

68. Susan Miller, *Women in Mark's Gospel,* Journal for the Study of the New Testament Supplement Series no. 259 (New York: T&T Clark International, 2004), 97. For example, Elijah prophesies that Jezebel will be eaten by dogs (1 Kgs. 21:23). In Matt. 7:6, Jesus teaches that his disciples should not throw that which is holy to dogs. Opponents and heretics are described as dogs in 2 Pet. 2:22, Phil. 3:2, and Rev. 22:15.

69. See chapter 2 for a discussion of the classical tradition's notion of divine *apatheia*.

that a Gentile woman could change the mind of the God incarnate, or that Jesus may have engaged in prejudicial behavior, is deeply at odds with dominant interpretive strands in the tradition. Instead, orthodox Christian readings have enhanced the "master" voice of Jesus and present the story as a myth of origin for Jesus' mission to the Gentiles. The woman's retort is read not as rejecting the label of a dog, but as that of humble acceptance of her sinful station and God's word. Schüssler Fiorenza explains, "The woman is seen as a proselyte who intercedes for the salvation of Gentiles, who are saved not through the encounter with the historical Jesus, but his word."[70] The Gentiles (of whom the Syro-Phoenician woman's faith is paradigmatic) accept the crumbs from the eucharistic table that the Jews first rejected and become children of God. This strategy of displacement and its anti-Jewish character has appeared repeatedly throughout the history of this passage's interpretation.[71] Moreover, as Kwok Pui-lan illustrates, "when the Gospel was brought to interact with other cultures in Asia, anti-Judaism and sexism further intersected with colonialism in the interpretation of this story."[72] Christian writers elaborated the salvation history motif so that the faith and humility of the Syro-Phoenician woman became a model for those colonized. "Just like the Gentile woman, colonized peoples were expected to be as subservient, obedient, and loyal as a 'devoted dog.'"[73] Until the latter half of the twentieth century, theological interpretations ignored rather than contested kyriocentric (master-centered) interpretive trends.

In order to interpret the dialogue that occurs between Jesus and the Syro-Phoenician woman and its christological import, one must attend to the dynamics of power and privilege within the narrative.

---

70. Schüssler Fiorenza, *But She Said*, 161.
71. Kwok, *Discovering the Bible*, 77.
72. Ibid., 78.
73. Ibid.

Such an analysis makes it difficult to argue that this passage is simply one about the willing conversion of the Gentiles to Christianity. Rather, it underscores the ways in which even the best of humanity (the incarnation of the Word) is not immune to ethnic prejudice and religious exclusivism. Such a statement does not take away from the fact that Jesus healed the sick, fed the poor, and cared for those who were downtrodden. Nor does it contest the ways in which Jesus fought against structural injustice. He and his disciples were killed for this. Yet the passage calls Christians to remember that even the body of Christ can become inscribed in structural sin, something that privileged interpreters often miss. Our idealization of Jesus has led privileged interpreters to excuse and overlook the ways in which christological discourse was never meant to be a monologue, an all-encompassing totality of divine Truth, preoccupied with matters of religious and doctrinal purity. Rather, it must be a living dialogue informed by the wisdom of those who occupy marginal sites.

Placing a Woman's Words at the Center: Insights from Feminist and Postcolonial Scholarship

By and large, feminist and postcolonial scholars have produced critical rereadings of the Markan and Matthean accounts emphasizing the Syro-Phoenician woman's wit, strength, and courage.[74] Western feminists have largely focused on deconstructing androcentric tendencies within the narrative and the history of its interpretation with the aim of "restor[ing] the history of Christian beginnings to women" and reinscribing the religious authority of women.[75] For

---

74. Female scholars from the Global South and feminist scholars have employed similar methods with other biblical passages. For example, see the essays in *Women and Christian Origins*, ed. Ross Shepard Kraemer and Mary Rose D'Angelo (New York: Oxford University Press, 1999) and *Feminist New Testament Studies: Global and Future Perspectives*, ed. Kathleen O'Brien Wicker, Althea Spencer Miller, and Musa W. Dube (New York: Palgrave MacMillan, 2005).
75. Schüssler Fiorenza, *In Memory of Her*, xx.

example, in *But She Said: Feminist Practices of Biblical Interpretation*, Schüssler Fiorenza sees the Syro-Phoenician woman representing "the biblical-theological voice of women, which has been excluded, repressed, or marginalized in Christian discourse."[76] In challenging Jesus' ethnocentrism, the woman becomes "a paradigm for feminists who transgress intellectual and religious boundaries in their movements toward liberation."[77] Women from the Global South have examined the ways in which constructions of gender intertwine with and are compounded by race, class, ethnicity, and empire in the narrative, noting similarities with the social situations of marginalized women in their own contexts. Ranjini Wickramaratne Rebera emphasizes the commonalities between the unnamed woman, as a single mother of a demon-possessed child, and the situation of women whose children have been wounded permanently through militarism, substance abuse, and HIV related illnesses.[78] She finds the woman a positive role model, whose "tenacity, commitment to her daughter's healing, and ability to use the 'power of the weak' in a positive and life-giving manner" render her an agent of social change who effects "a transformation in Jesus' own sense of identity and mission."[79]

In feminist and postcolonial readings, the Syro-Phoenician woman's words (not Jesus') are placed at the center of the dialogue and considered revelatory of God's *basileia*.[80] Gail R. O'Day argues, "The 'point' of the story rests in the change undergone by Jesus."[81]

---

76. Schüssler Fiorenza, *But She Said*, 11. The title for this book is taken from the woman's response to Jesus.
77. Ibid., 12.
78. Ranjini Wickramaratne Rebera, "The Syrophoenician Woman: A South Asian Feminist Perspective," in Levine and Blickenstaff, *A Feminist Companion to Mark*, 106.
79. Ibid., 107.
80. Musa Dube does not necessarily see the text as liberating in and of itself. Rather, in her research with women from African Initiated (Inland) Churches, many had to go beyond the text to come up with a liberative reading. See *Postcolonial Feminist Interpretation*, 194.
81. O'Day, "Surprised by Faith," 117.

The woman is the central protagonist in the pericope. She initiates the movement of the story with her petition and refusal to be silenced. In the end, "she leaves victorious, having been heard and answered by Jesus."[82] In contrast, Jesus' role is depicted as one of silence and refusal. Therefore, O'Day contends, "any attempt to classify this text by placing Jesus at its center will ultimately be inadequate."[83] Rather, it is the Syro-Phoenician woman's daring insistence that gives the text its distinct shape and form.

Highlighting similarities between the woman's words of petition and the cries of Israel in the lament psalms, O'Day likens the woman to Israel, "insistent, demanding, and unafraid to state her claims."[84] As discussed in the previous chapter, lamentations are prayers of longing, pleas for help that are strident, harsh, and heart rending. "They are profound interruptions and claims to attention."[85] In her petition, the woman gives "full voice to [her] fear, anger, and dismay, which are palpably present in life and in speech, and which contradict the settled claims of faith."[86] Similar to the lament of Israel, the woman demands that her suffering is indeed God's business. She boldly calls Jesus to account, appealing to his sense of vocation and mission.[87] Prior to this story, we hear of Jesus living a vocation of large vision and generosity. He has healed the sick and fed the five thousand. Jesus' denial of the Syro-Phoenician woman stands in stark contrast to the openness he has displayed to the needs of others.

In regard to the Markan account, Hisako Kinukawa asks if Jesus' mission is defined by care for the lowly, the poor, the sick, then how can he possibly "ignore a sick child while talking about feeding

82. Ibid., 118.
83. Ibid.
84. Ibid.
85. Bryan N. Massingale, *Racial Justice and the Catholic Church* (Maryknoll, NY: Orbis, 2010), 106.
86. Walter Brueggemann, *Introduction to the Old Testament: The Canon and Christian Imagination* (Louisville: WJK, 2003), 289.
87. O'Day, "Surprised by Faith," 123.

the 'children' of Israel?"[88] To deny this woman "bread" would be to contradict his own stated values. While she may be aware of the fact that she is from Tyre, "a city noted for robbing even the smallest bits of food from Galilean peasants," upon hearing Jesus "protect the 'others' in Galilee, she is made aware of the fact that she is also one of these 'others' in the society of Tyre."[89] The woman reminds Jesus that Tyre is also a hierarchical society, and she asks Jesus to be consistent in "giving primacy to the marginalized wherever they are and showing an egalitarian spirit toward those who are destitute."[90] In her response, the woman throws a mirror up to Jesus that reflects the ways in which his mission and vision has become mired in the trappings of ethnic prejudice and religious exclusivism. She reminds Jesus that there are others who also need to be fed.

Her tactic is similar to that of the martial art judo, whereby one uses the opponent's own power to defeat him or her.[91] Sharon Ringe explains, "Instead of confronting the insult, she turns the offensive label into a harmless one, and uses it to her advantage. 'Dog' moves from a label of contempt to a character in a domestic scene so familiar and so obvious that the logic cannot be refuted: children are always dropping food, and pets gobble it up almost before it hits the ground."[92] Therefore, she and her daughter will get what they need from the "crumbs that fall from the table," regardless of for whom it was intended. The woman's response brings "dogs" (persons considered unclean) into the house of God. She transfers a public metaphor to the domestic sphere, places the dogs right at the foot of

---

88. Hisako Kinukawa, "Biblical Studies in the Twenty-First Century: A Japanese/Asian Feminist Glimpse," in *Feminist New Testament Studies: Global and Future Perspectives*, ed. Kathleen O'Brien Wicker, Musa W. Dube, and Althea Spencer Miller (New York: Palgrave MacMillan, 2005), 148.

89. Kinukawa, "Decolonizing Ourselves as Readers," 142.

90. Ibid., 143.

91. Ringe, "A Gentile Woman's Story, Revisited," 90.

92. Ibid.

the table, and implies that they are members, albeit of low status, of the household.

The story points to a powerful reversal. For a moment, Jesus is no longer the master teacher. It is the woman who teaches Jesus something about the nature of discipleship and his own identity. In her response, the Syro-Phoenician woman refuses to take no for an answer and in doing so she uses the negative power of Jesus' remark to secure her own purposes. She calls into question Jesus' assumptions about her own identity and reminds him that even Tyrian society is a hierarchical one. She and her daughter are to be included in Jesus' mission to care for the poor and marginalized. "For a brief moment, she speaks in Jesus' place . . . as the normal subject of messianic discourse."[93] It is she, not Jesus, who evokes God's *basileia* as "a praxis of inclusive wholeness" whereby the measure of holiness is inclusivity and engendering wholeness in every human being.[94] Moreover, she does so from the subject position of an outsider. That is, in her speaking "for Christ," she maintains her own subjectivity.

In her reading of the narrative, Leticia A. Guardiola-Sáenz argues that the woman claims a place for herself at the table and demands to be considered as Other in her own right, breaking into empire. Contrary to other interpreters, Guardiola-Sáenz does not read the woman as identifying herself as a dog. "When she says, 'Yes, Lord,' she is agreeing with Jesus that it would be absurd to throw away the children's food to the dogs," when there are others, like herself, who are in need.[95] In so doing, her words open up the possibility of the "word of salvation issuing from an other who is 'not Christ,'" from the subject position of a marginalized outsider.[96] It is through the

93. Perkinson, "A Canaanitic Word," 80.
94. Schüssler Fiorenza, *In Memory of Her*, 120. As Schüssler Fiorenza illustrates, in the Gospels Jesus consistently claimed God's *basileia* vision for those who occupied marginal sites: the sick and crippled, the destitute and poor, and tax collectors, sinners, and prostitutes.
95. Guardiola-Sáenz, "Borderless Women," 78.

woman's speech, which emerges in a dialogue with Jesus, that healing issues forth.

What is remarkable about this biblical narrative is that the word of an "unclean" woman not only interjects a "christological word," but it also effects a change in Jesus. As Ringe asserts, "Her 'word' is credited for changing Jesus's mind and, implicitly, for the departure of the demon from her child."[97] Unlike any other Gospel narrative, at the end of the dialogue, Jesus does not have the upper hand. She beats Jesus at his own game and in so doing unmasks "[injustices] hidden beneath deep rationalizations of social and religious life."[98] She demands attention to suffering and injustice and interferes with "the way things are." When read in this manner, the story of the Syro-Phoenician woman becomes a powerful christological resource for privileged elites, raising questions not easily answered within our current theological frame and propelling us to new levels of truth seeking. In it, the reader finds an encounter between Jesus and a woman that "nudges us to dis-ease and dis-comfort,"[99] calling into question the apparent normalcy of skewed racial and gendered assumptions within the present-day *modus operandi* of Christian theology.

Throughout the history of Christian thought, sin, woundedness, and grace have been defined by the dominant elite. Today, this pattern continues as the contributions of womanist, feminist, black liberation, and queer theologies are still not taken seriously by the academy and the church. Women and men on the margins are speaking, but they often find few who are interested in listening. The

---

96. Perkinson, "A Canaanitic Word," 61.
97. Ringe, "A Gentile Woman's Story, Revisited," 83. Jim Perkinson makes a similar point in "A Canaanitic Word," 69ff.
98. Massingale, *Racial Justice*, 110.
99. M. Shawn Copeland, "Toward a Critical Christian Feminist Theology of Solidarity," in *Women and Theology*, ed. Mary Ann Hinsdale and Phyllis Kaminski, Annual Publication of the College Theology Society, vol. 40, (Maryknoll, NY: Orbis, 1994), 30.

failure to take seriously the work of those who name God from the margins is supported and justified by sociocultural norms about the inferiority (in terms of intellect and holiness) of nonwhites, women, and LGBTQ persons, which have been tacitly and explicitly adopted within the religious sphere.

At the end of the pericope, Jesus does not directly take credit for the healing of the Syro-Phoenician woman's daughter. He simply says, "For saying that, you may go—the demon has left your daughter" (Mark 7:29). This statement, as Ringe argues, leaves open the question as to whose word is salvific.[100] To use the language of Rita Nakashima Brock, Jesus is not a heroic figure, but a catalyst that "calls attention to brokenheartedness within the human community" and makes visible the grace of erotic power in the Christian community.[101] In this passage, redemption is not a monologue, but rather a *dialogos* supported by an encounter with the woman and Jesus.[102]

Engendering Christological Dis-Ease: Implications of Mark 7:24-30 for Contemporary Christians

We do not know what exactly happened in this narrative. The scene cannot be reconstructed. We have educated guesses based upon careful scholarship. What we can point to is the disruptive nature of the passage for contemporary christological understanding. In the text, the woman is a disruptive character. She not only interrupts Jesus' self-exile (or, hiding, if you will), but the discourse between her and Jesus calls into question assumptions about the nature of salvation (who it is meant for, who effects it, and who can partake of it). Her disruption bears fruit as it speaks messianic truth, calling Jesus and

100. Ringe, "A Gentile Woman's Story, Revisited," 83.
101. Brock, *Journeys by Heart*, 99.
102. The term *dialogos* belongs to Perkinson, "A Canaanitic Word," 72.

present-day Christians to account for the ways in which even the body of Christ itself can be inscribed in structural sin. This is at the literal and symbolic level.[103]

One's social identity is always an embodied identity. As cultural historian Jennifer Glancy illustrates, in order to grasp the complexity of the encounter between Jesus and the Syro-Phoenician woman, we have to consider the implications of embodiment: "In any given encounter, an individual is unlikely to keep intersecting facets of her identity 'in mind,' but without conscious analysis she will perform her complex identity 'in body.' The body is where cultural complexity takes place."[104] Glancy explains that "in the Roman Empire social identity was, inevitably, a kind of bodily knowledge, a knowledge that affected an individual's experience of being in the world and shaped his or her interactions with other people."[105] As a Jewish man in early Palestine, Jesus would not have been able to escape the reality of empire, social class, gender, or ethnicity. In his humanity, he would have been socialized into an environment that privileged maleness over femaleness, Jewishness over non-Jewishness, and held marked assumptions about ethnicity and race. As is the case today, religious people did not always subject these assumptions to critique. Therefore, it would not be unusual for social norms like the ones mentioned above to inform religious identity and moral imagining.[106] Given this reality, it is difficult for anyone in the narrative—even Jesus—to claim immunity from the reach of structural sin.

---

103. The reference of literal and symbolic is to James H. Cone, *God of the Oppressed*, rev. ed. (Maryknoll, NY: Orbis, 1997), 125.
104. Jennifer A. Glancy, "Jesus, the Syrophoenician Woman, and Other First Century Bodies" *Biblical Interpretation* 18 (2010): 343.
105. Ibid., 347.
106. Ibid.

Central to Christianity is the paradoxical holding together of "two apparently contrasting or even self-contradictory things . . . in order to express a possible truth."[107] In this sense, paradox is at the very heart of the Christian definition of the identity of God incarnate: one person two natures, fully divine and fully human in all things except sin. Yet, to be fully human means to share most deeply in human situatedness and embodiment, including the reality of structural sin. In exempting Jesus from participation in structural sin, we let Jesus' divinity "win out" in such a way that his humanity is truly diminished. We err on the side of docetism. Stating that the body of Christ is *inscribed* in social sin does not imply that Jesus is any less divine. Rather, it is to affirm Jesus' divinity while taking seriously his human contextualization in a way that does better justice to what must have been his own vulnerability and limitations, as exemplified by New Testament passages whereby he is taught and transformed by others. In reference to the pericope, James Martin SJ, suggests a similar interpretation: "Perhaps, however, Jesus needed to learn something from the woman's persistence: his ministry extended to everyone, not just Jews. Or maybe he was just tired. . . . Whatever the case ... both possibilities show Jesus's full humanity on display."[108] In this passage, we see Jesus, fully human, partaking in cultural processes whose harmful effects have not yet been fully examined, a process which has been repeated throughout human history.

As such, the passage bears marks of Jesus' own complicity in the ethnic and gender prejudice of his day. Jesus does not say to the woman, "I am sorry, I cannot help you." Nor does he disregard her outright as custom might have allowed. Rather, his response reminds the Syro-Phoenician woman of her "rightful" place in society by evoking the ancient link between women and the natural world.

---

107. Douglas, *What's Faith,* 19.
108. James Martin, SJ, *Jesus: A Pilgrimage* (New York: HarperOne, 2014), 3.

Alan Cadwallader, in his analysis of the text, notes that in Middle Platonic writing dating just prior to the Gospels, woman signified the material, the natural, over against the intellect.[109] "Animals were often the emblems of shame, women were similarly collated."[110] Further, "the uncontrolled license associated with harlots drew manifold connections with animals and provided demonstration of the 'natural' proclivities of women."[111] This is seen throughout the Bible: dogs are likened to male prostitutes (Deut. 23:18), evildoers (Ps. 22:16), and headstrong wives (Eccles. 26:25), and they are grouped with sorcerers, fornicators, murderers, and idolaters (Rev. 22:15). Jesus' response in Mark 7:27 not only bears the marks of ethnic prejudice and religious exclusivism but also patriarchy. As a barking dog must be restrained by a chain, this "shouting," "begging," and unclean woman needs to be restrained lest she wreak havoc on the rest of society.

The passage challenges assumptions about who Jesus is and where divinity is located. In this particular story, Jesus appears not to be the person we expect him to be: innocent, morally perfect, and one who takes sides with the oppressed. Rather, in his engagement with the Syro-Phoenician woman, Jesus appears to take sides with the oppressor, his actions mirroring present-day patterns of privileged escape, racism, and bullying. As such, the narrative calls into question dominant models of atonement whereby human salvation is predicated upon Jesus' perfect innocence, exempt from the trappings of structural sin. The notion that the body of Christ can be inscribed in social sin also holds significance at the symbolic level. In particular, the Syro-Phoenician story brings the church (as the body of Christ) face to face with its own complicity in structural injustice: racism,

---

109. Cadwallader, *Beyond the Word of a Woman*, 9.
110. Ibid.
111. Ibid.

heterosexism, homophobia, xenophobia, and misogyny. Similar to Jesus' response in the passage, the Christian church, through theological constructions and pastoral practice, has denied nonwhites, women, and LGBTQ persons full participation in the *basileia* of God, labeling them as polluted, unclean sinners who are unworthy of entering the household of God. As discussed in chapter 1, this can be seen in heteropatriarchal biblical and theological interpretation of the Fall of Adam and Eve. Yet, this also plays out in the alignment of the same-sex and gender-variant behavior with religious impurity. In the patristic period, early Christian writers described same-sex and gender-variant behavior as corrupting the entire human race. Patrick Cheng points to Philo's interpretation of Sodom and Gomorrah in *On Abraham*, which connects same-sex acts with collective punishment.[112] Prior to Philo, most references to the sin of Sodom involved inhospitality. Similar ideas have been expressed within contemporary Roman Catholic Church documents.[113] While the Roman Catholic Church names violence against homosexuals in speech or action as deplorable, it also holds that sexual orientation is not a "quality comparable to race, ethnic background, etc. in respect to non-discrimination."[114] Likening homosexuality to a contagious disease or mental illness, the Congregation of the Doctrine of Faith (the magisterial teaching office of the Roman Catholic Church) contends that restricting the basic rights of LGBTQ persons with

112. Patrick S. Cheng, *From Sin to Amazing Grace: Discovering the Queer Christ* (New York: Seabury, 2012), 44.

113. It is worth noting that it appears Pope Francis may change the tone of Catholic thinking on LGBTQ persons. In a recent interview, Pope Francis said that while the church has the right to express its opinions, it is not to judge or "interfere spiritually" in the lives of gays and lesbians. For more, see Antonio Spadaro, SJ, "A Big Heart Open to God: The Exclusive Interview with Pope Francis" *America: The National Catholic Review*, September 30, 2013, http://www.americamagazine.org/pope-interview.

114. Congregation for the Doctrine of the Faith, "Some Considerations Concerning the Response to Legislative Proposals on the Non-Discrimination of Homosexual Persons," July 24, 1992, par. 7 and 10, respectively.

respect to housing, employment, and care of children, may be crucial to "protect[ing] the common good."[115] The implication of this statement is that homogenital activity defiles the God-given moral and social order of society. In view of the prevalence of gay bashing and slut shaming, the religious labeling of gender-variant and same-sex activity as "unclean" is harmful. Fear of divine collective punishment fuels homophobia and misogyny in the United States.[116] For example, recall the earlier discussion of "Mix It Up at Lunch Day," whereby Christian Evangelical parents threatened to pull their children out of school for fearing that sharing a meal with LGBTQ students would compromise their child's integrity. While public attitudes and legislation surrounding gay marriage are changing, in the religious arena there is much to be done. Homophobia, and the accompanying misogyny, have real consequences to which heterosexual Christians are not immune. Narrowly defined gender roles often leave little room for self-expression, and those who defy traditional gender norms are often subject to scapegoating.

One can also draw a comparison, albeit inadequate, between Jesus' own display of ethnic prejudice and the history of race relations in the United Sates. White Christians have used the sexualization and demonization of black bodies to justify the enslavement, lynching, and segregation of nonwhite people. These stereotypes persist in the present-day polis. As Kelly Brown Douglas explains, the "Jezebel [stereotype] became the foundation for the idea of the Black woman as welfare mother/queen."[117] Welfare mothers continue to be portrayed "as promiscuous unmarried women who sit around, collect government checks, and give birth to a lot of children."[118] White

---

115. Ibid., par 12.
116. Cheng, *From Sin to Amazing Grace*, 40–41.
117. Kelly Brown Douglas, *Sexuality and the Black Church: A Womanist Perspective* (Maryknoll, NY: Orbis, 1999), 52–53.
118. Ibid., 53.

Christians have used this stereotype to deflect "attention away from white, Patriarchal, racist structures" to suggest that black women are not only the source of their impoverishment, but also to trumpet the value of the "hardworking" white family.[119] Conservative Christians in the political arena have long endorsed such attitudes.

Institutional racism has also infiltrated the Christian church. Jamie T. Phelps cites the long history of segregation, marginalization, and devaluation of nonwhites in Protestant and Catholic religious communions in the United States.[120] Phelps writes, "Black members were subjected to the same segregation, marginalization, and devaluation within the Church as they were accorded in society. The churches uncritically adopted the prevailing racist ideology and relegated the Christian principle of the unity of humankind exclusively to the spiritual realm."[121] Phelps points to the reluctance to include (and sometimes the outright exclusion of) nonwhites in seminaries and orders of women religious in the nineteenth and early twentieth centuries. Today, the devaluation of nonwhite voices and concerns continues in the church's tepid response to racial injustice. In the words of Bryan Massingale, through its practice and theology, "the U.S. Catholic Church has acted by omission and commission in ways that decisively allied it with the cultural of racial domination and caus[ing] it to be identified as 'white.'"[122] The church has been complicit in the racism, misogyny, and homophobia. By and large, the body of Christ has failed to acknowledge, much less recognize, the extent of its own participation in structural injustice. Speaking of white racial injustice, Karen Teel argues that to struggle effectively against whiteness, white Christians need "a Christology that renders

---

119. Ibid.
120. Jamie T. Phelps, "Communion Ecclesiology and Black Liberation Theology," *Theological Studies* 61 (2000): 680–81.
121. Ibid., 680.
122. Massingale, *Racial Justice*, 80

us uncomfortable in our skins."[123] Within the narrative of the Syro-Phoenician woman we find the stirrings of such a Christology. The derogatory remark Jesus utters, with its racial, ethnic, and gendered connotations, implicates the Christian church, as the body of Christ, in structural injustice. The Syro-Phoenician woman's response throws a mirror up to the Christian church, calling us to take seriously its own complicity in oppressive patterns of marginalization and dehumanization, making us squirm in our skins. This pertains to individuals who occupy sites of privilege, those who hold positions of ecclesial leadership, and the church as a whole.

While acknowledging Jesus' inscription in structural sin might offend the sensibilities of many contemporary Christians, in the context of heteropatriarchy and white supremacy, ignoring or diminishing Christian complicity with violence is too dangerous. The temptation to clean up the narrative signifies the ways in which elite Christians gloss over participation in structural injustice. In doing so, elite Christians respond to hegemony with a deafening silence. As is evident in the history of interpretation surrounding the passage, interpreters who occupy sites of cultural, racial, sexual, and socioeconomic dominance find it particularly difficult to acknowledge Jesus' own participation in structural sin. We want Jesus to be in solidarity with those of all races, to accord women a place at the table (and not just in the kitchen). We want Jesus to welcome LGBTQ persons with dignity and respect into the Christian communion. Yet, we champion these ideals as ideals, giving lip service to justice-making efforts without taking steps to relinquish power and privilege. In the context of structural violence, to engage in the work of bringing about God's *basileia* requires taking accountability for your own social location and for the ways

---

123. Teel, "What Jesus Wouldn't Do," 29.

in which "understanding [religious and secular] flows from that orientation."[124]

It is crucial to note that whole-making work cannot take place apart from a face-to-face encounter. Namely, we can theorize about people who are socially, economically, sexually, or racially different from ourselves. Theorizing, apart from flesh-and-blood encounter, is a form of systemic ignorance. It allows the dominant party (Jesus and his disciples) to construct a different reality about the lives of subjugated (Syro-Phoenician woman and her daughter)—"a reality that is not bound to be challenged or questioned if it is only part of a theory."[125] It is only through face-to-face encounter that we are really able to "listen to people's interpretations however different they are from one's own; and to see people as worthy of respect rather than helpless beings that require help."[126]

Perhaps the most astonishing aspect of the passage is that a conversation happens at all. Jesus and the Syro-Phoenician woman have a direct encounter, defying cultural, religious, and ethnic traditions that would justify the contrary. Instead of ignoring one another, they persist in the relationship. This flesh-and-blood encounter, while uncomfortable and messy, is where healing begins to take shape. It is in this sense that the passage invokes boundary crossing as a metaphor for salvation. We can say healing is a communal effort prompted by a face-to-face encounter between Jesus and the woman.

Similar to Brock's notion of Christa/Community, salvation is a dialogue, not a monologue. As Brock argues, in exorcising demons

---

124. George Yancy, *Black Bodies, White Gazes: The Continuing Significance of Race* (Lanham, MD: Rowman & Littlefield, 2008), 238. Yancy is quoting Lisa Heldke, "On Being a Responsible Traitor," in *Daring to be Good: Essays in Feminist Ethico-Politics*, ed. Bat-Ami On and Ann Ferguson (New York: Routledge, 1998), 98.

125. Mariana Ortega, "Being Knowingly, Lovingly Ignorant: White Feminism and Women of Color," *Hypatia* 21, vol. 3 (2006): 68.

126. Ibid., 69.

and healing the sick, Jesus is a catalyst of erotic power—restoring relations and facilitating the recreation of power in the community.[127] Through the metaphor of Christa/Community, Brock underscores the need to emphasize the communal nature of redemption and discipleship. To be a disciple of Christ is to be a person in relationship. Salvation does not reside in the hands of a single individual or elite group. Salvation arises out of "a commitment to restorative justice and steady, active love, embraced in a common life with all its difficulties and rewards."[128] In a parallel sense, in Mark 7:24-30 healing is effected as a result of the dialogue between the woman and Jesus. Jesus does not heal her daughter single-handedly.

Christ has been imprisoned by privilege.[129] We want Jesus to be just like us so as to see our own privilege and "supposed innocence" reflected back and reinscribed. White Christians often assume that Christ is white. Heterosexual Christians assume that Jesus is straight. And most of us have struggled to image God in female form. For a brief moment, Mark 7:24-30 asks us to suspend these assumptions. Here the divine *logos* is uttered not by Jesus. The divine *logos* comes forth from the mouth of a woman who occupies a marginal religious, gendered, and ethnic status. Salvific words are uttered in disruption of Jesus' own words and from a subject position not his.

In this way, Mark 7:24-30 disrupts dominant strands of christological discourse by recentering the words of those who occupy marginal sites in society as revelatory of God's *basileia* vision. Such a perspective is consonant with the work of scholars like James Cone, Elizabeth Johnson, Kelly Brown Douglas, and Justin Tanis. For example, in *God of the Oppressed*, black liberation theologian

---

127. Brock, *Journeys by Heart*, 81–82.
128. Rita Nakashima Brock, "The Cross of Resurrection and Communal Redemption," in *Cross Examinations: Readings on the Meaning of the Cross Today*, ed. Marit Trelstad (Minneapolis: Fortress Press, 2006), 25.
129. Grant, "Womanist Jesus," 8.

James Cone asks who would Jesus be if he were here today.[130] In posing this question, Cone does not suggest that exact correlations can be made between life in first-century Palestine and the present day. Rather, his point is that who Christians understand Christ to be informs their praxis (or action) in the world. Therefore, the "authority of the Bible for Christology" cannot reside in a literal interpretation; "it is found in its power to point to the One whom the people have met in the historical struggle of freedom."[131] Citing the ways in which the historical Jesus was present with the humiliated and weak, Cone argues that, in the context of racial injustice in the United States, God would assume the "flesh of a member of an oppressed group, not a privileged one."[132] As such, Cone argues that God is black. Using parallel logic, womanist theologian Kelly Brown Douglas contends that in the context of tridimensional oppression (race, gender, and class), Christ would be a black woman.[133] Likewise, transgender theologian Justin Tanis has written about a transgender Christ who challenges gender binaries of masculine and feminine.[134] These are but a few of many understandings of Christ by those who occupy marginal sites.

While concepts of whiteness, homosexuality and gender-variant behavior—as we understand them in the twenty-first century—cannot be directly applied to the world of first-century Palestine, the Syro-Phoenician woman's utterance of Jesus' messianic word begs the question of how we envision the *imago Christi* in a contemporary context. The reversal in this account suggests not only that God is incarnate in and among the voices of those who

---

130. Cone, *God of the Oppressed*, 99.

131. Ibid., 102.

132. Teel, "What Jesus Wouldn't Do,"27

133. Kelly Brown Douglas, *The Black Christ* (Maryknoll, NY: Orbis, 1993), chapter 5.

134. Justin Tanis, *Trans-Gendered: Theology, Ministry, and Communities of Faith* (Cleveland: Pilgrim, 2003), 138–43.

occupy sites deemed to be of "no account,"[135] but, in the context of radical inequality, God's saving word must be uttered in disruption of dominant strains of christological discourse. Namely, the story of the Syro-Phoenician woman points to the need for ongoing efforts to trouble the christological status quo and its import for shaping Christian theological imagination with respect to power and privilege. Such christological disruption cannot be a momentary pause or interjection with the intention of returning to former ways of being in the world.[136] Rather, it must be accompanied by a radically new way of being in relation to God, self, and one another that bespeaks a transformation of the social and religious order. In order to recognize and to hear God's word in our midst, privileged elites need to be jolted out of theological spaces of mindless conformity and complacency that assume the Christ would be just like us. Rather, God will be embodied among and in the voices of those who are most marginalized. This has profound implications for the meaning of Christian discipleship for privileged persons. Discipleship will involve facing up to our unearned privileges and taking responsibility for resisting them. Doing so means allowing our very subjectivity to be formed into something new: it evokes a *metanoia* wherein we turn away from denial, silence, passivity, and the advantage that privilege affords and turn toward active attempts to be in solidarity with those who are marginalized. Such a calling is not an easy one. It will mean making choices that are costly: professionally, personally, and financially. Perhaps this is what was meant in Luke 14:26—"Whoever comes to me and does not hate

135. The phrase "no account" is used by Letty M. Russell in *Just Hospitality: God's Welcome in a World of Difference*, ed. J. Shannon Clarkson and Kate M. Ott (Louisville: WJK, 2009), 2.

136. Homi K. Bhabha would mark the difference between a postmodern interruption and postcolonial disruption. A postmodern interruption would signify a pause, or an effort to make the present-day system better. As I am using the term here, *disruption* points to a radical transformation of the present-day order. For more, see *The Location of Culture* (New York: Routledge 1994), chapter 9. I am grateful to Gerald Boodoo for this insight.

father and mother, wife and children, brothers and sisters, yes, and even life itself, cannot be my disciple." Discipleship is costly. In following such a path, we are undoubtedly going to rock the boat and alienate people, even those we most admire.

Conclusion

The chapter that follows will construct a soteriology wherein grace is marked by the "dis-ease" and "dis-comfort" modeled in Mark 7:24-30. Yet, before doing so, it is worth noting the biblical story's own limitations for such a project. Thinking back to the narrative, one is left wondering how the story ended. What happened after the encounter? Did Jesus walk away embarrassed and return to hiding? Did he repent and thereafter extend greater hospitality to foreign Others? Or, was this a one-time deal? And what about the woman? What happened to her? How was she received in her community? Was she viewed as a traitor for "crossing over" to the other side? If she was an impoverished single mother, as Kinukawa and others suggest, does the exorcism signify a substantive change in her social status? If she was a wealthy widow, does she go forth and find ways to relinquish her own economic privilege?

One of the main limitations of the narrative is the lack of attention given to structural transformation. To a degree, this is a story about personal transformation, and in some sense, conversion to the Other. While personal conversion is vital to structural change, it is not enough. Addressing systemic injustice requires changes in structures at the level of policy, economics, and worldviews. Granted, in the context of Roman imperialism, the power of either character to effect such change is limited. However, the lack of reparations and repentance is problematic. In this narrative, Jesus humiliates the woman and her people. Regardless of socioeconomic standing, no one seeking help for a child deserves to be humiliated. In the passage, we do not see Jesus apologize or take back the insult. While some have conjectured that Jesus makes reparations by agreeing to heal the woman's daughter (or so it seems), he never explicitly acknowledges the harm done nor his own participation in this harm. In a contemporary context, given the Western tendency to seek a quick fix for structural injustice, this is highly difficult. Without an explicit acknowledgement of harm done and repentance, the text risks endorsing benevolent paternalism, wherein marginalized Others are viewed as helpless victims, lacking agency in their own right. For example, at the parish level, the term *social justice* is often exclusively applied to acts of charity: donations to food pantries, financial collections, and mission-based service trips. These well-intentioned efforts often end up further silencing, instead of empowering, the voices of those suffering and rarely cultivate lasting partnership among all parties involved. Instead, the operative assumption is that only privileged Christians have the skills, talent, and agency to devise a plan for healing and liberation.

While postcolonial and feminist readings of the passage point to a temporary reversal in power, the larger issue of structural injustice remains unaddressed. The woman may have "gained the upper hand" in the dialogue, but the issues of ethnic prejudice, religious exclusivism, patriarchy, and imperial reign remain. Moreover, as Ringe rightly notes, "when read in the canonical context as a Scripture of the Church," one has to seriously contend with the possibility of this passage "sanction[ing] the humiliation and verbal (as well as physical) abuse of women [and ethnic and religious nondominants] as a legitimate test of their faith."[137] Always lurking in the background are the practical ways in which this passage can be

---

137. Ringe, "A Gentile Woman's Story, Revisited," 99.

used to further justify the subjugation and colonization of those who are Other in terms of religion, gender, and ethnicity.

Finally, as I have noted, the encounter between the woman and Jesus does not take place on neutral ground. Each of the two figures occupies location of dominance and subordination. "Jesus, as a 'Jew' is under the colonial thumb of Rome, the comprador thumb of priest and scribe, the native-elite thumb of Herod, the economic thumb of Tyre."[138] The religious and political leaders of his day suspect that he may start a revolution. At the same, time he is also privileged by gender and race within the discourse in this narrative. It also possible that the woman holds a subordinate and dominant position. As a non-Jew, a single female without male representatives, and the mother of an afflicted child, she is triply polluted and stigmatized. Yet, the introduction of the term *hellenis* into the Markan account resists easy assumptions about the woman's social status. In this way, the Markan account highlights the complexity of social location in unearthing christological discourse. In this sense, the text resists easy simplification into dualistic categories of victim/oppressor and innocent/guilty, which historically (and presently) have served the interests of those who occupy social, cultural, economic, and gender sites of dominance. It is crucial to note, as Kwok suggests, "there is always the Other within the Other."[139] Therefore, the one who utters saving words, whether it is Jesus or the woman, to some degree occupies a site of privilege.

138. Perkinson, "A Canaanitic Word," 74.
139. Kwok, *Discovering the Bible*, 82.

5

Grace as Dis-ease: Toward a Soteriological Praxis for Bystanders

Heteropatriarchy and white supremacy are theological issues because they distort and deny Christianity's fundamental presupposition about the dignity of the human person.[1] Moreover, these particular forms of violence "have a theological base."[2] Speaking in the context of anti-gay bullying, Cody J. Sanders writes, "I find it difficult to believe that even those among us with a vibrant imagination can muster the creative energy to picture a reality in which anti-gay violence and bullying exist without the anti-gay religious messages that support them."[3] As Sanders rightly suggests, "These messages come in many forms, degrees of virulence, and volumes of expression."[4] From the angry chants and posters of groups like the

---

1. This statement is not meant to exclude other ways in which structural injustice are manifest in society. Rather, it is made in keeping with the central issues discussed in this book.
2. Cody J. Sanders, "Why Anti-Gay Bullying is a Theological Issue," *Religion Dispatches*, http://www.religiondispatches.org/archive/sexandgender/3479/why_anti-gay_bullying_is_a_theological_issue/. Sanders further elaborates this point in *Queer Lessons for Churches on the Straight and Narrow: What All Christians Can Learn from LGBTQ Lives* (Macon, GA: Faithlab, 2013), chapter 5.
3. Sanders, "Anti-Gay Bullying is a Theological Issue."
4. Ibid.

191

Westboro Baptist Church to more subtle forms of noninclusion in religious communions, homophobia and heterosexism continue to plague the body of Christ. So does white racism. White Christian complicity with the slavocracy and in black lynching lingers in the pristine sanctuaries of many segregated Christian communities. Undergirding noninclusion are dualistic and hierarchal conceptions of value and worth implicit within Christian theologies.[5] "The simplistic, black and white lines that are drawn between conceptions of good and evil make it all-too-easy to apply these dualisms to our binary divisions between groups of people. When theologies leave no room for ambiguity, mystery, and uncertainty,"[6] it becomes all too easy to fall prey to scapegoating tactics. Scapegoating does not work without the complicity of the crowd—that is, without the tacit and explicit acceptance of bystanders. We saw bystander complicity in the white men and women who cheered at the lynching of Richard Coleman (see chapter 2) and in present-day denials of white racial violence. The complicity of bystanders keeps gay bashing and slut shaming alive and well in our communities.

Heteropatriarchy and white supremacy are also soteriological issues. They are soteriological issues because human scapegoating, whether in the form of social-role surrogacy or anti-gay violence, bypasses the very heart of God's *basileia* vision.[7] As Robert E. Goss explains, in the Gospels, "Jesus used the symbol of God's reign to speak of liberating activity among people."[8] This vision of God's *basileia* was both "socially provocative" and "politically explosive."[9] It was socially provocative in that Jesus challenged the dominant

---

5. Ibid.
6. Sanders, *Queer Lessons*, 120–21.
7. See introduction, n11 for a definition of God's *basileia*. In this book, the use of the term *basileia* refers to the already but not-yet character of God's kingdom as justice for all.
8. Robert E. Goss, *Queering Christ: Beyond Jesus Acted Up* (Cleveland: Pilgrim, 2002), 154.
9. Ibid.

social structure of his day. God's coming *basileia* did not belong to the upper echelon of society. Rather, its place was among the least in the society: children (Matt. 18:4), the poor (Luke 6: 20), and the persecuted (Matt. 5:10).[10] Further, as Goss notes, God's *basileia* was politically explosive.[11] In placing God's *basileia* among the humiliated and marginalized of society, Jesus "gave them hope and the courage to resist the domination politics of first-century Palestine."[12] Jesus' social praxis around God's reign ignited a social movement that offered an alternative way of being in relationship: "discipleship of equals."[13] The Gospels testify to this. For, in enacting God's *basileia*, Jesus confronted Roman imperialism. "Jewish peasants were squeezed by a religious and political system of economic extraction."[14] Not only did Jesus criticize the systemic injustice of imperial hegemony, but in his ministry he modeled a new way of exercising power: power-in-relation.[15] The logic of God's *basileia*, as testified to by the Gospel writers, is not "the logic of social and political hierarchies built on a foundation of wealth, privilege, status, power, and force."[16] Rather, it is the logic of "an abundance that is shared" and characterized by mutuality in political, economic, social, and religious relations.[17]

---

10. Biblical references are Goss's, *Queering Christ*, 154–55.

11. Ibid., 155.

12. Ibid.

13. This phrase is Elisabeth Schüssler Fiorenza's. See *In Memory of Her: A Feminist Theological Reconstruction of Christian Origins* (New York: Crossroad, 1983), 140–50 for a full description.

14. Goss, *Queering Christ*, 157.

15. The notion of Jesus modeling power–in–relation (or erotic power) is a common leitmotif in feminist liberation theologies. Among the first to adopt this idea include Rita Nakashima Brock, *Journeys by Heart: A Christology of Erotic Power* (New York: Crossroad, 1988) and Carter Heyward, *Touching Our Strength: The Erotic as Power and the Love of God* (San Francisco: Harper, 1989). It has since been further developed in feminist and queer liberation theologies. Goss, for example, takes this concept up in *Queering Christ: Beyond Jesus Acted Up*.

16. Goss, *Queering Christ*, 158.

17. Ibid.

By staking a claim in the struggle for social and political liberation in history, one partakes in God's *basileia*. As James Cone prophetically states, "There can be no Christian theology that is not identified *unreservedly* with those who are humiliated and abused."[18] For Cone and many of the thinkers whose work we have examined thus far, to be a Christian is to take a public stand against all that denigrates and denies the divinely created humanity of another. Those who attempt to hide under the guise of neutrality for fear of "making waves" can hardly be considered Christian.[19] This is because the Christian God is not neutral regarding human affairs. In the Scriptures, we find a God who is "decidedly involved" in the world and radically opposed to human oppression.[20] When faced with tremendous sin and evil, Christians, too, must become a people of courageous decision. Our salvation depends upon it. If working against the social sins of heteropatriarchy and white supremacy has soteriological implications, we are beginning to work out our salvation.

Liberation theologians have long spoken about the kin-dom of God as being tied to the struggle for liberation. Gustavo Gutiérrez states, "Without liberating historical events, there would be no growth of the Kingdom. . . . We can say that the historical, political, liberating event *is* the growth of the Kingdom and *is* a salvific event; but it is not *the* coming of the Kingdom, not *all* of salvation."[21] While God's *basileia* extends beyond this world, it cannot and does not exist apart from liberation in history. The kin-dom is already and not yet. In the present, Christians partake in the kin-dom as they seek liberation in the world.

18. James H. Cone, *A Black Theology of Liberation*, 40th anniv. ed. (Maryknoll, NY: Orbis, 2010), 1. Emphasis mine.
19. Ibid.
20. Ibid., 6.
21. Gustavo Gutiérrez, *A Theology of Liberation*, trans. and ed. Sister Caridad Inda and John Eagleson, 15th anniversary ed. (Maryknoll, NY: Orbis, 1988), 104. Italics original.

What does it look like for privileged persons to participate in this process? What is the role of elites in the praxis of liberation, in the work of bringing about the kin-dom of God? This question is complicated, given the ways in which whiteness and heteronormativity continues to comprise a relational frame of domination-subjugation that remains largely unquestioned and invisible to most. Even for those who are aware of their own complicity within dynamisms of social privilege, engaging in liberative praxis is not as straightforward as one would like to think. As George Yancy explains in the context of white supremacy, "To be white in America is to be always already implicated in structures of power."[22] Therefore, even when "friends of the oppressed" or allies engage in actions that "bind" them to marginalized populations, "there is also a sense in which [allies as privileged people] simultaneously 'bind to' structures of power."[23] In other words, one cannot remove privilege as if it were a "knapsack."[24]

As I have suggested, the dominant theological modus encourages privileged Christians to turn to Jesus as a source of comfort. While visions of Jesus as a "rock" and "resting place" can be appropriate within certain pastoral contexts, in view of the violence that not only "surrounds us"[25] but operates within us, we need a soteriological vision that "jolts" us out of apathy and into spaces of compassionate witnessing. As privileged people, we are in need of christological "dis-ease" and "dis-comfort."[26] Such a process will entail a critical

---

22. George Yancy, *Black Bodies, White Gazes: The Continuing Significance of Race* (Lanham, MD: Rowman & Littlefield, 2008), 235.

23. Ibid., 235-6. The term *friends of the oppressed* is taken from Ada María Isasi-Díaz's *Mujerista Theology: A Theology for the Twenty-First Century* (Maryknoll, NY: Orbis, 1996), 95ff.

24. This reference is to Peggy McIntosh's essay "White Privilege: Unpacking the Invisible Knapsack." Barbara Applebaum makes this critique in *Being White, Being Good: White Complicity, White Moral Responsibility, and Social Justice Pedagogy* (Lanham, MD: Lexington, 2010), 31.

25. Yancy, *Black Bodies, White Gazes*, 238.

examination of the ways that structural sin is not only operative in the world, but also is written upon our bodies. I am not suggesting that those of us who occupy social sites of privilege by virtue of our race, gender, sexual orientation, class, or ethnicity are intrinsically bad people. As stated at the outset of this book, this would suggest that human beings are incapable of change and, therefore, ultimately not responsible for their own complicity in violence. In theological terms, such a claim would render human beings incapable of actualizing the fullness of their divinely created humanity. What I am suggesting is that privileged Christians and privileged soteriologies are in need of disruption in the form of "ambush."[27] As Jesus was ambushed by the woman from Tyre, so must we allow ourselves and our theologies to be ambushed by the divine speaking of those who are Other.

Drawing insight from Christian liberation theologies and George Yancy's work theorizing "whiteness as ambush," this chapter constructs a soteriology for bystanders, wherein grace bears the mark of "privileged ambush" and is often experienced as "dis-ease." Within such a theological framework, salvation is understood as a continuous project rooted in history that is connected to the concrete liberation of those who suffer injustice. Privileged participation in the work of liberation is rooted in a soteriological praxis that 1) is marked by vigilance and uncertainty, 2) embraces vulnerability and demystifies perfection, in an effort to 3) nurture personal and collective maturity within the body of Christ.

---

26. Karen Teel makes this point in "What Jesus Wouldn't Do," in *Christology and Whiteness: What Would Jesus Do?*, ed. George Yancy (New York: Routledge, 2012), 28–30.
27. This is George Yancy's term, as found in *Black Bodies, White Gazes*, 227–50.

Salvation History Is One

Historically,[28] churches have spoken of salvation as an otherworldly realm, characterized as "a cure for sin in this life," which "is in virtue of a salvation to be attained beyond this life."[29] Talk of salvation has concerned itself with what a person has to do in this life in order to get into heaven. (Even today, when I ask my students to diagram salvation on the board, Jesus appears floating among the clouds with the pearly gates off in the distance). Not only does such a view purport a spirituality marked by an individual's "flight from this world," but, in the context of structural injustice, it has also furthered narcissistic paternalism, whereby well-meaning Christians engage in acts of charity for the sake of securing their own salvation. As Gustavo Gutiérrez and others have argued, such theological naming (God-talk) has done more harm than good, for it encourages onlooking from a vantage point of power instead of genuine solidarity.

The following account, taken from Elie Wiesel's *Night,* poignantly illustrates this phenomenon.[30] As narrated by Wiesel, a train full of imprisoned and starving Jews stops in a German town: "A crowd of workmen and curious spectators had collected along the train. They had probably never seen a train with such a cargo. Soon, nearly everywhere, pieces of bread were being dropped into the wagons. The audience stared at these skeletons of men, fighting, one another to the death for a mouthful."[31] Here, bread was not cast as a sign of hospitality, as the German workmen did not see the Jews on the train as fully human. Instead of hospitality, the Jews were met with "staring

---

28. The phrase "salvation history is one" is a reference to Gustavo Gutiérrez, *A Theology of Liberation,* 86.

29. Ibid., 84.

30. Elie Wiesel, *Night* (New York: Batman Books, 1982).

31. Ibid., 113. Ronald Hecker Cram draws attention to this narrative in order to illustrate the phenomenon of onlooking in *Bullying: A Spiritual Crisis* (St. Louis: Chalice Press, 2003), 27.

from the vantage point of power."[32] As Wiesel recounts, no one tried to stop the train, nor did anyone present protest the imprisonment of Jews.

To stare from the vantage point of power is to be a privileged bystander. It is to collude with the interests of hegemony. For in staring, the one being stared at becomes a thing, an object for visual consumption. At first glance, the story recounted by Wiesel seems like a "far cry" from the experience of Western Christians today. Yet this is hardly the case. Most of us respond to violence in ways that parallel the German workmen. We stare at the suffering of others (e.g., Daisy Coleman, Tyler Clementi, Billy Lucas, and Trayvon Martin)[33] through the medium of our television sets, phones, tablets, and computers. We throw bread in the form of pity, condolences, and monetary aid. Yet we do little to stop the train of hegemonic violence to protest structural injustice. In doing so, we fail to offer hospitality to our neighbor, to witness to the *basileia* vision of God. Our failure affronts the Christian gospel as it thwarts the coming of God's kin-dom on earth.

The 1960s precipitated significant change in the ways in which theologians approached the questions and topics of theology. Using the tools of social analysis, liberation theologians in Latin America and in the United States began with the contention that the world was not how it should be (recall the discussion of structural sin in chapter 3) and argued that salvation is a transhistorical reality encompassing body and soul, the individual and society. Salvation "[implies] a historical liberation."[34]

Gustavo Gutiérrez published *A Theology of Liberation* following the 1968 Latin American bishops' conference in Medellín, Colombia.

---

32. Cram, *Bullying*, 28.
33. See the introduction of this book.
34. Gutiérrez, *A Theology of Liberation*, 97.

In the 1950s, neocolonialist economic policies made Latin America dependent upon foreign trade. The idea was that by adopting the capitalist systems of the more "economically developed" countries, Latin America would rise out of its "backward" ways and, ultimately, out of poverty.[35] This optimism faded in the 1960s when it became apparent that the gap between the rich and the poor in Latin America and around the world was only increasing. Moreover, social analysis illustrated that Latin America's poverty was a by-product of the social and economic policies of so-called first-world countries. Guerilla groups rose up in resistance, but this resistance was only met with more violence—and did little to liberate people in Latin America.[36] At the same time, Gutiérrez was frustrated with the church's silence regarding, and thus tacit complicity with, the various governmental policies that oppressed the people of Latin America.[37] Therefore, following the Second Vatican Council's call to "[read] the signs of the times" and to "[interpret] them in the light of the Gospel,"[38] Gutiérrez called for a united view of history in which salvation history and the secular history of Latin America (and the world) are inseparably linked through Christ's redemptive actions. In other words, salvation history is one.[39]

Gutiérrez argues that the work of building a just society is the work of God's *basileia*. The God who liberates the Israelites from slavery in Egypt is the same God who creates the earth and is present with us today. This God is not a neutral God in the face of oppression and human degradation. The God of Israel, as narrated in the biblical story of Exodus, is a divine being who is passionately engaged in

35. Ibid., 52.
36. Ibid., 55.
37. Ibid., 40–41.
38. Pope Paul VI, *Pastoral Constitution on the Church in the Modern World*, reprinted in *Vatican Council II: The Basic Sixteen Documents*, ed. Austin Flannery, OP, (New York: Costello, 1996), 165.
39. Gutiérrez, *A Theology of Liberation*, 86.

the world. This conviction contests any sublimation of the Christian salvation to "otherworldly concerns." Salvation is not simply the afterlife. Rather, it is justice in this life. As echoed in the words of James Cone, "Liberation as a future event is not simply *other* worldly but is the divine future that breaks into their social existence, bestowing wholeness in the present situation of pain and suffering."[40] Ultimately, for thinkers like Cone and Gutiérrez, for the gospel to be salvific it must lead to human action for justice in the present world. Therefore, christological questions cannot center around "what Jesus did, as if his behavior in first-century Palestine were an infallible ethical guide for our actions today," but rather must ask "what is [Jesus] doing" in history today.[41] Such a Christology leaves both oppressors and the oppressed without "the moral luxury of being on neither side."[42]

Injustice dehumanizes persons. This dehumanization informs the gaze of bystanders. It can also shape how the oppressed see themselves if dehumanization becomes internalized. The oppressed begin to believe that they are less than full and worthy human persons. The internalization of dehumanization is a powerful tool for reinforcing the subjugation of the oppressed. Therefore, the first step in liberation and thus salvation is the education and empowerment of those who are marginalized. Liberation cannot be initiated by those who have the power to dominate. "In order for liberation to be authentic and complete, it has to be undertaken by the oppressed themselves and so must stem from the values proper to them."[43] For those who suffer under the weight of social injustice, participation in God's *basileia* begins with what Paulo Freire terms *conscientization*, wherein "the

40. James H. Cone, *God of the Oppressed*, rev. ed. (Maryknoll, NY: Orbis, 1997), 146. Italics original.
41. Ibid., 204.
42. Ibid., 201.
43. Gutiérrez, *A Theology of Liberation*, 57.

oppressed reject the oppressive consciousness which dwells within them, become aware of their situation, and find their own language."[44] Conscientization is not "something that happens once and for all."[45] Rather, it is a continuous task on the part of humanity to exercise our "creative potential" and to "assume responsibility" for the present and the future.[46]

For those who benefit from social privilege, the possibility of a liberative response also begins with conscientization. Oppressors must become aware of their own role in contributing to the suffering of others. Such awareness cannot come apart from efforts to "establish dialogue and mutuality with the oppressed."[47] In other words, the conscientization of the oppressor depends on entering into solidarity with the oppressed. Solidarity is not an easy road to love and harmony. Compassionate solidarity is truly a "wrenching task."[48] It is "an achievement of community" that defies the "dynamism of domination."[49] As such, solidarity on the part of the privileged cannot be approached from the vantage point of benign paternalism, pity, kindness, or sympathy. Rather, true solidarity has as its goal radical social transformation and emerges in the practices of mutuality and compassion.

Solidarity as the *Sine Qua Non* of Salvation

Salvation is entering into communion with God and others. While "salvation is gratuitously given by God; it flows from the very essence

---

44. Ibid. Also see Paulo Freire, *Pedagogy of the Oppressed*, trans. Myra Bergman Ramos, 30th anniv. ed. (New York: Bloomsbury Academic, 2000).

45. Isasi-Díaz, *Mujerista Theology*, 95.

46. Ibid.

47. Ibid.

48. M. Shawn Copeland, "Toward a Critical Christian Feminist Theology of Solidarity," in *Women and Theology*, ed. Mary Ann Hinsdale and Phyllis H. Kaminski (Maryknoll, NY: Orbis, 1994), 31.

49. Ibid, 29.

of God: love," it is "worked out through the love between God and each human being and among human beings."[50] This love relationship is the "goal of all life—it constitutes the fullness of humanity."[51] Ada María Isasi-Díaz names solidarity as the *sine qua non* of salvation. She explains, "Salvation depends upon love of neighbor, and because love of neighbor should be expressed through solidarity, solidarity can and should be expressed as the *sine qua non* of salvation."[52] Such an assertion, however, requires that the privileged are clear on two things: 1) who is our neighbor and 2) what is meant by solidarity. In order to answer the first question, Isasi-Díaz turns to the Scriptures, where the parables of Jesus point to our neighbor as the one who is least among us (Matthew 25), a sworn enemy (Luke 10:25-37), and those who are humiliated, despised, and disabled (Luke 14:12-14). The neighbors with whom we are called to be in solidarity with are the poor, the oppressed, and persons who are denigrated and marginalized in our society. Theologies of liberation see the poor and the oppressed as the special locus of God's revelation and argue that without their liberation, God's kin-dom will not be realized on earth or in heaven. There can be "no salvation outside the poor."[53]

But what exactly does it mean for privileged persons to be in solidarity with the oppressed? For many Christians in the Western world, the words *solidarity* and *love of neighbor* ring hollow, echoing nothing more than agreement: supporting a cause or being inspired by a group of people.[54] For Isasi-Díaz such sentiments are, at best, "distant cousins" of solidarity in that they do little "to bind"

---

50. Isasi-Díaz, *Mujerista Theology*, 89.
51. Ibid.
52. Ibid., 88.
53. Jon Sobrino, "Extra Pauperes Nulla Salus," in *No Salvation Outside the Poor: Prophetic-Utopian Essays* (Maryknoll, NY: Orbis, 2008), 35–76.
54. Isasi-Díaz, *Mujerista Theology*, 89.

communities and persons together. To speak of solidarity is to speak of intimate and passionate relationships that are "grounded in 'common responsibilities and interests,' which necessarily arouse shared feelings and lead to joint action."[55] To speak of solidarity is to speak of responsible relationships that are born of compassionate commitment to the liberation and full flourishing of all. In practice, such a vision requires that there is a real understanding of "the interconnections between oppression and privilege, between the rich and the poor, the oppressed and the oppressors."[56] On the part of the oppressed, there must be ongoing efforts toward conscientization, including awareness of the causes of the oppression and the need to change them. For those who wish to become "friends of the oppressed" there must also be an illumination of one's own complicity in oppression and a willingness to leave "their role as oppressors behind,"[57] or a *kenosis* [emptying] of privilege. To grasp this concept of solidarity as *kenosis*, it is helpful to turn to the work of Shawn Copeland.

Copeland locates the Christian praxis of solidarity beneath the cross. Not only does the cross "expose our pretense to historical and personal innocence, to social and personal neutrality," but it also "uncovers the limitation of all human efforts and solutions to meet the problem of evil."[58] Solidarity can never be separated from self-giving love, human and divine.[59] In view of the crosses of history, only those who are willing to "struggle on the side of the exploited, despised, and poor 'will discover [Christ] at their side.'"[60] If Christ is found among the oppressed, then to be at-one with Christ is to

55. Ibid.
56. Ibid.
57. Ibid., 96.
58. M. Shawn Copeland, *Enfleshing Freedom: Body, Race, and Being* (Minneapolis: Fortress Press, 2010), 99.
59. Ibid.
60. Ibid.

be at-one with those who are poor and marginalized. For Copeland, "solidarity begins in *anamnesis*—the intentional remembering of the dead, exploited, despised victims of history."[61] While she cautions that this remembering cannot be a "pietistic or romantic memorial," as history is always fraught with ambiguities, the practice of *anamnesis* calls us to shoulder responsibility "for the ways in which oppression is both a reality of the present and a fact of history."[62] Present-day injustices cannot be separated from historical atrocities. (For example, racism continues to shape race relations today.) The practice of solidarity entails a profound reckoning with the "enormity of suffering, affliction, and oppression" as well as our "own complicity and collusion in the suffering, affliction, and oppression of others."[63] There are no easy outs. In and through the praxis of solidarity, Christians must come to terms with the crucified Christ and "shoulder responsibility" for the struggle for justice, even when doing so involves a great cost to us.[64] It is important to note that the "shouldering of responsibility" is not an individual project. Rather, it is the work of whole communities. Within these communities, the responsibilities and roles must differ according to the place one occupies in relation to the cross (suffering). For privileged bystanders, solidarity is going to involve a *kenosis* of privilege itself.[65]

Speaking in the context of his work with the LGBTQ community, Larry Kent Graham describes his own experience of being a straight ally as one of "decentering heterosexual privilege."[66] In his own words, "To be a straight ally is not only to mediate affirming

---

61. Ibid., 100.
62. Ibid., 100–101.
63. Copeland, "Critical Christian Feminist," 29.
64. Copeland, *Enfleshing Freedom*, 101.
65. Ibid., 126, and "Critical Christian Feminist," 25.
66. Larry Kent Graham, "The Role of Straight Allies in Pastoral Care of Lesbians and Gays," *Out of the Shadows into the Light: Christianity and Homosexuality*, ed. Miguel A. De La Torre (St. Louis: Chalice, 2009), 109.

acceptance, but it is to participate in constructing a new social order and a new command structure by which all lives are enriched and set free."[67] Doing so requires that white straight allies find ways to decenter power gained from heterosexual and racial privilege. In practice this means more than simply regarding "one another as equals under the gospel."[68] It means that those who occupy social sites of privilege step back and take our "lead" from those who suffer injustice. To be a straight or cisgender ally is to allow lesbian, gay, bisexual, and transgender friends to become our teachers, guides, and critics. To be a white ally is to resist the tendency to declare colorblindness and to acknowledge that whites do not understand what it means to be nonwhite. It is to engage in humble, attentive, active listening. As Graham rightly notes, in doing so, allies often experience "inconvenience, discomfort, and discrimination."[69] Such discomfort might mean being shunned by family members, friends, and colleagues (after all, solidarity is a public practice, not a private practice), but also coming to terms with the ways in which our actions might be "inadequate, misguided, and even, insensitive, and offensive."[70] In this way, solidarity rooted in true compassion is an uncomfortable task that often sheds an "unflattering light on our need to dominate others and our collusion in the structural causes of unjust suffering."[71]

Power and privilege cannot be undone by merely casting off biased beliefs and attitudes, nor is it the work of one person. Rather, the systemic nature of privilege and oppression calls for transformation: at the collective level of social systems and at the individual level

---

67. Ibid.
68. Ibid.
69. Ibid.
70. Ibid.
71. Maureen H. O'Connell, *Compassion: Loving Our Neighbor in an Age of Globalization* (Maryknoll, NY: Orbis, 2009), 146.

for those who wish to become allies in the struggle for justice. For dominant elites, engaging in the praxis of solidarity—the work of redemption itself—will often mean finding oneself ambushed.

Privileged Ambush and the Possibility of Transformation

Comedian Michael Richards (known as the character "Cosmo Kramer" on the sitcom *Seinfeld*) may not have realized the significance of his insight when he attempted a televised apology for his explosive racist tirade at the Laugh Factory in 2006. Pointing to a group of Blacks in the audience who allegedly had been talking during his performance, with a great deal of anger and vitriol he shouted: "Shut-up. Fifty years ago, we'd have you upside down with a fucking fork up your ass. You can talk, you can talk, you can talk. You brave motherfucka!. . ." After this tirade, people actually began to leave the show. On his way out, one of the Black men shouted back at Richards, saying how unfair it was that he used such language. Richard responded, "That's what happens when you interrupt a white man, don't you know?"[72]

Shortly after the incident, Richards appeared on the *Dave Letterman Show* and offered the following words of apology: "I'm not a racist. That's what's so insane about this. . . . And yet, it's said. It comes through. It fires out of me."[73]

This incident and its lasting impact on Richards's career is recounted by George Yancy in *Black Bodies, White Gazes: The Continuing Significance of Race* in order to illustrate the experience of white ambush.[74] The experience challenged Richards's own understanding of himself as a "good white." While Richards may not think of himself as "a racist—perhaps because he has Black friends and other 'friends of color' and does not use the notorious 'n-word' on a daily basis, and because he does not identify as a skinhead or

---

72. As recounted by George Yancy in *Black Bodies*, 231. It is worth noting that Richards went on for a quite some time after this and used the N-word six times.
73. Ibid., 232.
74. Ibid.

associate with Klan groups," his rant at the comedy club exposed the ways in which racism and white privilege continue to permeate his own identity.[75] As Yancy explains, "Being a good white does not mean one has *arrived*. In fact, being antiracist does not mean that the white self has arrived."[76] For many whites, the notion of oneself as a "good white" or "antiracist white" actually works to obstruct "the necessary deeper critical work required to unearth the various ways in which one is complicit in racist behavior."[77] In other words, the assumption that one has "arrived" at a nonracist self denies the complexity and ambiguity that shrouds antiracist work itself. Racism cannot be undone in a single action or by a single person. Rather, white involvement in the project of dismantling racism must be an ongoing project that is marked by continuous vigilance.[78]

In America, there is no such thing as white innocence, as whiteness continues to be a structural and systemic reality that governs actions and relations rather than an aggregate of personal or individual racist behaviors. As revealed by Richards's response to the black patron who challenged his racist remarks, the prevailing social order is one marked by the dually constructed presumption of white entitlement to dominate and nonwhite subjugation and oppression. "To interrupt a white man, to look a white man in the eyes, to disagree with a white man, is to forget one's place in the natural scheme of things."[79] While most white people do not engage in outbursts similar to Richards, the white racial frame is not something that white people can just step outside of. The *white racial frame* (Joe Feagin's term) refers not only to racist stereotyping and ideology, but a "set of deep emotions and visceral elements, even language accents and sounds"

75. Ibid.
76. Ibid.
77. Ibid.
78. Ibid., 233.
79. Ibid., 231.

that have been essential to the maintenance of white superiority and nonwhite inferiority.[80] This set of ideas and emotions is often tacitly and unconsciously passed along to future generations. Whiteness continues to shape white subjectivity. White privilege, like white racism, is a systemic (or structural) reality. Whites cannot step outside of white privilege, even as they engage in antiracist work. This complicates what it means to be a white ally.

Each semester, I teach a course on theological anthropology to undergraduate students. One of the central learning objectives of this course is to examine the ways in which our own social situatedness informs the experience of sin and grace. Included among the readings assigned are a number of pieces authored by self-identified queer, black liberation, mujerista, womanist, and feminist theologians. As we work our way through the material, students often insist on their own attitudes of tolerance toward marginalized groups. For example, in the context of a discussion about queer theology, the majority of self-identified heterosexual students will say things like, "I think gay people should be free to love whomever they want," or "I have a friend who is gay." As students declare attitudes of "loving" acceptance (more appropriately tolerance) toward LGBTQ persons, the remainder of the class nods their heads as if to signify agreement. A similar thing happens within the context of classroom conversations about race and white racism. Unfortunately, declarations of a tolerant attitude make it difficult to get to the heart of the matter: white racial privilege and heterosexual privilege, which exist and continue to perpetuate injustice regardless of tolerant attitudes.[81]

---

80. Joe R. Feagin, *The White Racial Frame: Centuries of Racial Framing and Counter-Framing*, 2nd ed. (New York: Routledge, 2013), ix. For more descriptive detail and examples, see chapter 1 of Feagin's book.

After sitting through a particularly "politically correct" semester of classroom discussions, a group of nonwhite students decided to say the unsaid. For their final project, they chose to focus on their own experience of race and racism on campus. Utilizing technology that allowed them to disguise the voices and identity of those speaking, they crafted a video in which students of color voiced experiences of racism on campus: "never feeling like you really fit in;" tokenism—being expected to speak on behalf of the all people of color; the pressure to excel so as not to make "my own race look bad"; and being told point-blank that the "only reason you got that scholarship is to fulfill a diversity quota."

As the video played, a palpable shame and anger filled the classroom space. Leaving the classroom, one white student audibly muttered, "I am not going to listen to this crap." The remaining students sat there stunned, red-faced. They had been ambushed. The video, alongside the personal testimony of their classmates, had the impact of unnerving student beliefs about their own "acceptance" or "tolerance" of others. It challenged their self-identification as "good," white Christian people.[82] This was a pedagogical experience that I, a white female professor, could not plan or implement. Privileged ambush does not originate from a member of the dominant group. Privileged ambush usually arises out of the words or experiences of members of the nondominant group. Similar to the situation involving Michael Richards, this word often takes the form of an interruption, or disruption, jolting us out of spaces of complacency. To be ambushed is to have been confronted with one's own complicity in injustice. It is a profound experience of dis-ease. While we are taught at a young age that to interrupt or disrupt someone

81. It is worth noting that the student population at the university where I teach is predominantly white. While there are a number self-identified gay, lesbian, and bisexual students on campus, the campus environment is not particularly supportive of expressions of sexual diversity.
82. As recorded in student writing after the video.

is impolite or rude, in the context of apathy that is an accomplice to violence, interruption or disruption can be life-saving. Hegemony thrives in environments marked by apathy. It is therefore critical that privileged Christians "take notice" of injustice and "decide to undertake the struggle against it."[83] The experience of ambush can be a powerful tool in this regard. In an encounter of ambush, not only is the valorization and normalization of hegemonic violence called into question, but elites are confronted with the ways in which privilege is at work with themselves.[84] For example, in watching the video and hearing the testimony of their classmates, white students in my class were faced with the fact that their whiteness renders them participants in a dominant racial group on campus, which as an institution excludes their nonwhite peers. Many of my students experienced a visceral reaction when confronted with the pain of their nonwhite peers. As my white students were faced with the question—"To what degree am I complicit in the pain of this person, this group?"—their sense of self-certainty regarding their own goodness and innocence was momentarily suspended.

Ambush in the form of surprise presents privileged elites with an opportunity for *metanoia* (conversion). In coming face to face with one's own complicity in violence, there is always the possibility of outright denial, invalidation, or minimization—namely, of uttering an apology merely for the sake of saving one's own face and continuing on as if nothing happened. (This appears to be what has happened in the case of Michael Richards.)[85] Indeed, such a response would be in keeping with the dominant moral and religious ethos of this country. Yet, the more authentic Christian response to ambush is

83. Teel, "What Jesus Wouldn't Do," 22.

84. Yancy, *Black Bodies*, 238.

85. Kate McDonough, "Michael Richards Unsuccessfully Apologizes for Being Racist," *SALON*, http://www.salon.com/2012/09/28/michael_richards_unsuccessfully_apologizes_for_being_racist.

personal conversion, or *metanoia*. Ambush provides "the opportunity for creative intervention, for assuming the subject position of an ally."[86] In assuming the "subject position of ally," privileged elites are called to "engage in a form of relationality that requires a suspension of self-certainty, arrogance, fear, and other blaming."[87] Doing so requires that privileged elites regard the experience of ambush in and of itself as valuable to their own growth, and a call to change. As Yancy rightly observes, all too often those who occupy sites of social dominance view critique as a sign of defeat and respond defensively.[88] Yet, in order for ambush to lead to conversion, privileged elites must adopt a posture of "openness to having one's world transformed and cracked."[89] Nurturing these "cracks and fissures" demands a commitment to social praxis that is accompanied by a radical shift in values. Change, vulnerability, uncertainty, and interdependence must be regarded as intrinsic to our livelihood and our redemption. Such valuing will require new ways of imaging divine grace and salvation.

Grace as Interruption, Grace as Ambush

Divine grace has often been described in terms that express surprise, astonishment, and even disruption of the present order. For example, thinkers like Hans Urs von Balthasar and Karl Barth speak of grace as having an event-like quality. The in-breaking of the divine Word awakens the Christian community, calling us to conversion. In the encounter with the Word of God, the human person is interrupted, taken back, and caught up within the power of divine grace. As Balthasar writes, "It is not we ourselves who determine on our part what is heard and place it before us as object in order to turn our

---

86. Yancy, *Black Bodies*, 241.
87. Ibid.
88. Ibid., 240.
89. Ibid.

attention to it when it pleases us; that which is heard comes upon us, without our being informed in advance, and it lays hold of us without our being asked. We cannot look out in advance and take up our distance."[90] Ultimately, for Balthasar, "the basic relationship between the one who hears [the Word] and that which is heard [the Word] is thus the relationship of defenselessness on the one side and of communication on the other."[91] It is God who speaks and human beings who listen. Balthasar's insistence on this particular dynamism is reflective of a larger methodological concern: preservation of the self-authenticating and self-interpreting nature of divine revelation. This methodological conviction, which is shared by his mentor and contemporary, Karl Barth, was largely motivated by concern about the turn to the subject within the nineteenth-century liberal theologies (á la Friedrich Schleiermacher) and their potential to authorize Christian participation in hegemony.

Karl Barth, writing in Europe during the first half of the twentieth century, witnessed firsthand Christian complicity with hegemonic violence. In 1914, ninety-three German intellectuals signed a manifesto in support of the war policy of Kaiser William II at the onset of World War I. As he writes, "Among them I found to my horror nearly all my theological teachers whom up to then I had religiously honored."[92] For Barth, this moment signified "the failure of the ethics of modern theology."[93] In Barth's eyes, the situation

---

90. Hans Urs von Balthasar, *Spouse of the Word*, vol. 2 of *Explorations in Theology*, trans. A.V. Littledale et al. (San Francisco: Ignatius, 1991), 475.

91. Ibid., 475–76. This dynamism of receptivity and activity is present throughout Balthasar's corpus and thoroughly gendered. For more, see Lucy Gardner and David Moss, "Something Like Time; Something Like the Sexes—An Essay in Reception," in *Balthasar at the End of Modernity* (Edinburgh: T&T Clark, 1999), 69–137.

92. Barth as quoted by Thomas F. Torrance in *Karl Barth: An Introduction to His Early Theology 1910–1931* (Edinburgh: T&T Clark, 1962/2000), 38. Barth makes a similar point in "The Humanity of God," in *God, Grace, and Gospel*, trans. James Strathearn McNab, *Scottish Journal of Theology*, Occasional Papers no. 8 (London: Oliver and Boyd LTD, 1959), 33.

93. Karl Barth, "The Humanity of God," 33–34.

dictated nothing less than a radically new methodological approach. No longer could God be accommodated to the needs and wants of society. Theology was not to be judged by whether it conformed to criteria adopted by the other sciences. Rather, theology was to be based on the Word of God, which stands over and against human philosophies.[94] The Word of God escapes all human speculation and stands as wholly Other, infinitely different from creatures.[95]

While Barth's metaphysical turn may have been prompted by well-placed concern about the inadequacy of certain forms of Christian theological method to address the problem of Christian complicity with violence,[96] as I have argued, high christologies are also subject to abuse. The emphasis on divine sovereignty has been misappropriated in order to justify Christian imperialism and limits the Christian moral imagination within contexts marked by privileged apathy by locating the work of redemption exclusively within the suffering of a divine Other.[97] In this framework, Jesus alone can atone for human sin and bring about divine justice (whether this justice is understood as liberation of the oppressed or personal conversion). Jesus is a divine

94. Karl Barth, *The Doctrine of the Word of God, Church Dogmatics* 1/1, ed. G. W. Bromiley and T. F. Torrance, trans. G. W. Bromiley (New York: T&T Clark, 1936/1975), 4.

95. Karl Barth, *The Doctrine of God, Church Dogmatics* 2/2, ed. G. W. Bromiley and T. F. Torrance, trans. G. W. Bromiley et al. (New York: T&T Clark, 1957), 94–145.

96. This line of interpretation of Barth's work is subject to debate. One of the first to make this point was Friedrich-Wilhelm Marquardt. See "Socialism in the Theology of Karl Barth," in *Karl Barth and Radical Politics*, ed. and trans. George Hunsinger (Philadelphia: Westminster, 1976), 19–46. For further discussion of the contribution of Barth's work for political theology, see Timothy J. Gorringe, *Karl Barth: Against Hegemony* (New York: Oxford University Press, 1999).

97. In all fairness, both Barthian and Balthasarian theological paradigms seek to bridge the divide between God and humanity in their own right. Barth himself writes that "human freedom is not realized in solitary detachment of an individual in isolation from his fellow men." See Karl Barth, *The Humanity of God* (Richmond: John Knox, 1960), 77. Yet this being said, Barth makes it clear that this freedom is freedom for relationship with God. Human freedom exists within the freedom of God. God is sovereign, "perfecter of history." Hans Urs von Balthasar makes a similar point and is indebted to Barth on this point to a degree. For more on the relationship of Barth and Balthasar see, Stephen D. Wigley, *Karl Barth and Hans Urs von Balthasar: A Critical Engagement* (New York: T&T Clark, 2007).

superhero who "does what no other human can do."[98] In the words of Susie Paulik Babka, "Jesus can perform extraordinary actions because he is divine and as such manifests an unattainable humanity: his apparent celibacy means that he is beyond sexuality, he manipulates nature by calming storms and walking on water, and he never makes a mistake or says anything wrong."[99] This makes it nearly impossible for human beings to emulate Christ in our own lives and suggests that God "can only act externally toward the repair of the world, as an outsider, but not as one of the world."[100] Such a construction is one that renders human beings passive and impotent in the face of injustice, and allows for the justification of apathy regarding our own complicity in sin.

God's Word does irrupt in human history. In view of privileged complacency in the evil of structural injustice, such interruption is vital to the liberation of the world. Yet "God's advancement of justice and liberation of the oppressed are not external to the particular workings of finite existence established by God."[101] Human beings are participants within the life of God and, therefore, within the work of bringing about God's *basileia*. Salvation history is one.[102] Therefore, it is necessary to set forth another paradigm for grace as interruption. In the context of privileged apathy, the former, at best, signifies a momentary pause in the status quo as opposed to its radical transformation.

Returning to the story of the Syro-Phoenician woman (Mark 7:24-30), we find the christological basis for a new understanding of the surprising, disrupting character of divine grace.[103] In this

---

98. Susie Paulik Babka, "Arius, Superman, and the *Tertium Quid*: When Popular Culture Meets Christology," *Irish Theological Quarterly* 73 (2008): 129.

99. Ibid.

100. Ibid., 131.

101. Ibid., 132.

102. Gutiérrez, *A Theology of Liberation*, 86.

103. Refer to chapter 4 above for a full discussion of the narrative.

narrative, Jesus is ambushed by Syro-Phoenician woman, who calls attention to the ways in which the body of Christ is inscribed within social sin. As I have argued in chapter 4, the dialogue between Jesus and the woman calls into question privileged christological complacency surrounding the nature of salvation (who it is meant for, who effects it, and who can partake of it). In the narrative, it is a foreign woman, not Jesus, who utters the Good News of God's kindom. In doing so, she calls Jesus to account for the ways in which his mission and vision have become caught up in ethnic prejudice and religious exclusivism. This ambush, which takes the form of an utterance of God's messianic vision, "Sir, even the dogs under the table eat the children's crumbs," becomes a catalyst for healing in that it calls the Christian church to conversion in light of its own complicity in structural injustice.

As in the story of the Syro-Phoenician woman, we need to begin to see privileged ambush as a form of divine speech, of divine grace. All too often we look for God in the wrong places. We think we will find God's Word within places of safety, security, and economic prosperity. Yet, time and time again, the gospels tell us that God's Word does not dwell there. The Word of God dwells among the humiliated, oppressed, despised, and forsaken. It can be heard in the anguish of all who suffer daily harassment and torment because of their sexual orientation or gender identity. It echoes in the cry from the lynching tree, among the floodwaters of Katrina, and in the cultural humiliation of nonwhites in America. The Word of God can be heard in the silent shame of women raped, battered, and abused. The Word of God dwells among those crucified in history.

Racism, heterosexism, and sexism are sinful. They distort our relationship with one another, God, and ourselves. For many elites, apathy tends to be the rule, not the exception, in responding to these sins. Privileged ambush opens the door to the possibility of redemption by calling elites to conversion and repentance and creating the opportunity for our own participation in the work of social transformation. In the experience of ambush, privileged persons are presented with the opportunity to learn more about themselves, and the way in which their own identity participates in the subjugation of others.[104] In this way, ambush can be seen as a form of redeeming grace, opening pathways for privileged persons to enter into solidarity with the oppressed. This is particularly so when we respond to the grace of ambush with a posture of humble thankfulness.

Humble thankfulness on the part of those privileged functions as a "bridge to others,"[105] to self, and to the divine: fostering communion that seeks to make the bodies of those who are crucified visible. In this way, the grace of ambush invites privileged elites to partake in what Shawn Copeland has called eucharistic solidarity.[106] The Eucharist evokes the paschal mystery in its entirety: the life, death, and resurrection of Jesus. As it points toward "a body that carries the marks of violence,"[107] the Eucharist orients the Christian community to the suffering of those who have been and continue to be crucified by structural injustice. As such, the Eucharist is evocative of an embodied social praxis. Copeland explains,

> Commitment to intentional and conscious Eucharistic living initiates a change of direction in the personal and social living of an individual as well as the living of many. Eucharistic solidarity challenges us in living out the implications and demands of discipleship. Prerogatives rooted in socially constructed disparities are deconstructed. We become aware of ourselves as striving to realize concretely the fruitful insights of practical intelligence and rectitude.[108]

104. Yancy, *Black Bodies*, 240.
105. Ibid., 241.
106. Copeland, *Enfleshing Freedom*, 127.
107. Ibid.
108. Ibid., 127–28.

Through the bringing together of broken bodies, we are given the opportunity to respond in ways that reflect an ongoing commitment to God's *basileia*. It is in this sense that the eucharistic thanksgiving calls forth Easter hope.[109]

Such a hope must have a practical meaning. For privileged people, this involves more than self-reflection on one's own complicity in violence. The praxis of eucharistic solidarity requires outward attempts toward social solidarity, including active welcome and public advocacy. For example, in the context of heterosexism, such attempts might include "joining in corporate endeavors [already begun by LGBTQ persons] to normalize and make visible the experience of lesbians and gays," using one's own influence and power to "to create venues where power and influence can be shared," promoting public policies that provide equal access to employee benefits within the workplace, and challenging heterosexist theologies and pastoral practice.[110] In the context of white supremacy, the effort to undo whiteness would include finding ways to redistribute wealth and power; making visible the experience of nonwhites within the secular and sacred public spheres; education surrounding immigration and work toward its reform; challenging racist theologies and pastoral practice; and active attempts to desegregate day-to-day existence.[111] These are a just a few examples among many.

The work of social justice is an ongoing task. God's *basileia* is not a once-and-for-all reality. In the Gospels, Jesus likens the kin-

---

109. Goss, *Queering Christ*, 163–65.

110. Graham, "Role of Straight Allies," 117. Also see Goss, *Queering Christ*, 163–69, for additional examples.

111. For further examples countering whiteness, see chapters 8 and 9 of Feagin's *White Racial Frame*. For examples in Christian contexts, see chapter 3 of Bryan N. Massingale's *Racial Justice and the Catholic Church* (Maryknoll, NY: Orbis, 2010) as well as the essays in *Disrupting White Supremacy from Within: White People on What We Need to Do*, eds. Jennifer Harvey, Karin A. Case, and Robin Hawley Gorsline (Cleveland: Pilgrim, 2004).

dom of God to a mustard seed (Mark 4:31) or yeast (Matt. 13:33), both of which need tending to grow. Christian churches seek out the kin-dom of God and promote its growth. In contexts marked by privileged apathy, cultivating the kin-dom of God will necessarily involve nurturing privileged ambush, placing ourselves in situations that challenge biases and prejudicial exclusivism. At the personal level, this means cultivating a form of "double-consciousness" whereby one maintains "a self-reflexive posture" that tries to "understand what it means to be" the other and how we ourselves might be perceived through others' eyes.[112] Such "double-consciousness" is always subject to distortion and, therefore, requires constant vigilance informed by an ongoing commitment to learn and to be critiqued by those who are different. At the collective level, nurturing privileged ambush involves a commitment to asking the really hard questions. Is the body of Christ really a place where all are welcome? Does our interpretation of church teaching contribute to theology and pastoral practice that stresses the importance of structural change as much as charity? Is it possible to justify hate speech or other practices of relational aggression in our interpretation of texts and traditions? These questions must not only be asked among a group of our likeminded peers, but they must also give way to an ongoing dialogue that invites all to the table. In other words, religious communities must take responsibility for creating environments that welcome critical questioning and, in doing so, attentively seek out the voices and concerns of those who are marginalized.

In view of the propensity of privileged apathy to define what counts for "Christian" behavior, the grace of ambush must be nurtured. Our salvation depends upon it. Let me be clear, it is not the

---

112. Yancy, *Black Bodies*, 240.

responsibility of the poor, marginalized, and dispossessed to ambush those who are privileged. *Heteropatriarchy and white supremacy are the problems of privileged people.*[113] In other words, one cannot be white, heterosexual, or male without receiving the benefits of these categories. Therefore, it is the responsibility of the privileged to work out their own salvation, by accepting "graciously all the help that is offered, and [using] it to figure out how to 'rescue'" themselves.[114] As Karen Teel suggests, this might sound harsh. Yet, it is consistent with the way that Jesus spent the bulk of his time and attention in his ministry. "In the gospels, Jesus' engagement with the powerful may well be no more than a footnote to his main work of redemption among the marginalized."[115] Perhaps we might expect the same in an encounter with the risen Christ today.

Toward a Soteriological Praxis for Privileged Bystanders

If we are to take seriously Ada María Isasi-Díaz's claim that solidarity is the *sine qua non* of salvation, then, for privileged bystanders, the pathway to salvation must extend beyond mere rhetoric. Our redemption will be worked out through a liberative praxis marked by compassionate solidarity. While conversion to solidarity "cannot be willed, neither can it be manipulated. It *is* possible, when we place ourselves in the way of change's possibility, when we open ourselves to difference."[116] For privileged elites, placing ourselves in the "way of change's possibility" begins by pausing long enough to take notice of other human beings in our midst. While this statement may affront

---

113. W. E. B. Du Bois was first to turn the question, "How does it feel to be a problem?" back on white people themselves. See *The Souls of Black Folk* (New York: Penguin, 1996), 3–4. Originally published (New York: A.C. McClurg & Company, 1903). Since then a number of scholars have taken up Du Bois's charge and applied it to their own context.
114. Teel, "What Jesus Wouldn't Do," 28.
115. Ibid., 29.
116. Copeland, "Critical Christian Feminist," 23. Italics original.

our academic sensibilities in its simplicity, in a violent world, the practice of "witnessing" to one another is easier said than done.[117]

To be human is to be a person in relation. It is be involved in the lives of others. To return to the words of Archbishop Desmond Tutu, "'My humanity is caught up, is inextricably bound up, in yours.' We belong in a bundle of life."[118] Our ability to respond to others and the ethical obligation to do so (response-ability) defines our agency in the world. It is constitutive of our identity. We do not know who we are apart from relationship with others.

From the day that we enter this world, we are highly dependent upon others for physical, emotional, and spiritual sustenance. We rely on the earth and those who tend the land for food, water, and the electric power to heat our homes. For most in the Western world, our access to these vital resources is purchased off the backs of many who labor under unjust working conditions. The companionship of good friends and intimate partners and healthy family relationships are vital to our own emotional well-being. Meaningful work, where our skills, talents, and personhood are valued, is critical to the development of a healthy sense of self. Having a religious community "to call home," should we so choose, is an important aspect of spiritual growth. Yet, all too often we take our dependence on others for granted, becoming only aware of their importance when one or more is lost.

For privileged people, the propensity to sin is rooted in the tendency to lose sight of this fundamental relatedness. To quote Sallie McFague, sin is "living disproportionately, falsely, inappropriately

---

117. In the words of Kelly Oliver, "Subjectivity is responsibility: it is the ability to respond and to be responded to. Responsibility, then, has the double sense of opening up the ability to respond—response-ablity—and ethically obligating subjects to respond by virtue of their very subjectivity itself. *Witnessing beyond Recognition* (Minneapolis: University of Minneapolis Press, 2001), 91.

118. Desmond Mpilo Tutu, *No Future without Forgiveness* (New York: Doubleday, 1999), 31.

within this space, refusing to accept the limitations and responsibilities of our place."[119] Such near-sightedness is tied to the relatively isolated and segregated lives we live. As discussed in chapter 1, violence is hidden from view by social norms that privilege a few at great cost to many, and this hiddenness itself also precipitates violence. Facebook, Instagram, and Twitter allow us to connect with persons across the globe. Yet, they also normalize distance in relationships. Given the propensity to dehumanize persons and communities within the United States, this distance is pernicious, for it allows us to close our eyes to violence and the suffering it causes. Most of us are ignorant of how our food is produced or how our clothing is made. We do not know our next door neighbors, much less those who occupy social sites different than our own. The loss of relationality, of genuine solidarity across difference and similarity, is to our own detriment. It prevents us from actualizing the fullness of our divinely created humanity. Toward this end, I outline three "soteriological" praxes for privileged people.[120] These praxes are not an exhaustive list. They are simply meant to be starting points as we stumble together on the journey to wholeness. I have named them "soteriological" because, along with divine grace, they open us to the power of conversion—to more authentic relationships with God, self, and one another.

In Christian tradition, to speak of redemption is to speak of a process of becoming at-one with God, self, and others. While part

---

119. Sallie McFague, *The Body of God: An Ecological Theology* (Minneapolis: Fortress Press, 1993), 115.

120. I am hardly the first person to speak of soteriological praxis. This concept is explicitly developed in the work Ignacio Ellacuría. See Michael E. Lee, *Bearing the Weight of Salvation: The Soteriology of Ignacio Ellacuría* (New York: Crossroad, 2009). Delores Williams also speaks of Jesus emulating a soteriological praxis in *Sisters in the Wilderness: The Challenge of Womanist God-Talk* (Maryknoll, NY: Orbis, 1993), 163–66. Miguel A. De La Torre also speaks of the saving role of praxis for the privileged in *Doing Christian Ethics from the Margins*, 2nd ed., rev. and expanded (Maryknoll, NY: Orbis, 2014), 32–37. He draws insight from the contributions of Juan Luis Segundo and Gustavo Gutiérrez.

of the process of at-one-ment involves freedom from sin, liberation from sin is for the purpose of relationship with the divine and each other. It is for the sake of wholeness of relationship. Such wholeness is not found by chasing after a dream of unattainable perfection. Wholeness, as suggested by the poetic vision of womanist theologian Emilie Townes, seeks the concrete material and spiritual well-being of those of who are suffering.[121] Wholeness is found in the difficult space of making choices for the common good in local communities. This is a wholeness that harnesses human potential by forming relationship among real individuals. Here, in this place of "mundane agency," of "everydayness," redemption is found.[122]

Privileged Vigilance

In chapter 2, I spoke about silence as a double-sided coin. In the context of white supremacy and heteropatriarchy, silence can and does signify privileged disengagement. (Recall my own silent disengagement in Kenya.) Yet, silence can also create space for deep listening: to one another, God, and ourselves. This kind of silence is hardly foreign to Christian tradition. For example, in centering prayer, a practical method of contemplation, Christians are invited into silence as a way of deepening their relationship with God. The idea is that in emptying our minds of habitual thought patterns (usually by mediating on a word or a phrase), our inner world begins to change. As we center our attention on the divine within, we begin to notice God's presence elsewhere.[123] Thomas Keating describes this as follows: "By turning off the ordinary flow of thoughts [and really listening to God within], which reinforce one's habitual way

121. Emilie M. Townes, *In a Blaze of Glory: Womanist Spirituality as Social Witness* (Nashville: Abingdon, 1995), 49.
122. Ibid., 47.
123. Thomas Keating, "Cultivating the Centering Prayer," in *Finding Grace at the Center* (Still River, MA: St. Bede, 1978), 24.

of looking at the world," we come to know God and ourselves in a deeper way.[124] In particular, the kind of deep listening promoted by centering prayer requires that we "pause" long enough from the demands of daily life to be quiet and stay awake. In other words, the "listening" of centering prayer is kind of a silent vigilance, where one is still but attentive. The deep listening of contemplative prayer is not something that one comes to overnight. It requires daily practice and commitment.

The practice of deep listening is necessary for privileged elites in their efforts to become allies in the work of bringing about the kindom.[125] This is not only in the sense of individual contemplation, but also in the sense of "active and attentive listening" to the voices of men and women whose suffering is conjoined to our own privilege. In the words of Copeland, "To negotiate the borders of race and social class, ears, minds, and hearts must become attuned to vocabularies, grammars, syntaxes, scales, and tones."[126] In so doing, we are called upon to enact a "new and bold expression of the virtue of humility."[127] The humility of which Copeland speaks is not the humility of polite silences or ineffective guilt. It is a humility that is negotiated in and through conversations marked by fits and starts, uncomfortable silences, and most of all an effort and desire to understand. Like the deep listening of contemplative prayer, listening across borders is an ongoing effort requiring practice and commitment. Given the ways in which violence continues to be hidden under the guise of social norms, deep listening will not likely

---

124. Ibid., 25.
125. There are strong links between contemplation and social action in the Catholic tradition. Prominent examples include Theresa of Avila, Thomas Merton, and Dorothy Day. For more, see Susan Rakoczy, *Great Mystics and Social Justice: Walking on the Two Feet of Love* (Mahwah, NJ: Paulist, 2006) and Grace M. Jantzen, *Power, Gender, and Christian Mysticism* (Cambridge, UK: Cambridge University Press, 1996).
126. Copeland, "Critical Christian Feminist," 25.
127. Ibid.

be the result of happenstance. Rather, it must be the result of a conscious decision to pay attention: "to look and listen and check and question."[128] In order to pay attention, the sense of certainty that couches privileged elites' view of the world must be exposed. We must continually question our own understanding as well as the judgments we have made.[129] From the kinds of "knowing" that we consider credible, to unjust governmental structures that we are willing to accept simply because they "do no harm to us," to assertions of colorblindness, and mere tolerance of sexual diversity, we must become vigilant about our own presumption of innocence. Privileged folks must always be on the lookout for the ways in which heteropatriarchy and white supremacy negatively impact the well-being of others, while simultaneously supporting our own "interests, desires and loathings."[130] Such vigilance is a difficult task that extends beyond the work of an individual. Rather, this kind of deep listening necessitates the use of social analysis—unearthing the ways in which power and privilege are operative within the sociocultural contexts in which we live and have our being—as well as finding new ways to embrace our vulnerability.

Embracing Vulnerability and Demystifying Perfection

To be human is also to be vulnerable. To acknowledge this reality is to really be honest with ourselves and God. While it may not always be prudent or appropriate to expose our vulnerability, it is an important soteriological praxis in releasing us from the sin of hiding. As originally formulated by Valerie Saiving, the sin of hiding refers to a loss of self to the extent that one fails to take responsibility for

128. Marilyn Frye, "In and Out Of Harm's Way: Arrogance And Love," in *The Politics of Reality: Essays in Feminist Theory* (Freedom, CA: Crossing, 1983), 75.
129. Copeland makes this point in "Critical Christian Feminist," 16.
130. Frye, *Politics of Reality*, 75.

one's own life.[131] In hiding, we live an alienated existence. Shielded by fear and insecurity, our relationships deceive us of our God-given capacity for relational power. Hiding can be death dealing, particularly when it bears the mark of mindless, or even pressured, conformity to the status quo. Recall (chapter 1) that hiding is not just about a lack of self-assertion. It is also about segregation and cultures of violence that encourage escapism from the suffering of others and privileged complicity.

We have to stop hiding to embrace our vulnerability. While the reasons for hiding are complex, it is in part tied to the cultural glorification of the value system linked to hegemonic masculinity: rampant individualism and cutthroat competiveness where life is a zero-sum game. In such a system there can only be one "top dog." Making it to the top of the social or economic ladder defines success in a way that rests upon the denigration of others. Furthermore, the ability "to put others down" is interpreted as a sign of personal strength. We live in a culture that not only prizes radical self-sufficiency, but also views weakness with contempt. And, really, why shouldn't we? From Superman to Jesus Christ, our cultural, moral, and religious heroes embody perfection as dynamic overcomers of adversity. (Or at least their personal failings are swept under the rug in the wake of a new success.) Yet, such is not the lot of our existence. More often our lot is one of stumbling, tripping, and falling. Ours is a life of imperfection.

As my students will attest, the pressure to be perfect is tremendous. We all want to get straight As, to have the perfect body (yes, even men), to be a part of the "right" social group, and sport trendy clothing and accessories. While some of this pressure dissipates with age, I can say that as a thirty-something mother who works outside

---

131. Valerie Saiving Goldstein, "The Human Situation: A Feminine View," *The Journal of Religion* 40, no. 2 (1960): 100–12. See chapter 3 of this book for further discussion of sin as hiding.

of the home, I often find myself succumbing to it. For example, I agonize over child-care decisions and often feel guilty about serving mac 'n' cheese for dinner instead of organic quinoa. This grasping for perfection (in my case to be the "perfect" parent) is a plea for control, one that is unattainable. Michelle Saracino poignantly remarks, "The path to perfection is the road to destruction."[132] For perfectionism "restricts our freedom to be creative, imaginative, and open to genuine vulnerability."[133] In laboring after a life of perfection, we live life in rigid boxes, afraid to step outside of them and enter life in its messiness and ambiguity.

The practice of exposing and honoring vulnerability means letting go of the need to be right, to stop pretending that we have all the answers. In particular, I am referring to those of us who are so "set in our ways or judgments that we assume we 'have' it politically, intellectually, or spiritually."[134] In letting go of the façade of perfection, we open ourselves up to the possibility of cultivating healthy and appropriate ways of dealing with our limitations and failings. We also open ourselves up to the possibility of learning from each other. Letting go of perfectionism opens up space for the grace of ambush.

Embracing vulnerability is a liberative spiritual praxis, as it models for future generations a new way of being in relation: one that is marked by courageous hope instead of fear. Vulnerability appropriately unmasked has the power to stop unbridled competitivism in its tracks. It does so by changing the rules of the game. James Alison gives the example of a parent teaching a child

---

132. Michelle Saracino, *Clothing*, Christian Explorations in Daily Living, series ed. David H. Jensen (Minneapolis: Fortress Press, 2012), 53. Saracino speaks of a number of themes discussed here in on 19–25.

133. Ibid., 61.

134. Carter Heyward, *Saving Jesus from Those Who Are Right: Rethinking What It Means to Be Christian* (Minneapolis: Fortress Press, 1999), 11.

how to play tennis.[135] In this context, the playing field is not equal, as the parent clearly has more power and skill than the child. One approach would be for the parent to teach the child to how to win, by gradually sharpening the competitive edge. Allison explains, "The parent is never going to humiliate the child by beating them unduly easily, but nor are they going to let themselves be beaten, because what they want the child to do is to want to win."[136] In this case, the parent models winning as the ideal. The other option would be for the parent to teach the child simply how to play, in other words, "being a sparring partner for the child at the level of the child's strength, but also learning the greater skill of actually being able to lose without patronizing the child."[137] Being able to lose is actually the greater skill because it "sets us free from the compulsion to win in order to actually enjoy playing."[138] Embracing our vulnerability frees us from the dynamism of viewing each person as a potential rival or competitor and for the possibility of entering into friendship with one another.

Embracing vulnerability also teaches us how to deal with our failings. Learning how to lose is a forgotten art. Many of the young adults with whom I work do not know how to deal with failure, either at a personal or collective level. On the personal level, protecting our children from failure (or our students through grade inflation) robs them not only of a genuine sense of accomplishment, but also of the opportunity to learn from their mistakes. In the collective sense, finding healthy and appropriate ways to address our failings and the failings of previous generations is vital to contesting the problem of privileged apathy. Instead of pushing systemic violence under the proverbial rug through patterns of denial and

135. James Alison, *On Being Liked* (London: Crossroad, 2003), 39.
136. Ibid., 39–40.
137. Ibid., 40.
138. Ibid.

systemic ignorance, privileged people need to own the damage done by our own complacency and the complacency of our ancestors. White people are responsible for white racism and the harm it causes. Heterosexual people are responsible for heterosexism and the harm that it causes. In embracing our vulnerability (instead of shunning it or hiding it) we open ourselves to the possibility of repentance and conversion. In so doing, we come to understand that our salvation is tied to the salvation of others. Salvation no longer becomes a matter of "my flourishing," it becomes a question of "our flourishing." For privileged folks, the enactment of such soteriological understanding requires embracing our own vulnerability—acknowledging the "limitations and responsibilities" of our place.[139]

At the theological level, vulnerability as a soteriological praxis is suggestive of a new christological vision. The tradition has always held that Jesus is like us in everything but sin. It is not my intent to contest this doctrine, but rather to suggest that our understanding of that teaching has led to confusion. We need a soteriological vision that blends our understanding of divine perfection and immutability with a sensibility that makes a place for a sinful and changeable people who play a role in their own salvation. As I have argued, christological visions that rest upon God's immutability and impassibility give way to hierarchal and authoritarian ways of relating. In view of privileged bystanding, I find it more helpful to see Christ as one who models appropriate vulnerability, by allowing himself to be ambushed by a marginal Other and in refusing to claim sole ownership in the task of proclaiming God's *basileia*. In the story of the Syro-Phoenician woman, Jesus is not a miracle-worker per se, but a "catalyst" in the healing of the woman's daughter.[140] Recall

139. McFague, *Body of God*, 115.
140. Rita Nakashima Brock, *Journeys by Heart: Christology of Erotic Power* (New York: Crossroad, 1989), 99.

that in the Markan version of this narrative, Jesus does not take credit for Syro-Phoenician woman's daughter's exorcism. Instead, he links her own word to her daughter's healing. "For saying that, you may go—the demon has left your daughter" (Mark 7:29). It is through her encounter with Jesus that the woman realizes her own power to heal. This does not suggest that the work of salvation lies solely in human hands. Instead, salvation is a continuous project that is realized in history. In and through the encounter with the divine word, we are empowered to effect our own healing and participate in the healing of others. In doing so, we partake in the in-breaking of God's *basileia*. To use the language of scholasticism, we cooperate with divine saving grace.[141] In the context of privileged apathy, such cooperation with divine grace depends upon our recognition of the divine word and our willingness to come out of hiding. God's saving word is often found in unexpected places and uttered by persons deemed to be of no account. As privileged persons we must be willing to do some border crossing of our own, allowing the word of God to interrupt not only our lives, but ourselves. This must be our prayer. In it the seeds of our salvation can be found.

Responsible Freedom: Cultivating Collective and Personal Maturity

One of the great ironies of life is that in order to acknowledge our interdependence and vulnerability, we have to develop a sense of self. An important part of taking responsibility for our lives means getting clear on who we are (our identity) and what we are about (our mission). Mindless conformity—simply going along with the crowd for the sake of fitting in—is often a sign of immaturity. Conformity is not always a bad thing. Yet, very often it mutes our ability to

---

141. Thomas Aquinas, *Summa Theologica*, II.1, Question 111, article 2, accessed at http://www.newadvent.org/summa/2111.htm.

appreciate the value of uniqueness, whether our own and that of others. This is especially the case when conformity becomes habitual. For privileged people to enter into the work of solidarity, we must have a clearly demarcated sense of self. One has to know what one stands for and be willing to risk the consequences of standing up for one's beliefs. For instance, recall the narratives of gay bashing and slut shaming recounted in the first chapters of this book. Within the contexts marked by heteropatriarchal violence, maturity means publicly siding with those who are ostracized by the community, and thereby taking on the risk of being marginalized oneself. While self-development is the responsibility of the individual, it also belongs to the whole community. As parents, educators, and mentors, we are called to participate in the creation of healthy environments conducive to growth and self-exploration. To do so is an act of faith and justice.[142]

Immaturity is also evidenced in a false sense of security regarding one's own knowledge and worldview. It is the refusal to change: the failure or inability to acknowledge that one does not always have the whole story. Sometimes this manifests itself in the form of temper tantrums. For my two-year-old daughter, this means lying down in the middle of a drugstore kicking and screaming because she is not allowed to have a pack of chewing gum, a choking hazard. In adults, tantrums often take the form of emotional manipulation: shutting people out or threatening them. The critical difference is that my two-year-old does not have the cognitive capacity to understand why she is being denied what she wants, much less the self-control to deal with her own frustration. In adults, though, immaturity can be culpable. Most adults do have the cognitive capacity to acknowledge

---

142. The Roman Catholic Church, for example, has stressed the importance of instilling "the essential values of human life" in children and orienting the family toward the common good. Julie Hanlon Rubio, *Family Ethics: Practices for Christians* (Washington, DC: Georgetown University Press, 2010), 55.

the limitations of our own point of view and to take responsibility for the ways in which it shapes our relationships with others. We may not always be able to see this apart from the critique of others, but we can take ownership for our own growth by cultivating a spirit of openness to difference and by respectfully placing ourselves in relation to those who differ according to race, class, gender, or sexual orientation. To return to the insight of George Yancy (in the context of white racism): "Whites who are open to life-affirming and transformative transactions with people of color are not simply waiting defensively in fear of new information that may threaten to destabilize their sense of self. Rather, there is an openness to having one's world transformed and cracked."[143] We cannot grow without change. Sometimes change is a painful process that entails letting go of habitual ways of thinking and being in the world.

To mature is to reach one's full potential, to be fully developed.[144] To use a term attributed to Karl Rahner, maturity involves responsible freedom.[145] Maturity is "the courage and resolve to make decisions and to take responsibility for them."[146] The actualization of our divinely created humanity rests upon cultivating personal and collective maturity. This growth to maturity (or responsibility in freedom) is both a spiritual and a political praxis that points toward an eschatological vision. Growth to maturity is a life-long journey

---

143. Yancy, *Black Bodies,* 240.

144. According to the Oxford English Dictionary, maturity in persons is "the state of being physically and mentally mature; fullness or perfection of growth or development. Also: the state of being of age." See "maturity, n.". *OED Online.* September 2013. Oxford University, http://www.oed.com/view/Entry/115126?redirectedFrom=maturity.

145. Karl Rahner, *Foundations of the Christian Faith: An Introduction to the Idea of Christianity* (New York: Seabury, 1978), 94. Also see Karl Rahner, "The Mature Christian," *Theological Investigations,* trans. Hugh M. Riley, ed. Paul Imhof, SJ, vol. 21 (New York: Crossroad, 1988), 118.

146. Rahner, "Mature Christian," 119. Rahner goes on to say that maturity often involves the price of loneliness as, in taking responsibility for freedom, one often finds oneself going against the grain.

wherein we ultimately decide about ourselves, who we are in relation to the divine, and who we are in relation to the world.[147]

God's grace sustains our being and our doing in the world. In the words of Rahner, God is "the absolute and ultimate horizon within which human existence is lived out in freedom, knowledge and action."[148] Creation is enfolded within the divine being. We are not our own. At the same time, we are creatures who are endowed with freedom and we are responsible for our lives. Therefore, freedom is not the power to do this or that. Freedom is the power to decide about ourselves.[149] It is the power to actualize our very being, a "capacity of subjectivity."[150] When faced with the offer of divine grace (or God's self-gift), human beings have the choice to say yes or no. This choice is not a one-time decision. Rather, it is throughout the course of our whole lives (in our work, in our relationships with others, in our relationship with God) that we say yes or no to the invitation of grace. The goal of human freedom is to be in solidarity (or communion) with God and others.[151] In responding affirmatively to the offer of divine grace, we allow ourselves to be "'defined' by [our own] actions and desires, but also by the Mystery of God who desires to be the atmosphere, the horizon, and final goal of all [our] life experiences."[152] Ultimately, for Rahner, human freedom opens out into eschatology. God's future, and our own, arises out of the present. When we say yes to the divine self-gift, we are choosing to be in loving relation with God—now and in eternity.

147. Karl Rahner, *Foundations of the Christian Faith*, 94.
148. Ibid., 73.
149. Ibid., 94.
150. Ibid., 95.
151. Brian McDermott, "The Bonds of Freedom," in *A World of Grace: An Introduction to the Themes and Foundations of Karl Rahner's Theology*, ed. Leo J. O'Donovan (New York: Crossroad, 1981), 53.
152. Ibid., 54.

The actualization of our humanity in freedom is also a political reality.[153] To speak of God's future is to speak of wholeness of relationship in the present and in what is yet to come. Eschatology is not a "once and for all" transformation at the end of time. It is also understood as the collective struggle for justice, which is "a never ending task, to be renewed constantly, for the global community on earth."[154] To speak of the kin-dom of God is to speak of the liberation of the future.[155] It is to live life in anticipation of "messianic righteousness and justice."[156] Such an understanding not only has ethical consequences for the ways in which we live our lives, but it also determines our subjectivity. As Jürgen Moltmann writes, "The future in which God comes is described by the word *advent*, and is distinguished from the future time, which we call 'future.' Advent is expected—future develops. But the future always develops out of what we expect. What comes to meet us determines what we become."[157] God's future determines who we are and the horizon of our freedom. The horizon of our freedom is tied to the freedom (liberation) of others. In other words, to be responsible is to not only allow oneself to be addressed by God and others, but it is to take the content of that address and to make a decision against domination, against oppression, against apathy. It is to choose to love.

---

153. Certainly, Rahner's own reflections on human freedom include an understanding of the collective, as we do not make decisions in social contexts. Yet this point comes out much stronger in the works cited below.

154. Peter C. Phan, "Woman and the Last things: A Feminist Eschatology," in *In the Embrace of God: Feminist Approaches to Theological Anthropology,* ed. Ann O'Hara Graff (Maryknoll, NY: Orbis, 1995), 213. Other scholars have made this point as well. For example, see Rosemary Radford Reuther, *Sexism and God-Talk: Toward a Feminist Theology* (Boston: Beacon, 1983), 235–58; Sallie McFague, *The Body of God: An Ecological Theology* (Minneapolis: Fortress Press, 1993), 197–212; and the essays in *Liberating Eschatology: Essays in Honor of Letty M. Russell,* eds. Margaret A. Farley and Serene Jones (Louisville: WJK, 1999).

155. Jürgen Moltmann, "Liberating and Anticipating the Future," in Farley and Jones, *Liberating Eschatology,* 197.

156. Ibid., 202.

157. Ibid., 189. Italics original.

In a world that continues to be marked by division, dehumanization, and oppression, to choose love—to respond affirmatively to God's self-gift with one's life—is to actively resist violence.

Religious institutions can do this by cultivating a clear sense of mission and identity that is informed by God's *basileia* vision of wholeness and radical inclusivity, as well as by taking responsibility for living out this mission and identity in the world.[158] In view of the problem of social privilege, this kind of clarity of mission and identity requires ongoing introspection into the church's own participation in violence and discrimination. Personal and collective maturity, as the body of Christ, calls us to account for the ways in which we have been silent or active supporters of violence. As we stand before those who have been crucified by violence, we must ask ourselves, "What have I done to crucify them? What am I doing to take them down from their cross? What ought I to do that a crucified people may rise again?"[159] This introspection must be propelled into an investment of time and resources (at the local and global level) aimed to effect structural change. As expelling the bully from school does not resolve the problem of school violence, communities have to make a commitment to work toward systemic change—within both social and religious spheres. We must teach our children that violence is wrong while modeling nonviolent behavior ourselves. This includes actively working to cultivate environments that debunk patriarchy, heterosexism, racism, and xenophobia in all its forms and to actively promote God's welcome.

While religious institutions may not be directly liable for individual acts of violence perpetrated against nonwhites, LGBTQ persons, or women, they are culpable in the sense of "creating an

158. Letty M. Russell, *Just Hospitality: God's Welcome in a World of Difference*, ed. J. Shannon Clarkson and Kate M. Ott (Louisville: WJK, 2009), 118.
159. Jon Sobrino, *The Principle of Mercy: Taking the Crucified People from the Cross* (Maryknoll, NY: Orbis Books, 1994), 96.

atmosphere in which [these] acts of violence" are thinkable.[160] As Sanders suggests (in the context of LGBTQ violence), "The persistence with which Christian Churches have portrayed LGBTQ people as unnatural, dangers to society, predators of our children, and gender objects of disgust and derision—emblematic of the 'evil' which 'good' Christians are to stand against—weaves a perverse web of violence within which we must live our lives."[161] The role religious ideology plays in shaping the Christian moral imagination surrounding LGBTQ, racial, and other forms of gender-based violence is unique to its own context; common among them, however, is the eroticization of power and control, which disrespects the body, the natural world, and the feminine, and authorizes heteropatriarchal control.[162] As Kelly Brown Douglas has argued, this legacy has worked to suppress nonwhites throughout Western Christian religious history as well.[163] To reiterate, I am not suggesting that Christian churches bear sole responsibility for the existence of heteropatriarchy and white supremacy within the Christian West. However, the Christian churches cannot declare innocence, as their theologies and pastoral practices have created a great source of pain for men and women.

In recent years, a number of Christian churches have made strides toward healing. For example, the General Synod of the United Church of Christ has made a commitment to open their doors to LGBTQ persons and clergy and to educate those preparing for ministry on issues surrounding sexual justice.[164] In the Roman

160. Sanders, *Queer Lessons*, 128.
161. Ibid., 128.
162. Refer to chapter 1 of this book for a full discussion of this point.
163. Kelly Brown Douglas, *What's Faith Got to Do with It? Black Bodies/Christian Souls* (Maryknoll, NY: Orbis, 2005), chapters 4 and 5.
164. United Church of Christ, General Synod Resolution, 1985, Calling on United Church of Christ Congregations to Declare Themselves Open and Affirming (ONA), Adopted by General Synod XV, UCC, Ames, Iowa, July 2, 1985, http://www.ucc.org/education/polity/pdf-folder/ona-resolution-1985.pdf. This adoption of ONA does not mean that all UCC Churches abide

Catholic communion, Pope Francis has encouraged Church leadership to embody God's welcome by changing the question surrounding Catholic identity and mission. Since his election to the papacy, Francis has called the Church to focus on concern for the poor and social justice instead of hot-button topics like abortion, contraception, and gay marriage. While Francis's leadership includes a welcome change in tone, it does not replace the need for a formal apology for the harm done by the exclusion of women, nonwhites, and LGBTQ persons, nor the need for structural change. In practice, most American churches fail to take seriously social issues like LGBTQ equality, racial justice, and violence against women.[165] It is here, within the body of Christ, that the grace of ambush is most desperately needed.

It takes a lot of courage to admit to the person or persons you harmed that you were wrong and, then, to make reparations. To be very clear, I am not talking about the repentance of a private confessional. I am talking about the public confession of sin done in the spirit of reconciliation. To be truly repentant and to seek forgiveness is a hopeful posture. It is hopeful in the sense that in repenting for sin, one is placing a bet on the possibility of transformation and change. Organizations that see themselves as timeless, unchanging, and static are precluded from the possibility of repentance because one cannot truly repent apart from a willingness

by it. This is because individual UCC congregations are autonomous and, therefore, not bound to the recommendations of the General Synod. As reported by the Human Rights Campaign, the Open and Affirming office reports more than 20 percent of all UCC Churches are officially listed as participants in ONA. Moreover, the Religious Institute is reporting that every United Church of Christ Affiliated Seminary adheres to its criteria for sexual justice education. See "Every United Church of Christ–Affiliated Seminary is Sexually Healthy and Responsible, Lauds Religious Institute," *Religious Institute*, http://www.religiousinstitute.org/every-united-church-of-christ-affiliated-seminary-is-sexually-healthy-and-responsible-lauds-religious-institute/.

165. Sanders makes this point with respect to LGBTQ issues in *Queer Lessons*, 130. Bryan N. Massingale makes a similar point in *Racial Justice*, 75–80.

to change. (Perhaps this is why the Catholic Church has apologized so few times throughout history.) To repent is to express confidence in our capacity for positive growth. It is to recognize the harm done and to "go forth and sin no more." It is to acknowledge the ways in which heterosexist church teaching and pastoral practice continue to precipitate emotional, spiritual, and physical harm to LGBTQ persons and women and, then, to do some serious listening to the experiences and wisdom of those harmed in an effort to reform church teaching and pastoral practice and to heal wounds. Despite being named as sinful in church documents, white racism continues to be operative within the body of Christ and is still not taken seriously as moral or theological issues.[166] To repent is to acknowledge the ways in which white racism and white silence surrounding white racism is radically at odds with God's *basileia* vision and to take concrete steps toward its elimination in society and in the church.

When we repent, we express confidence in the relationship: namely, that it is worth staying around for the long haul despite the discomfort one might encounter along the way. To repent is to care. Repentance is an expression of love. I am not suggesting that repentance will always be met with forgiveness (nor that it should be), nor claiming that past harms should be forgotten. Rather, embracing change is intrinsic to growth. Christian tradition has always spoken about change in terms of conversion or *metanoia*. Through conversion of heart, we openly contest fatalism and place a strong bet on hope.

---

166. Massingale, *Racial Justice*, 77. Massingale characterizes the Roman Catholic Church's stance on racism as "tepid, lukewarm, and half-hearted." The USCCB names racism as an evil that "endures in the Church and society." See USCCB, "Brothers and Sisters to Us: U.S. Catholic Bishops Pastoral Letter on Racism," 1979, http://www.usccb.org/issues-and-action/cultural-diversity/african-american/brothers-and-sisters-to-us.cfm.

For Christians, hope in God's future must be more than wishful thinking. It is the very foundation of our faith. After witnessing Jesus' public shaming and violent execution and coming to terms with their silence in view of Jesus' persecution, the community of disciples "refused to let death defeat them."[167] At the crucifixion of Jesus, violence did not have the last word. In the midst of fear, insecurity, and disappointment, the first Christians found the courage to continue the work of bringing about God's *basileia*. While the challenges the church faces in the twenty-first century differ from those in first-century Palestine, the task of faith is similar. In the midst of violence, persecution, and torture, we are called to reject silent indifference, apathy, and ineffective guilt and to choose that which promotes wholeness and fullness of life for all of God's creation. It is here, in the midst of our strivings, that hope is found.

167. Brock, *Journeys by Heart*, 100.

Conclusion

We live in a society that is all too willing to tolerate violence. Violence, a communal problem, impacts the flourishing of all involved: victims, perpetrators, and bystanders. Violence desecrates the image of God as it dehumanizes and fractures communion among all God's people.

Throughout this book, I have focused on the problem of bystander complicity in violence and what to do about it. I have argued apathy in violent contexts is culpable. This is true when an individual observes a violent situation and fails to call for help. It is also seen in collective manifestations of privileged apathy discussed in chapter 2 (i.e., systemic ignorance, denial, and permission to escape). Apathy fuels oppression. In our efforts to escape suffering, we isolate ourselves, erecting physical, geographical, economic, and emotional barriers. These barriers create distance, making it easier to rationalize violence against persons and communities who are deemed to be of "no account."[1]

While apathy can touch the lives of all, it is a problem of special importance to those who occupy social sites of power and privilege.

---

1. Letty M. Russell uses the phrase "no account" to refer to those who occupy marginal social sites. See *Just Hospitality: God's Welcome in a World of Difference*, ed. J. Shannon Clarkson and Kate M. Ott (Louisville: WJK, 2009), 2.

The poignant words of Dorothee Sölle bear repeating: "Apathy flourishes in the consciousness of the satiated."[2] In nations where "private prosperity obscures public poverty," where whiteness covers up the dehumanization and degradation of white racism, and where heteropatriarchy works to normalize violence against women and LGBTQ persons, suffering remains hidden from view.[3] As history has shown, apathy has an interest in triumphalism, not compassion.

Apathy is a Christian problem not only because Christians too often have chosen to be bystanders in the face of violence, but also because Christian theology has played a role in the social conditioning of privileged apathy. Christological narratives that give pride of place to divine immutability and omnipotence, especially when paired with individualized notions of sin-talk, work to affirm hegemonic patterns of violence in the United States today. Often such violence remains invisible to dominant elites.

Apathy is contrary to Christian identity. As the Gospel writers testify, Jesus lived a life of compassionate involvement in the world, evidenced in his ministry with the marginalized and outcast and in his critique of hegemonic forces of his day. Ultimately, it was Jesus' passion for life that led to his death on the cross. As Christians, we are continually called to reckon with what it means to be passionately engaged in the world today. For privileged Christians, this means not only opening our eyes and ears to the violence that surrounds us but also operates within us.

The way beyond apathy (for privileged persons) is not easy. It involves a willingness to enter into compassionate solidarity with those who are marginalized. Genuine solidarity is hard work. As Shawn Copeland reminds us, "to contest the gravitational pull of domination" in "the midst of affluence and comfort" is indeed "a

2. Dorothee Sölle, *Suffering*, trans. Everett R. Kalin (Philadelphia: Fortress Press, 1975), 40.
3. Ibid.

wrenching task."[4] Such a task does not exist apart from a practical hope. Until we are able to envision a world without violence and our own participation in the creation of such a world, it will never become a reality.

In 2000, the National Alliance to End Homelessness (NAEH) released "A Plan: Not a Dream; How to End Homelessness in Ten Years," which sought to address the systemic causes and social changes that have led to widespread homelessness in the United States.[5] The NAEH's goal is for "America to change its thinking and pursue steps that seek—not just to manage—but to permanently end the problem within ten years."[6] Typically the approach to homelessness has been one of pointing people to soup kitchens or overnight shelters. However, as the NAEH points out, such an approach not only has a greater cost to cities in the long run, but it also fails to address larger structural issues surrounding homelessness. Putting an end to homelessness requires planning that focuses on the outcome of ending homelessness. Such an outcome will only be achieved through an investment in prevention: social service agencies have to be given the incentive to care for those with the most complex problems (including mental and physical illness), affordable permanent supportive housing must be built, and an infrastructure to offer opportunities for income and housing must be created.[7] The NAEH plan is bold. At the time of its release some even called it naively utopian. (Some still do. After all, it has been fifteen years and homelessness still exists.) In an interview a few after years its release,

4. M. Shawn Copeland, "Toward a Critical Christian Feminist Theology of Solidarity," in *Women & Theology*, ed. Mary Ann Hinsdale and Phyllis H. Kaminski, Annual Publication of the College Theology Society 40 (Maryknoll, NY: Orbis, 1994), 29–30.

5. For more, see National Alliance to End Homelessness, "A Plan: Not a Dream; How to End Homelessness in Ten Years, Executive Summary," http://b.3cdn.net/naeh/b970364c18809d1e0c_aum6bnzb4.pdf. Published on the NAEH website at http://www.endhomelessness.org/pages/ten-year-plan.

6. Ibid.

7. Ibid.

Patricia Crowley, OSB, a member of the team that drafted the City of Chicago's NAEH plan, remarked,

> I think we have just gotten into the habit of accepting [homelessness]. We don't think it's good, but we say, "Well, there will always be people who are homeless." I think we need to change the way we think about it. . . . When we were writing the plan, we asked ourselves that question [was it realistic?] for weeks on end. The way I see it, reality is formed by the way we imagine things and the way we talk about things. That's why it's important to talk about an end to homelessness. If we continually say, "It'll always be there," we'll never get rid of it.[8]

For Crowley and others like her, the first step in the creation of a world without homelessness is imagining a world without homelessness. Those who cannot envision a world without homelessness and their own participation in that world will never be able to see the necessary steps to get there. It is important to note that Crowley is a realist. For more than twenty years, Crowley was the director of Deborah's Place, an organization that provides supportive housing for women in Chicago.[9] In her tenure there, she witnessed homelessness, poverty, and abuse firsthand. She knows how difficult it is to break this cycle and has done much by the way of "opening the back door."[10] Her hope can hardly be chalked up to naive optimism. Rather, it is rooted in a profound conviction about the power of the human spirit and the possibilities for human conversion. But, as she cautions, "we act on what we're passionate about, and we're only passionate about what touches us personally."[11] Perhaps the most

---

8. "Ending Homelessness as We Know It: An Interview with Sister Patricia Crowley O.S.B," *U.S. Catholic* 69, no. 2 (Feb 2004): 25. Around the time this piece was released, Sr. Pat came and gave a similar presentation at Amate House, a postcollege volunteer program in Chicago, where I was working as a program coordinator. Deborah's Place has long been a volunteer placement site.

9. For more on the mission and work of Deborah's Place, see http://www.deborahsplace.org/.

10. Opening the back door refers to helping people to exit the system as quickly as possible by finding permanent housing and employment solutions.

11. "Ending Homelessness," 27.

important thing Christians can do is build relationships with those whom we consider strangers. Crowley explains, "When I was first going to a soup kitchen, I found it much easier to stand behind the soup pot than to actually talk with the people."[12] Building relationships across differences is not an easy or straightforward process. It takes an investment of time and energy on the part all parties involved. These relationships, like God's *basileia,* must be nurtured.

We are graced with the capacity to be agents of social change—to partake in the work of bringing about God's *basileia.* When we engage in liberative praxis, our lives reflect the hope of the resurrection. Such hope is not fanciful or easy. To engage in the praxis of Christian hope, we must stretch. Through the praxis of hope we are called to go beyond ourselves: to go outside our "comfort zone" and beyond our current situation. To hope is to take a stand, with one foot firmly planted in the present (already) and the other in the (not yet) future. What we think about God's future matters. Our eschatological assumptions shape our praxiological commitments, the urgency of our desires, and the ways in which we communicate those desires. They shape what we believe is possible and the way in which we plan out our lives, as imperfect as this plan and its execution may be.

The Word of God continues to irrupt throughout history. As privileged elites, we often fail to hear God's Word because our hearts are hardened to the ones who speak it. As in the story of the Syro-Phoenician woman, a foreign woman of "no account" who utters God's *basileia* vision, so, today, privileged Christians must listen for the divine *logos* being spoken by marginalized persons and communities. Such listening rests upon nurturing soteriological

12. Ibid.

praxis that welcomes and recognizes grace in the form of privileged ambush. This requires a radical reordering of esteemed values (theological and otherwise) and a restructuring of the accompanying norms and dictums that govern relationships and structures in the United States.

Relatedness must take pride of place over individualism, especially given the latter's propensity toward objectification and dehumanization. In practical terms, this means adopting theological models and pastoral practices that reflect the interdependence of all creation and the divine being. Such a reckoning would not only radically reorient our prayer and worship,[13] but it would also change the terms of our academic scholarship and theological education. The voices and concerns of those who suffer injustice would become the center of our prayer, study, and action.

We also desperately need new ways of honoring vulnerability, that of our own as well as the fragility of all creation. We continue to live in ways that treat bodies as indispensable products for our consumption. Such practices are emblematic of Western narcissism and they leave future generations bereft of resources. In embracing our vulnerability, we open ourselves up to pathways of empathy, repentance, and compassion.

Finally, the body of Christ, as a whole, needs to actively deepen Christian maturity. To quote Karl Rahner again, "Maturity means courage for greater freedom and this freedom means greater responsibility."[14] As Christians, we not only need to engage in healthy self-criticism, but we must also welcome it and the change it brings. To mature is to resist the easy path of mindless conformity.

---

13. Throughout her writing, Carter Heyward offers a number of examples. For example, see the liturgical resources at the back of *Saving Jesus from Those Who Are Right: Rethinking What It Means to Be Christian* (Minneapolis: Fortress Press, 1999), 204–15.

14. Karl Rahner, "The Mature Christian," in *Theological Investigations* trans. Hugh M. Riley, vol. 21 (New York: Crossroad, 1988), 128.

Such growth takes courage, as it often makes "human beings lonely in a certain sense. They have to make decisions by themselves, without being told in advance what to do."[15] It requires actively cultivating a sense of identity and mission, and finely honing the skills of discernment of the spirit. These are just starting points along the journey. Indeed, there is much more work to be done.

Fifteen years after the NAEH's Ten Year plan was first introduced, homelessness continues to be an issue in large cities like Chicago. This does not mean that the efforts of Crowley and all involved in implementing the NAEH plan were a failure. In fact, there is quite a bit of evidence to the contrary.[16] What it does mean is that the journey to putting an end to violence is an ongoing project in continual need of renewal. Like a garden, the kin-dom of God needs tending. Part of the natural cycle of growth involves planting, fertilizing, watering, and pruning before one can reap its fruits. So too must we understand our participation in the work of bringing about God's *basileia*.

Justice, and the necessary transformation that accompanies it, is not going to happen overnight. For privileged folks, the journey from passive bystander to compassionate witness is a life's work. Coming to terms with one's own complicity in violence and finding ways to enter into the dialogue as a "friend of the oppressed" requires a commitment to justice that is willing to bear the risk of the cross itself. As privileged bystanders, we have the responsibility to find ways to respectfully join others in solidarity on this journey. While our efforts may be far from perfect, may we find courage to take risks,

---

15. Ibid.
16. The long-term effects of Chicago's NAEH on its homeless population have been studied by members of the Center for Urban Research and Learning at Loyola University of Chicago. For a summative analysis, see Michael R. Sosin, Christine George, Susan F. Grossman, Julie Hilvers, and Koonal Patel, "Final Wave Survey Results: A Preliminary Evaluation of Chicago's Ten Year Plan to End Homelessness," *Chicago Alliance to End Homelessness*, August 2011, http://www.allchicago.org/sites/default/files/archive_files/Final Wave Report 8-31-11.pdf.

to make mistakes and to take responsibility for them, and, most of all, to remain in the relationship even when we feel di-ease and discomfort. For in this, redemption will be found.

Bibliography

Abelard, Peter. "Exposition of the Epistle to the Romans." Reprinted in *Readings in the History of Christian Theology*, edited by William C. Placher. Louisville: WJK, 1988.

Ackermann, Denise M. *After the Locusts: Letters from a Landscape of Faith.* Grand Rapids: Eerdmans, 2003.

———. "Lamenting Tragedy from 'the Other Side'." In *Sameness and Difference: Problems and Potentials in South African Civil Society,* edited by James R. Cochrane and Bastienne Klein, 213–42. Washington DC: Council for Research, 2000.

Ahmed, Sara. "Declarations of Whiteness: The Non-Performativity of Anti-Racism." *Borderlands* 3, no. 2 (2004), http://www.borderlands.net.au /vol3no2_2004/ahmed_declarations.htm.

Alison, James. *On Being Liked.* London: Crossroad, 2003.

Alonso, Pablo. *The Woman Who Changed Jesus: Crossing Boundaries in Mk 7, 24-30.* Leuven: Peeters, 2011.

Andolsen, Barbara Hilkert. *Daughters of Jefferson, Daughters of Bootblacks: Racism and American Feminism.* Macon, GA: Mercer University Press, 1986.

Anselm of Canterbury. "Why God Became Man." In *Anselm of Canterbury: The Major Works,* edited by Brian Davies and G. R. Evans, 260–356. New York: Oxford University Press, 1998.

Applebaum, Barbara. *Being White, Being Good: White Complicity, White Moral Responsibility, and Social Justice Pedagogy*. New York: Lexington Books, 2010.

Augustine of Hippo. *The Trinity*. Translated by Edmund Hill, OP. New York: New City, 1991.

Aulén, Gustaf. *Christus Victor: An Historical Study of the Three Main Types of the Idea of Atonement*. Translated by A. G. Herbert. New York: MacMillan, 1969.

Babka, Susie Paulik. "Arius, Superman, and the *Tertium Quid*: When Popular Culture Meets Christology." *Irish Theological Quarterly* 73 (2008): 113–32.

Banyard, Victoria L., Elizabeth G. Plante, and Mary M. Moynihan. "Bystander Education: Bringing a Broader Community Perspective to Sexual Violence Prevention." *Journal of Community Psychology* 32 (2004): 61–79.

Barth, Karl. *The Doctrine of God, Church Dogmatics* 2/2. Edited by G. W. Bromiley and T. F. Torrance. Translated by G. W. Bromiley et al. New York: T&T Clark, 1957.

———. *The Doctrine of the Word of God, Church Dogmatics* 1/1. Edited by G. W. Bromiley and T. F. Torrance. Translated by G. W. Bromiley. New York: T&T Clark, 1936/1975.

———. *The Humanity of God*. Richmond, VA: John Knox, 1960.

Bartky, Sandra Lee. *"Sympathy and Solidarity" and Other Essays*. Lanham, MD: Rowman & Littlefield, 2002.

Bazelon, Emily. *Sticks and Stones: Defeating the Culture of Bullying and Rediscovering the Power of Character and Empathy*. New York: Random House, 2013.

Bentley, Sarah. "Bringing Justice Home: The Christian Challenge of the Battered Women's Movement for Christian Social Ethics." In *Violence against Women and Children: A Christian Theological Sourcebook*, edited by Carol J. Adams and Marie M. Fortune, 151–71. New York: Continuum, 1995.

Beste, Jennifer. *God and the Victim: Traumatic Intrusions on Grace and Freedom*. New York: Oxford University Press, 2007.

Bhahba, Homi K. *The Location of Culture.* New York: Routledge, 1994.

Boff, Leonardo. *Jesus Christ Liberator: A Critical Christology for Our Times.* Maryknoll, NY: Orbis Books, 1978.

Brock, Rita Nakashima. "The Cross of Resurrection and Communal Redemption." In *Cross Examinations: Readings on the Meaning of the Cross Today,* edited by Marit Trelstad, 241–51. Minneapolis: Fortress Press, 2006.

———. "Ending Innocence and Nurturing Willfulness." In *Violence against Women and Children: A Christian Theological Sourcebook,* edited by Carol J. Adams and Marie Fortune, 71–84. New York: Continuum, 1995.

———. *Journeys by Heart: Christology of Erotic Power.* New York: Crossroad, 1989.

Brock, Rita Nakashima, and Rebecca Ann Parker. *Proverbs of Ashes: Violence, Redemptive Suffering, and the Search for What Saves Us.* Boston, MA: Beacon Press, 2002.

Brown, Joanne Carlson and Rebecca Parker. "For God So Loved the World?" In *Christianity, Patriarchy, and Abuse: A Feminist Critique,* edited by Joanne Carlson Brown and Carole R. Bohn, 1–30. New York: Pilgrim, 1989.

Brown, Robert McAfee. *Religion and Violence.* 2nd ed. Philadelphia: Westminster, 1987.

Brueggemann, Walter. *Disruptive Grace: Reflections on God, Scripture, and the Church.* Edited by Carolyn J. Sharp. Minneapolis: Fortress Press, 2011.

———. *Introduction to the Old Testament: The Canon and Christian Imagination.* Louisville: WJK, 2003.

———. *Israel's Praise: Doxology against Idolatry and Ideology.* Philadelphia: Fortress Press, 1988.

———. *Mandate to Difference: An Invitation to the Contemporary Church.* Louisville: WJK, 2007.

———. *Message of the Psalms: A Theological Commentary.* Minneapolis: Augsburg Press, 1984.

———. *The Psalms and the Life of Faith.* Edited by Patrick D. Miller. Minneapolis: Fortress Press, 1995.

Burkill, T.A. "The Historical Development of the Story of the Syrophoenician Woman (Mark vii: 24-31)." *Novum Testamentum* 9 (1967): 161–77.

Cadwallader, Alan. *Beyond the Word of a Woman: Recovering the Bodies of the Syrophoenician Woman.* Adelaide: ATF Press, 2011.

Cassidy, Laurie M. and Alex Mikulich, eds. *Interrupting White Privilege: Catholic Theologians Break the Silence.* Maryknoll, NY: Orbis Books, 2007.

Cheng, Patrick S. *From Sin to Amazing Grace: Discovering the Queer Christ.* New York: Seabury Press, 2012.

Coloroso, Barbara. *The Bully, the Bullied, and the Bystander.* Rev. ed. New York: HarperCollins, 2008.

Cone, James H. "Black Liberation Theology and Black Catholics: A Critical Conversation." *Theological Studies* 61 (2000): 731–47.

———. *A Black Theology of Liberation.* 20th anniversary ed. Maryknoll, NY: Orbis Books, 1990.

———. *The Cross and the Lynching Tree.* Maryknoll, NY: Orbis Books, 2012.

———. *God of the Oppressed.* Rev. ed. Maryknoll, NY: Orbis Books, 1997.

———. "Theology's Greatest Sin: Silence in the Face of White Supremacy." In *Soul Work: Anti-Racist Theologies in Dialogue*, edited by Marjorie Bowens-Wheatley and Nancy Palmer Jones, 1–15. Boston, MA: Skinner House, 2002.

Connell, R.W. *Masculinities.* 2nd ed. Berkeley: University of California Press, 2005.

Cooper-White, Pamela. *The Cry of Tamar: Violence against Women and the Church's Response.* 2nd ed. Minneapolis: Fortress Press, 2012.

Copeland, M. Shawn. *Enfleshing Freedom: Body, Race, and Being.* Minneapolis: Fortress Press, 2010.

———. "Toward a Critical Christian Feminist Theology of Solidarity." In *Women and Theology*, The Annual Publication of the College Theology Society, volume 40, edited by Mary Ann Hinsdale and Phyllis Kaminski, 3–38. Maryknoll, NY: Orbis, 1994.

Cram, Ronald Hecker. *Bullying: A Spiritual Crisis.* St. Louis: Chalice, 2003.

De La Torre, Miguel A. *Doing Christian Ethics from the Margins*. 2nd ed, rev. and exp. Maryknoll, NY: Orbis, 2014.

———. ed. *Handbook of Theologies of Liberation*. St. Louis: Chalice, 2004.

———. "Mad Men, Competitive Women, and Invisible Hispanics." *Journal of Feminist Studies in Religion* 28, no. 1 (2012): 121–26.

Douglas, Kelly Brown. *The Black Christ*. Maryknoll, NY: Orbis, 1993.

———. *Sexuality and the Black Church: A Womanist Perspective*. Maryknoll, NY: Orbis, 1999.

———. *What's Faith Got to Do With It? Black Bodies/Christian Souls*. Maryknoll, NY: Orbis, 2005.

Dovidio, John F., Samuel L. Gaertner, Kerry Kawakami, and Gordon Hodson. "Why Can't We All Just Get Along: Interpersonal Biases and Interracial Distrust." *Cultural Diversity and Ethnic Minority Psychology* 8, no. 2 (2002): 88–102.

Du Bois, W. E. B. *The Souls of Black Folk*. New York: Penguin, 1996. Originally published New York: A. C. McClurg & Company, 1903.

Dube, Musa W. *Postcolonial Feminist Interpretation of the Bible*. St. Louis: Chalice, 2000.

Engel, Mary Potter. "Evil, Sin, and Violation of the Vulnerable." In *Lift Every Voice: Constructing Christian Theologies from the Underside*, edited by Susan Brooks Thistlethwaite and Mary Potter Engel, 159–71. Rev. ed. Maryknoll, NY: Orbis, 1998.

Farley, Margaret A. and Serene Jones, eds. *Liberating Eschatology: Essays in Honor of Letty M. Russell*. Louisville: WJK, 1999.

Feagin, Joe R. *The White Racial Frame: Centuries of Racial Framing and Counter-Framing*. 2nd ed. New York: Routledge, 2013.

Feimster, Crystal Nicole. *Southern Horrors: Women and the Politics of Rape and Lynching*. Cambridge: Harvard University Press, 2009.

Field, Juliane E., Jered B. Kolbert, Laura M. Crothers, and Tammy L. Hughes. *Understanding Girl Bullying and What to Do about It: Strategies to Help Heal the Divide*. Thousand Oaks, CA: Corwin, 2009.

Fischer, Peter, Joachim I. Krueger, Tobias Greitemeyer, Claudia Vogrincic, Andreas Kastenmüller, Dieter Frey, Moritz Heene, Magdalena Wicher, and Martina Kainbacher. "The Bystander-Effect: A Meta-Analytic Review on Bystander Intervention in Dangerous and Non-Dangerous Emergencies." *Psychological Bulletin* vol. 137, no. 4 (2011): 517–37.

Fortune, Marie M. *Sexual Violence: The Sin Revisited.* Cleveland: Pilgrim, 2005.

Freire, Paulo. *Pedagogy of the Oppressed.* Translated by Myra Bergman Ramos. 30th anniversary ed. (New York: Bloomsbury Academic, 2000).

Frye, Marilyn. *Difference and the Politics of Reality: Essays in Feminist Theory.* Freedom, CA: Crossing, 1983.

Galtung, Johan. "Violence, Peace, and Peace Research." *Journal of Peace Research* 6, no. 3 (1969): 167–91.

Garbarino, James. *Lost Boys: Why Our Sons Turn Violent and How We Can Save Them.* New York: Free, 1999.

———. *Raising Children in a Socially Toxic Environment.* San Francisco: Jossey-Bass, 1995.

García-Rivera, Alejandro. *The Community of the Beautiful.* Collegeville, MN: Liturgical, 1999.

Gebara, Ivone. *Longing for Running Water: Ecofeminism and Liberation.* Minneapolis: Fortress Press, 1999.

———. *Out of Depths: Women's Experience of Evil and Salvation.* Translated by Anne Patrick Ware. Minneapolis: Fortress Press, 2002.

Gibbs, Jewelle Taylor and Joseph R. Merighi. "Young Black Males: Marginality, Masculinity, and Criminality." In *Just Boys Doing Business? Men, Masculinities, and Crime,* edited by Tim Newburn and Elizabeth A. Stanko, 64–68. New York: Routledge, 1994.

Girard, René. "Sacrifice as Sacral Violence and Substitution." In *The Girard Reader,* edited by James G. Williams, 69–93. New York: Crossroad, 1996.

———. *Things Hidden Since the Foundation of the World.* Translated by Stephen Bann and Michael Metteer. Stanford, CA: Stanford University Press, 1987.

Glancy, Jennifer A. "Jesus, the Syrophoenician Woman, and Other First Century Bodies." *Biblical Interpretation* 18 (2010): 342–63.

Gorringe, Timothy J. *Karl Barth: Against Hegemony.* New York: Oxford University Press, 1999.

Goss, Robert E. *Queering Christ: Beyond Jesus Acted Up.* Cleveland: Pilgrim Press, 2002.

Graham, Larry Kent. "The Role of Straight Allies in Pastoral Care of Lesbians and Gays." In *Out of the Shadows into the Light: Christianity and Homosexuality,* edited by Miguel A. De La Torre, 104–20. St. Louis: Chalice, 2009.

Grant, Jacquelyn. "The Sin of Servanthood: And the Deliverance of Discipleship." In *A Troubling in My Soul: Womanist Perspectives on Evil and Suffering,* edited by Emilie M. Townes, 199–218. Maryknoll, NY: Orbis, 1993.

———. "Womanist Jesus and the Mutual Struggle for Liberation." *Journal of the Interdenominational Theological Center* 30, nos. 1–2 (Fall/Spring 2003–2004): 3–33.

Greider, Kathleen J. *Reckoning with Aggression: Theology, Violence, and Vitality.* Louisville: WJK, 1997.

Guardiola-Sáenz, Leticia A. "Borderless Women and Borderless Texts: A Cultural Reading of Matthew 15:21-28." *Semeia* 78 (1997): 69–81.

Gudorf, Christine E. *Victimization: Examining Christian Complicity.* Philadelphia: Trinity International, 1992.

Gutiérrez, Gustavo. *A Theology of Liberation.* Translated and edited by Sister Caridad Inda and John Eagleson. 15th anniversary ed. Maryknoll, NY: Orbis, 1988.

Harrison, Beverly Wildung. "The Power of Anger in the Work of Love." In *Making the Connections: Essays in Feminist Social Ethics,* edited by Carol S. Robb, 3–21. Boston: Beacon, 1985.

Harvey, Jennifer. "What Would Zacchaeus Do? The Case for Disidentifying with Jesus." In *Christology and Whiteness: What Would Jesus Do?,* edited by George Yancy, 84–100. New York: Routledge, 2012.

———. *Whiteness and Morality: Pursuing Racial Justice through Reparations and Sovereignty.* New York: Palgrave MacMillian, 2007.

Harvey, Jennifer, Karin A. Case, and Robin Hawley Gorsline, eds. *Disrupting White Supremacy from Within: White People on What We Need to Do.* Cleveland: Pilgrim, 2004.

Heyward, Carter. *Our Passion for Justice: Images of Power, Sexuality, and Liberation.* New York: Pilgrim, 1984.

———. *The Redemption of God: A Theology of Mutual Relation.* Washington, DC: University Press of America, 1982.

———. *Saving Jesus from Those Who Are Right: Rethinking What It Means to Be Christian.* Minneapolis: Fortress Press, 1999.

Hobgood, Mary Elizabeth. *Dismantling Privilege: An Ethics of Accountability.* Rev. ed. Cleveland: Pilgrim, 2009.

———. "White Economic and Erotic Disempowerment: A Theological Exploration in the Struggle against Racism." In *Interrupting White Privilege: Catholic Theologians Break the Silence,* edited by Laurie M. Cassidy and Alex Mikulich, 40–55. Maryknoll, NY: Orbis, 2007.

hooks, bell. *Feminist Theory: From Margin to Center.* 2nd ed. Cambridge: South End Classics, 2000.

Horsley, Richard A. *Hearing the Whole Story: The Politics of Plot in Mark's Gospel.* Louisville: WJK, 2001.

Hunt, Mary E. "Lovingly Lesbian: Toward a Feminist Theology of Friendship." In *Sexuality and the Sacred: Sources for Theological Reflection,* edited by Marvin M. Ellison and Kelly Brown Douglas, 183–96. 2nd edition. Louisville: WJK, 2010.

Isasi-Díaz, Ada María. *Mujerista Theology: A Theology for the Twenty-first Century.* Maryknoll, NY: Orbis, 1996.

Jantzen, Grace M. *Power, Gender, and Christian Mysticism.* Cambridge, UK: Cambridge University Press, 1996.

Jennings Jr., Theodore W. "Reconstructing the Doctrine of Sin." In *The Other Side of Sin: Woundedness from the Perspective of the Sinned-Against,* edited by Andrew Sung Park and Susan L. Nelson, 105–22. Albany, NY: SUNY Press, 2001.

Joh, Wonhee Anne. *The Heart of the Cross: A Postcolonial Christology.* Louisville: WJK, 2006.

Johnson, Allan G. *Privilege, Power, and Difference*. 2nd ed. New York: McGraw-Hill, 2006.

Johnson, Elizabeth A. *She Who Is: The Mystery of God in Feminist Theological Discourse*. New York: Crossroad, 1992.

Jones, Serene. *Trauma and Grace: Theology in a Ruptured World*. Louisville: WJK, 2009.

Katz, Jackson. *The Bystander Approach*. Enola, PA: National Sexual Violence Resource Center, 2011.

Keating, Thomas. "Cultivating the Centering Prayer." In *Finding Grace at the Center*, 23–34. Still River, MA: St. Bede, 1978.

Keller, Catherine. *From a Broken Web: Separation, Sexism, and Self*. Boston: Beacon, 1988.

Hisako Kinukawa, "Biblical Studies in the Twenty-First Century: A Japanese/Asian Feminist Glimpse." In *Feminist New Testament Studies: Global and Future Perspectives*, edited by Kathleen O'Brien Wicker, Althea Spencer Miller, and Musa W. Dube, 137–50. New York: Palgrave MacMillian, 2005.

———. "Decolonizing Ourselves as Readers: The Story of the Syro-Phoenician Woman as a Text." In *Distant Voices Drawing Near: Essays in Honor of Antoinette Clark Wire*, edited by Holly E. Hearon, Marvin L. Chaney, and Antoinette Clark Wire, 131–44. Collegeville, MN: Liturgical, 2004.

———. *Women and Jesus in Mark: A Japanese Feminist Perspective*. Maryknoll, NY: Orbis Books, 1994.

Kirk-Duggan, Cheryl A. *Misbegotten Anguish: A Theology and Ethics of Violence*. St. Louis: Chalice, 2001.

———. *Refiner's Fire: A Religious Engagement with Violence*. Minneapolis: Fortress Press, 2001.

Klein, Jessie. *The Bully Society: School Shootings and the Crisis of Bullying in American Schools*. New York: New York University Press, 2012.

Koswic, Joseph, Emily A. Greytak, Mark J. Bartkiewicz, Madelyn J. Boesen, and Neal A. Palmer. *The 2011 National School Climate Survey: The*

Experiences of Lesbian, Gay, Bisexual and Transgender Youth in Our Nation's Schools. New York: GLSEN, 2012.

Kraemer, Ross Shepard and Mary Rose D'Angelo, eds. *Women and Christian Origins*. New York: Oxford University Press, 1999.

Kwok, Pui-lan. *Discovering the Bible in the Non-Biblical World*. Maryknoll, NY: Orbis, 1995.

Lamb, Sharon. *The Trouble with Blame: Victims, Perpetrators, and Responsibility*. Cambridge, MA: Harvard University Press, 1996.

Latané, Bibb and John M. Darley. *The Unresponsive Bystander: Why Doesn't He Help?* Englewood Cliffs, NJ: Prentice-Hall, 1970.

Lee, Michael E. *Bearing the Weight of Salvation: The Soteriology of Ignacio Ellacuría*. New York: Crossroad, 2009.

Levine, Amy-Jill. *Social and Ethnic Dimensions of Matthean Salvation History*. Lewiston, NY: Edwin Mellen, 1988.

Lorde, Audre. "The Uses of Anger: Women Responding to Racism." Reprinted in *Sister Outsider: Essays and Speeches*, 124–33. Berkeley: Crossing, 2007.

Marquardt, Friedrich-Wilhelm. "Socialism in the Theology of Karl Barth." In *Karl Barth and Radical Politics*, translated and edited by George Hunsinger, 19–46. Philadelphia: Westminster, 1976.

Martin, SJ, James. *Jesus: A Pilgrimage*. New York: HarperOne, 2014.

Massingale, Byran N. *Racial Justice and the Catholic Church*. Maryknoll, NY: Orbis, 2010.

McFague, Sallie. *The Body of God: An Ecological Theology*. Minneapolis: Fortress Press, 1993.

McIntosh, Peggy. "White Privilege and Male Privilege: A Personal Account of Coming to See Correspondences through Work in Women's Studies." Reprinted in *Critical White Studies: Looking behind the Mirror*, edited by Richard Delgado and Jean Stefancic, 291–99. Philadelphia: Temple University Press, 1997.

McKernan, Signe-Mary, Caroline Ratcliffe, Eugene Steuerle, and Sisi Zhang. "Less Than Equal: Racial Disparities In Wealth Accumulation." *Urban*

Institute, http://www.urban.org/UploadedPDF/412802-Less-Than-Equal
-Racial-Disparities-in-Wealth-Accumulation.pdf.

Miles, Margaret R. *Carnal Knowing: Female Nakedness and Religious Meaning in the Christian West.* New York: Random House, 1989.

———. *Practicing Christianity: Critical Perspectives for an Embodied Spirituality.* New York: Crossroad, 1988.

Miller, Susan. *Women in Mark's Gospel.* Journal for the Study of the New Testament Supplement Series 259. New York: T&T Clark International, 2004.

Mills, Charles W. *The Racial Contract.* Ithaca, NY: Cornell University Press, 1997.

———. "White Ignorance." In *Race Epistemologies of Ignorance*, edited by Shannon Sullivan and Nancy Tuana, 11–38. Albany, NY: SUNY Press, 2007.

Moltmann, Jürgen. "Liberating and Anticipating the Future." In *Liberating Eschatology: Essays in Honor of Letty M. Russell,* edited by Margaret A. Farley and Serene Jones, 189–208. Louisville: WJK, 1999.

Morton, Nelle. *The Journey is Home.* Boston: Beacon, 1985.

Moynihan, Mary M. and Victoria L. Banyard. "Educating Bystanders Helps Prevent Sexual Violence and Reduce Backlash." *Sexual Assault Report* 12 (2009): 49–50, 52, 57, 60–62, 64.

Nelson, Jacqueline K., Kevin M. Dunn and Yin Paradies. "Bystander Anti-Racism: A Review of the Literature." *Analyses of Social Issues and Public Policy* 11 (2011): 263–84.

Nelson Dunfee, Susan. *Beyond Servanthood: Christianity and the Liberation of Women.* New York: University Press of America, 1989.

———. "The Sin of Hiding: A Feminist Critique of Reinhold Niebuhr's Account of the Sin of Pride." *Soundings* 65, no. 3 (1982): 316–27.

Niebuhr, Reinhold. *Human Nature.* Vol. 1 of *The Nature and Destiny of Man.* New York: Charles Scribner's Sons, 1941.

Nilson, Jon. *Hearing Past the Pain: Why White Catholic Theologians Need Black Theology.* Mahwah, NJ: Paulist, 2007.

O'Connell, Maureen H. *Compassion: Loving Our Neighbor in an Age of Globalization.* Maryknoll, NY: Orbis, 2009.

———. "No More Time for Nostalgia: Millennial Morality and a Catholic Tradition Mash-Up." In *Handing on the Faith*, edited by Matthew Sutton and William Portier, 75–87. Maryknoll, NY: Orbis, 2014.

O'Day, Gail R. "Surprised by Faith: Jesus and the Canaanite Woman." In *A Feminist Companion to Matthew*, edited by Amy-Jill Levine with Marianne Blickenstaff, 114–25. Sheffield: Sheffield Academic, 2001.

Oliver, Kelly. *Witnessing: Beyond Recognition.* Minneapolis: University of Minnesota Press, 2001.

Olweus, Dan. "Bullying at School: Basic Facts and Effects of a School Based Intervention Program." *Journal of Child Psychology and Psychiatry* 35, no.7 (1994): 1171–90.

Ortega, Mariana. "Being Knowingly, Lovingly Ignorant: White Feminism and Women of Color." *Hypatia* 21, vol. 3 (2006): 56–74.

Park, Andrew Sung and Susan L. Nelson, eds. *The Other Side of Sin: Woundedness from the Perspective of the Sinned-Against.* Albany, NY: SUNY Press, 2001.

Perkinson, Jim. "A Canaanitic Word in the Logos of Christ; Or the Difference the Syrophoenician Woman Makes to Jesus." *Semeia* 75 (1996):61–84.

———. *White Theology: Outing White Supremacy in Modernity.* New York: Palgrave MacMillan, 2004.

Phan, Peter C. "Woman and the Last Things: A Feminist Eschatology." In *In the Embrace of God: Feminist Approaches to Theological Anthropology,* edited by Ann O'Hara Graff, 206–28. Maryknoll, NY: Orbis, 1995.

Phelps, Jamie T. "Communion Ecclesiology and Black Liberation Theology." *Theological Studies* 61 (2000): 672–99.

———. "Joy Came in the Morning Risking Death for Resurrection: Confronting the Evil of Social Sin and Socially Sinful Structures." In *A Troubling in My Soul: Womanist Perspectives on Evil & Suffering*, edited by Emilie M. Townes, 48–64. Maryknoll, NY: Orbis, 1993.

Plaskow, Judith. *Sex, Sin, and Grace: Women's Experience and the Theologies of Reinhold Neibuhr and Paul Tillich.* Washington, DC: University Press of America, 1980.

Poling, James N. *Deliver Us from Evil: Resisting Racial and Gender Oppression.* Minneapolis: Fortress Press, 1996.

Pope Paul VI. *Pastoral Constitution on the Church in the Modern World.* Reprinted in *Vatican Council II: The Basic Sixteen Documents,* edited by Austin Flannery, OP, 163–282. New York: Costello, 1996.

Rahner, Karl. *Foundations of the Christian Faith: An Introduction to the Idea of Christianity.* New York: Seabury, 1978.

———. "The Mature Christian." In *Theological Investigations,* translated by Hugh M. Riley, vol. 21, 115–29. New York: Crossroad, 1988.

Rakoczy, Susan. *Great Mystics and Social Justice: Walking on the Two Feet of Love.* Mahwah, NJ: Paulist, 2006.

Ray, Kathleen Darby. *Deceiving the Devil: Atonement, Abuse and Ransom.* Cleveland: Pilgrim, 1998.

———. "Tracking the Tragic: Augustine, Global Capitalism, and a Theology of Struggle." In *Constructive Theology: A Contemporary Approach to Classical Themes,* edited by Serene Jones and Paul Lakeland, 135–39, 141–43. Minneapolis: Fortress Press, 2005.

Rebera, Ranjini Wickramaratne. "The Syrophoenician Woman: A South Asian Feminist Perspective." In *A Feminist Companion to Mark,* edited by Amy-Jill Levine with Marianne Blickenstaff, 101–10. Sheffield: Sheffield Academic, 2001.

Rieger, Joerg. *Christ & Empire: From Paul to Postcolonial Times.* Minneapolis: Fortress Press, 2007.

Ringe, Sharon H. "A Gentile Woman's Story, Revisited: Rereading Mark 7:24-31A." In *A Feminist Companion to Mark,* edited by Amy-Jill Levine with Marianne Blickenstaff, 79–100. Sheffield, UK: Sheffield Academic, 2001.

Rivera, Mayra. "Incarnate Words: Images of God and Reading Practices." In *They Were All Together in One Place? Toward Minority Biblical Criticism,* edited by Randall C. Bailey, Tat-siong Benny Liew, and Fernando F. Segovia, 313–30. Atlanta: SBL, 2009.

Roper, Lyndal. *Oedipus and the Devil: Witchcraft, Sexuality, and Religion in Early Modern Europe.* New York: Routledge, 1994.

Rubio, Julie Hanlon. *Family Ethics: Practices for Christians.* Washington, DC: Georgetown University Press, 2010.

Ruether, Rosemary Radford. *Sexism and God-Talk.* 2nd ed. Boston: Beacon, 1992.

Russell, Letty M. *Just Hospitality: God's Welcome in a World of Difference.* Edited by J. Shannon Clarkson and Kate M. Ott. Louisville: WJK, 2009.

Saiving Goldstein, Valerie. "The Human Situation: A Feminine View." *The Journal of Religion* 40, no. 2 (1960): 100–12.

Salmavalli, Christina. "Bullying and the Peer Group: A Review." *Aggression and Violent Behavior* 15 (2010): 112–20.

Sanders, Cody J. *Queer Lessons for Churches on the Straight and Narrow: What All Christians Can Learn from LGBTQ Lives.* Macon, GA: Faithlab, 2013.

Sands, Kathleen M. *Escape from Paradise: Evil and Tragedy in Feminist Theology.* Minneapolis: Fortress Press, 1994.

Saracino, Michelle. *Clothing.* Christian Explorations in Daily Living, series ed. David H. Jensen. Minneapolis: Fortress Press, 2012.

Schüssler Fiorenza, Elisabeth. *But She Said: Feminist Practices of Biblical Interpretation.* Boston: Beacon, 1992.

———. "The Ethics of Biblical Interpretation: Decentering Biblical Scholarship," *JBL* 107 (1988): 3–17.

———. *In Memory of Her: A Feminist Theological Reconstruction of Christian Origins* New York: Crossroad, 1983.

Schwartz, David, Laura J. Proctor, and Deborah H. Chien. "The Aggressive Victim of Bullying: Emotional and Behavioral Dysregulation as a Pathway to Victimization by Peers." In *Peer Harassment in School: The Plight of the Vulnerable and Victimized,* edited by Jaana Juvonen and Sandra Graham, 147–74. New York: Guilford, 2001.

Segovia, Fernando F. "'And They Began to Speak in Other Tongues': Competing Modes of Discourse in Contemporary Biblical Criticism." In *Reading From this Place,* edited by Fernando F. Segovia and Mary Ann Tolbert, vol. 1, 1–32. Minneapolis: Fortress Press, 1995.

Smith, Christian, with Kari Christoffersen, Hilary Davidson, and Patricia Snell Herzog. *Lost in Transition: The Dark Side of Emerging Adulthood.* New York: Oxford University Press, 2011.

Smith, Holly. "Culpable Ignorance." *The Philosophical Review* 92, no. 4 (1983): 543–71.

Sobrino, Jon. *Christology at the Crossroads.* Maryknoll, NY: Orbis, 1978.

———. "Extra Pauperes Nulla Salus." In *No Salvation Outside the Poor: Prophetic-Utopian Essays,* 35–76. Maryknoll, NY: Orbis, 2008.

———. *Jesus the Liberator: A Historical-Theological View.* Maryknoll, NY: Orbis, 1993.

———. *The Principle of Mercy: Taking the Crucified People from the Cross.* Maryknoll, NY: Orbis, 1994.

Sölle, Dorothee. *Stations of the Cross: A Latin American Pilgrimage.* Translated by Joyce Irwin. Minneapolis: Fortress Press, 1993.

———. *Suffering.* Translated by Everett R. Kalin. Philadelphia: Fortress Press, 1975.

Suchocki, Marjorie Hewitt. *The Fall to Violence: Original Sin in Relational Theology.* New York: Continuum, 1995.

Sue, Derald Wing. *Microaggressions in Everyday Life: Race, Gender, and Sexual Orientation.* Hoboken, NJ: Wiley, 2010.

Swinton, John. *Raging with Compassion: Pastoral Responses to the Problem of Evil.* Grand Rapids, MI: Eerdmans, 2007.

Tabachnick, Joan. "Engaging Bystanders in Sexual Violence Prevention." *National Sexual Violence Resource Center.* Enola, PA: NSVRC, 2008.

Tanenbaum, Leora. *Slut! Growing Up Female with a Bad Reputation.* New York: Seven Stories, 1999.

Tanis, Justin. *Trans-Gendered: Theology, Ministry, and Communities of Faith.* Cleveland: Pilgrim, 2003.

Teel, Karen. *Racism and the Image of God.* New York: Palgrave MacMillan, 2010.

———. "What Jesus Wouldn't Do." In *Christology and Whiteness: What Would Jesus Do?,* edited by George Yancy, 19–35. New York: Routledge, 2012.

Terrell, JoAnne Marie. *Power in the Blood? The Cross in the African American Experience*. Maryknoll, NY: Orbis, 1998.

Thandeka. *Learning to Be White: Money, Race, and God in America*. New York: Continuum, 2007.

Theissen, Gerd. *The Gospels in Context: Social and Political History in the Synoptic Tradition*. Translated by Linda M. Mahoney. Minneapolis: Fortress Press, 1991.

Thistlethwaite, Susan Brooks. "Militarism in North American Perspective." In *Women Resisting Violence: Spirituality for Life*, edited by Mary John Mananzan, Mercy Amba Oduyoye, Elsa Tamez, J. Shannon Clarkson, Mary C. Grey, and Letty M. Russell, 119–25. Eugene OR: Wipf and Stock, 2004, 1996.

———. *Sex, Race, and God: Christian Feminism in Black and White*. New York: Crossroad, 1989.

Thurston, Bonnie Bowman. *Preaching Mark*. Minneapolis: Fortress Press, 2002.

Townes, Emilie M. *In a Blaze of Glory: Womanist Spirituality as Social Witness*. Nashville, TN: Abingdon, 1995.

———. "Living in the New Jerusalem: Rhetoric and Movement of Liberation in the House of Evil." In *A Troubling in My Soul: Womanist Perspectives on Evil & Suffering*, edited by Emilie M. Townes, 78–91. Maryknoll, NY: Orbis, 1993.

Turkle, Sherry. *Alone Together: Why We Expect More from Technology and Less from Each Other*. New York: Basic, 2012.

Tutu, Desmond Mpilo. *No Future without Forgiveness*. New York: Doubleday, 1999.

Twale, Darla J., and Barbara M. De Luca. *Faculty Incivility: The Rise of the Academic Bully Culture and What to Do About It*. San Francisco: Jossey-Bass, 2008.

Twemlow, Stuart W., and Frank C. Sacco. *Why School Antibullying Programs Don't Work*. Latham, MD: Jason Aronson, 2008.

Van den Bergh, Linda, Eddie Denessen, Lisette Hornstra, Marinus Voeten, and Rob W. Holland. "Implicit Prejudiced Attitudes of Teachers:

Relations to Teacher Expectations and the Ethnic Achievement Gap" *American Educational Research Journal* 47, no. 2 (June 2010): 497–527.

Von Balthasar, Hans Urs. *Spouse of the Word.* Vol. 2 of *Explorations in Theology.* Translated by A. V. Littledale and Alexander Dru. San Francisco: Ignatius, 1967/1991.

Wainwright, Elaine. "Not Without My Daughter: Gender and Demon Possession in Matthew 15.21-28." In *A Feminist Companion to Matthew,* edited by Amy-Jill Levine with Marianne Blickenstaff, 126–37. Sheffield: Sheffield Academic, 2001.

Weingarten, Kaethe. *Common Shock: Witnessing Violence Everyday.* New York: Penguin, 2003.

West, Traci C. *Wounds of the Spirit: Black Women, Violence, and Resistance Ethics.* New York: New York University Press, 1999.

Whitfield, Charles L., Robert F. Anda, Shanta R. Dube and Vincent J. Felitti. "Violent Childhood Experiences and the Risk of Intimate Partner Violence in Adults: Assessment in a Large Health Maintenance Organization." *Journal of Interpersonal Violence* 18, no. 2 (2003): 166–85.

Wiesel, Elie. *Night.* New York: Batman, 1982.

Wigley, Stephen D. *Karl Barth and Hans Urs von Balthasar: A Critical Engagement.* New York: T&T Clark, 2007.

Wiley, Tatha. *Original Sin: Origins, Developments, Contemporary Meanings.* New York: Paulist, 2002.

Williams, Delores S. "Christian Scapegoating." *The Other Side* 29 (May–June 1993): 43–44.

———. *Sisters in the Wilderness: The Challenge of Womanist God-Talk.* Maryknoll, NY: Orbis, 1993.

Wright, George C. *Racial Violence in Kentucky, 1865–1940: Lynchings, Mob Rule, and "Legal Lynchings."* Baton Rouge, LA: Louisiana State University Press, 1990.

Yancy, George. *Black Bodies, White Gazes: The Continuing Significance of Race.* Lanham, MD: Rowman & Littlefield, 2008.

———, ed. *Christology and Whiteness: What Would Jesus Do?* New York: Routledge, 2012.

Young, Iris Marion. "Responsibility, Social Connection, and Global Labor Justice." In *Global Challenges: War, Self-Determination, and Responsibility for Justice,* 159–86. Malden, MA: Polity, 2008.

Index

1-1. Process...

CPSIA information can be obtained
at www.ICGtesting.com
Printed in the USA
FFOW02n1317071017
40761FF